TWENTIETH-CENTURY ENGLISH LITERATURE

Twentieth-Century English Literature

1901-1960

A. C. Ward

METHUEN & CO LTD
11 NEW FETTER LANE EC4

First published 1928 as
Twentieth-Century Literature 1901–1925
Reprinted five times
Seventh edition 1940
Reprinted five times
Twelfth edition 1956
Reprinted 1959
Thirteenth edition (paperback for ELBS) 1963
Fourteenth edition 1964, revised and reset as
Twentieth-Century English Literature 1901–1960
Reprinted 1966

Printed and bound in Great Britain by
Butler & Tanner Ltd, Frome

PREFACE TO THE 1964 EDITION

This book was first published in 1928 as *Twentieth-Century Literature 1901–1925: The Age of Interrogation*. It was revised and enlarged for the seventh printing in 1940, and again for the twelfth edition in 1956. For the present edition I have provided a largely new opening chapter and added comments on some of the writers who have come into prominence since the previous revision. What I wrote in the 1940 preface, retained on the next page, applies in the main to this latest revision, though I have made further excisions and modifications in the material as first written.

If my scepticism concerning certain current reputations should arouse indignation, younger readers will have the advantage of living to know, decades hence, whether or not the voice of fashion was trustworthy.

Throughout, my belief is as unfashionable as that of Bacon, with whom I hold that 'Studies serve for delight' and not primarily for any academic or material advantage.

May 1964 A. C. W.

PREFACE TO THE 1940 EDITION

While renewing my acquaintance with this book during the preparation of this later and enlarged edition, it became evident to me that in 1940 I have fewer enthusiasms and fewer animosities than I had in 1928. I was therefore inclined, while making revisions and additions, to bring the following pages into line with my current way of thinking. In a few instances this led to a substantial modification of opinions expressed earlier, but where my former interest in any particular writer had gone beyond recovery I allowed the views of my departed self to prevail. It is probable that if this survey had been first written at the present date I should have omitted entirely some names that seemed worth including in 1928. I retain most of these, however, since reputations moribund at the moment will not necessarily remain so and others that now flourish may wither away.

A. C. W.

CONTENTS

CHAPTER I

THE SETTING

Little more than half a century separated the end of Queen Victoria's reign from the beginning of Elizabeth II's, yet in that first fifty years of the twentieth century the human race moved faster – forward *and* backward – than during perhaps fifty generations in the past. Man's growing mastery of the physical world and its material resources is a story of ever-accelerating progress accompanied in its later phases by an unprecedented moral and spiritual relapse. Progress and regress, both, are fruits of the Scientific Revolution which has been the outstanding feature of this century. The perfecting of the internal combustion engine made possible the aeroplane and other means of mass slaughter in two world wars, with nuclear power to follow, bringing the threat of universal destruction though also the possibility of world protection by reason of the nations' saving fear of mutual annihilation. In peacetime the motor car and motor cycle gave almost unlimited mobility to millions, a large proportion of them young people thus enabled to travel far from their homes and elude natural parental guidance and control. Among the several revolutions within the Scientific Revolution the revolt of youth has been as notable as any and its distant repercussions are unpredictable. All that could be said currently was that the ease with which the mass manipulation of youth could be organized had been shown in such movements as the Hitler Youth and similar political bodies elsewhere. It was no new thing in Continental and Eastern countries to utilize students as active political partisans, but in Britain until the middle of the present century it had been accepted that the first duty of students is to study, not to agitate – agitation being, indeed, the chief source of disablement for study. Political demonstrations by untutored youth (mentally untutored, that is, and therefore easily susceptible to emotional conditioning) are unlikely to lead either to wise reforms or to effective revolution. When unharmful they are invariably pathetic and futile; if productive, their end could be mob rule.

In the study of literature few things are more interesting than to consider the periodic changes of outlook which sway the human mind and spirit, and to observe those recurrent fluctuations of values which cause the truths and certainties of one generation to appear as superstitions and baseless conventions in the eyes of generations following. Young men and young women during the twentieth century looked back upon the Victorian Age as dully hypocritical. Victorian ideals appeared mean and superficial and stupid. This mood was part cause and part consequence of changes, effected or impending, in the literature of the first quarter of the twentieth century. From 1901 to 1925 English literature was directed by mental attitudes, moral ideals, and spiritual values at almost the opposite extreme to the attitudes, ideals and values governing Victorian literature. The old certainties were certainties no longer. Everything was held to be open to question. Standards of artistic craftsmanship and of aesthetic appreciation began to change fundamentally. What the Victorians had considered beautiful their children and grandchildren thought hideous. The treasured bric-à-brac of Victorian mantelshelves and whatnots was thrown into Edwardian and Georgian dustbins, though before the reign of George V was out many of the rejects had become 'antiques' and collectors' pieces.

But however much the post-Victorian generation disliked the furnishings of Victorian households, they were even more contemptuous of the furnishings of Victorian minds. In the Victorian Age there was a widespread and willing submission to the rule of the Expert; the Voice of Authority was accepted in religion, in politics, in literature, in family life. When the orthodox Voice was not heeded, it was usually because a rival voice spoke more persuasively to individual ears. To some, the Voice of Darwin in *The Descent of Man* sounded more credible and more authoritative than the Voice of God in the Book of Genesis. It was not the acceptance of any single body of doctrine that distinguished the Victorian, but his insistent *attitude* of acceptance, his persistent belief in (but rare examination of) the credentials of Authority, his innate desire to affirm and conform rather than to reject or to question. Yet whatever weakness underlay the Victorian spirit of acceptance and affirmation was for the most part an innocent weakness, a readiness to accept phrases at face value without critical examination. Victorian faith and morality may have been unflawed on the surface, but to early twentieth-century minds they seemed often to lack any core of personally realized conviction – to be mere second-hand clothing of the mind and spirit.

A further characteristic of Victorianism was a firm belief in the permanence of nineteenth-century institutions, both temporal and spiritual. The Victorians seemed to themselves to be living in a house built on unshakable foundations and established in perpetuity. The Home, the Constitution, the Empire, the Christian religion – each of these, in its own form and degree, was taken as a final revelation. It was not allowable even to hint that, in the course of natural processes of change, any or all of these institutions might be displaced or superseded.

Among early twentieth-century writers, the Victorian idea of the permanence of institutions was displaced by the sense of a universal mutability. H. G. Wells spoke of 'the flow of things',[1] and elsewhere described a company of people as 'haunted by the idea that embodies itself in the word "Meanwhile" '. He goes on: 'In the measure in which one saw life plainly the world ceased to be a home and became the mere site of a home. On which we camped. Unable as yet to live fully and completely.' Later, he speaks of 'all this world of ours being no more than the prelude to a real civilization'.[2]

If the cost of seeing life plainly is that the world no longer appears to be a home but only the site of a home, the Victorians would have listened with composure to the charge that they did not see life plainly. The change of outlook that came with the twentieth century was due to the growth of a restless desire to probe and question. Bernard Shaw, foremost among the heralds of change, attacked with vigour the 'old superstition' of religion

[1] *The World of William Clissold* (1926). [2] *Meanwhile* (1927).

and the 'new superstition' of science, not because he was antagonistic to either religion or science as such, but because, in his view, every dogma is a superstition until it has been personally examined and consciously accepted by the individual believer. *Question! Examine! Test!* – these were the watchwords of his creed. He let slip no opportunity to challenge the Voice of Authority and the Reign of the Expert. With equal assurance he interrogated economists, artists, doctors, educationists, politicians, scientists, religionists; and the effect of his writings was to spread abroad for at least a generation the interrogative habit of mind. Thousands who had been brought up to regard religion and morality as subjects to be spoken of with reverently lowered voices, heard, as though it were a trumpet-call, Andrew Undershaft's declaration in Shaw's *Major Barbara*: 'That is what is wrong with the world at present. It scraps its obsolete steam engines and dynamos; but it won't scrap its old prejudices and its old moralities and its old religions and its old political constitutions.' The effect of this was invigorating to some; but others might have expressed their sensations in the words of Barbara herself, 'I stood on the rock I thought eternal; and without a word it reeled and crumbled under me.'

The revolt from Victorianism – from its sense of stability, its striving for order, its consciousness of dignity – created for the multitude only a spiritual vacuum. But Victorianism was bound to die, of its own excess. In its middle years, as early as 1869, Meredith was writing in one of his letters, 'Isn't there a scent of damned hypocrisy in all this lisping and vowelled purity of the *Idylls* [of Tennyson]?' Hardy, simultaneously, was murmuring in his earliest poems against the 'purblind doomsters' whose 'crass Casualty' seemed to him to hold the universe in purposeless and automatic bondage. And by 1872 Samuel Butler had begun, in *Erewhon*, that attack on Victorianism which he was to conduct with vehemence for the remainder of the nineteenth century. In the eighteen-nineties the gravity of the Victorians was further shaken by the so-called Decadents, impatient 'to eat of the fruit of all the trees in the garden of the world'.[1] Victorianism outlived the Decadents; but at the turn of the new century came a succession of writers with power-

[1] Oscar Wilde, *De Profundis* (1905).

fully sceptical minds untouched by reverence for custom or the established order. These writers had grown up during the 'nineties, but they had not conformed to the current doctrine of 'art for art's sake'. Their creed was 'art for life's sake' or, at least, for the sake of the community.

At this point, however, there is need to distinguish between two groups of writers: the group that was already established in the first decade of the present century; and the group that had not so far begun to produce, but was shaping its ideas largely in conformity with a work which had had no public impact, G. E. Moore's *Principia Ethica* (1903). These latter writers coalesced in what came to be known as the Bloomsbury Group[1] which went some way to restoring, though with a difference, the art-for-art's-sake principle. Their older contemporaries, who might be styled the Fabian Society group, included few, if any at all, who would have dissented from Shaw's 'for art's sake alone' he would not have written even a single sentence.[2]

The Fabian Society had been founded in 1884 for 'the general dissemination of knowledge as to the relation between the individual and society in its economic, ethical, and political aspects', and the end-result of this dissemination was to be 'the spread of Socialist opinions, and the social and political changes consequent thereon'. From the first the Society attracted authors into its ranks, and though Shaw and Wells (the latter soon defected) were the most prominent creative writers among its early members, with the foundation of *The New Statesman* as its mouthpiece in 1913 a host of younger literary men, also, either advocated its principles or were more or less influenced by them.[3] But the prime movers were animated by sociological and political motives, and literature as such was secondary to these.

[1] See below, pp. 11 f. [2] See below, p. 97.

[3] *New Statesmanship* (edited by Edward Hyams, 1963), an anthology drawn from contributions to the paper during its first fifty years, includes material by (besides Shaw and Wells) Arnold Bennett, D. H. Lawrence, George Orwell, J. B. Priestley, C. P. Snow, Angus Wilson, Virginia Woolf and many others. The Literary Editors of the paper included J. C. Squire, Desmond MacCarthy, Raymond Mortimer, David Garnett, V. S. Pritchett. It was common knowledge, or at least a well-circulated joke, that many buyers of *The New Statesman* in the 1940s and 1950s read it backwards, starting at the end with the literary articles and abandoning it midway on reaching she often sour political pages.

The triumph of orthodox Fabianism was attained through the influence on the recently founded Labour Party of those indefatigable researchers Beatrice and Sidney Webb, whose imposing histories of local government, and more particularly Mrs Webb's famous Minority Report on poor-law reform (1909), were essential manuals for Socialists. The Webbs' indispensable instrument for government was State control, a vast administrative machine designed to ensure the welfare of the massed millions. When it came into partial operation later in the century, it proved to be a machine which in practical working could not avoid treating individual men and women as punched cards passing through the entrails of a computer. That the Webbs' tireless labours subsequently issued in unprecedented material and physical benefit to millions cannot be questioned. In not unimportant respects they were the architects of the Welfare State[1] which they barely lived to see in being, and they must be given credit for its virtues and take blame for some at least of its defects. In their rightful concern for the under-privileged many, the Webbs were blind to the leaven in the social lump – the exceptional, the eccentric, the individually independent-minded, the nonconforming. In any system of State socialism such blindness to the individual is inevitable. It is impracticable to legislate for the odd-man-out, or to pay particular attention to any minority section that lacks numerical power to sway elections.

A prominent American politician rejoiced during the Second World War that this is 'the century of the Common Man'. In the decade following the war, however, it became evident that it was not the Common Man – not the individual 'little man' as H. G. Wells had conceived him early in the century in Arty Kipps and Mr Polly – but Mass Man that dominated the scene. Although horizons had stretched to infinity through the universality of air travel, the British found themselves almost claustrophobic in a rapidly shrinking Empire, soon to be no Empire at all as one after another of the former overseas possessions dropped away to assume

[1] This term, which gained general currency after 1945, seems to have originated with William Temple (Archbishop of Canterbury from 1942): 'We have . . . seen that in place of the conception of the Power-State we are led to that of the Welfare-State.' (In *Citizen and Churchman*, 1941.)

the responsibilities and burdens of self-government. With the dissolution of the Empire the British by tens of thousands lost most of the opportunities for enterprise and adventure that had been for centuries open to their forebears, while the coincident decline of Christianity at home and abroad closed foreign missionary fields which had offered service of another sort. Thus, while the insularity of the British appeared to be lessened by their growing predilection for holidays abroad and by the large-scale influx of migrants from overseas bringing unfamiliar manners and customs, Great Britain nevertheless became morally and mentally frustrated.

Other and more debilitating causes contributed to the sense of enclosement.

Throughout the period between the two world wars, the growth of mass-production methods in industry created deep concern among sociologists who recognized that a lifetime of work on assembly-line processes was destructive of interest in the objects produced and a threat of death to craftsmanship. By the middle of the century individual skill and craftsman's pride had almost vanished. Simultaneously there developed a widespread indifference – and in some quarters a positive antagonism – to form and style in writing. The approved novels and plays of the 1950s either ignored or of set purpose flouted literary craftsmanship. Art gave place to 'anti-Art', and under the anti-Art banner chaotic production needed no apology or defence: chaos had indeed come again, bringing its high priests and devotees.

Though Samuel Beckett's *Waiting for Godot* (1955) might be taken as the pattern play of the decade, it is necessary to look farther back for the origins of the 'new' literature – to 1922, the year of James Joyce's *Ulysses* and T. S. Eliot's *The Waste Land.* With the appearance of these, literature left the highroad of communication and retreated into an esoteric fastness. In the preceding years of the century the leading writers – Hardy, Kipling, Shaw, Wells, Arnold Bennett, Galsworthy – had been respected by critics (except by those whose political convictions were at odds with those of Kipling on one wing and with Shaw's on the other) and were also enjoyed by the general body of averagely intelligent readers. The writer who was almost certainly the greatest novelist of the first decades of the century, Joseph Conrad, though less quickly accepted by a large reading public, made no claim to write for a specifically intellectual audience. The surprising outburst of poetry during the First World War was also intelligible and attractive to the common reader,[1] and though in the post-1922 period it became fashionable among *avant garde* critics and their followers to denigrate the Georgian poets of the 1914–18 period, these held a firm place in anthologies[2] during the next half-century, while the collected poems of Rupert Brooke remained in steady demand notwithstanding the disfavour expressed by commentators who accepted the new orthodoxy of intellectualism. Nothing in the field of reviewing and criticism could be more remarkable than critics' real or assumed unawareness of publishing facts and bookshop experience. While it was being repeatedly said that 'Nobody reads Galsworthy now', *The Forsyte Saga* progressed steadily towards its fiftieth impression with no aid from paperback sales. For a book to become an immediate best-seller is not evidence of worth; many such perish year by year. It is, however, a sign if not a guarantee of enduring merit to retain widespread interest for half a century or so, as Galsworthy's *Saga* has done.

The exponents of the new-style criticism based on 'close textual analysis' claimed that their methods were a fulfilment of or an improvement on Matthew Arnold's principle that literature should provide a 'criticism of life'; but that phrase remained a phrase, since the handicap borne by the professional academic scholar is his isolation from 'life' as it is lived by the community at large. If literature is to dwindle to the point where it becomes little but raw material for university exercises, literature can have no future as an enrichment of life. Academic criticism and study whose productive end is simply the multiplication of academics *ad infinitum* is no more than a process of professional inbreeding, a kind of cerebral incest.[3]

[1] I use 'common reader' here to denote a person of average education and intelligence, even though Virginia Woolf's admirable essays in her volumes entitled *The Common Reader* are certainly addressed to those of uncommon education and intelligence.

[2] Although 'anthology pieces' came to be used as a term of reproach by some critics, enduring merit is the common requirement for admission to anthologies.

[3] See below, pp. 210 ff.

Much of this misapplied critical approach has centred on Shakespeare, with the particular purpose of demolishing the theory that drama is pre-eminently a conflict of character, as it was taken to be in, notably, A. C. Bradley's *Shakespearean Tragedy* (1904). Yet if for the great majority of theatregoers and readers during more than three hundred years Shakespeare's plays had not been accepted as pre-eminently concerned with conflict of character, Shakespeare would long since have disappeared from the stage. Equally untenable is the scholastic argument that his characters are not to be viewed as 'real' people, for it is the primary function of a playwright through the power of imagination to create a fuller 'reality' than is offered by common experience.

The dictatorial intellectualism which dates from the year of *Ulysses* and *The Waste Land* was rooted in contempt for normal intelligence, as is shown by the attitude of one of the pioneer interpreters of James Joyce. In the first edition (1930) of his commentary on *Ulysses* Stuart Gilbert wrote:

> In the seven years which Mr Joyce devoted to the construction of this monument of literature, well-planned and strongly built, he never once betrayed the authority of intellect to the hydra-headed rabble of the mental underworld.

Though this passage was omitted from the 1952 edition, the following words were retained concerning the character Stephen Dedalus, generally held to be a projection of Joyce himself:

> Stephen is still an intellectual exile, proudly aloof from the mediocrity of his contemporaries, and he still displays an ironic disdain for their shoddy enthusiasms.

In an end-note to volume I of *The Criterion*, which he directed influentially from 1922 to 1939, T. S. Eliot wrote:

> Those . . . who affirm an antimony between 'literature', meaning any literature which can appeal only to a small and fastidious public, and 'life', are not only flattering the complacency of the half-educated, but asserting a principle of disorder.

The footnotes to *The Waste Land* displayed the breadth of Eliot's learning, yet in proportion to the totality of knowledge, or even in relation to the individual specialized knowledge of a skilled craftsman in some different field, he might himself be thought to display 'the complacency of the half-educated'. As a branch of the Humanities, literature has a recreative function which intellectual arrogance can only blight. Close scholarly investigation of literary texts has its own, different and subordinate, function. While such a breathtaking adventure in textual detective work as Professor Hinman's tracking down[1] of the different compositors, individual typefaces, formes and presses involved in the production of the 1623 collection of Shakespeare's plays is beyond praise, it is nevertheless only a bibliographical tool – though an invaluable tool – in the scholar's workshop. It clears up a handful or two of doubts and verbal problems, but makes only a minor contribution to the proper enjoyment and understanding of Shakespeare.

The booby-traps that lie in the path of the textual critic are amusingly indicated by another leading American bibliographer, Professor Bowers, in reference to certain observations on T. S. Eliot's 'Whispers of Immortality' by Professor William Empson in *Seven Types of Ambiguity* (1930), a book taken as gospel by a generation of students:

> . . . when a critic arrives at conclusions about the point of a poem that are reached through the interpretation of printer's errors in the text, we may see how readily white may be made black, and black white, and we may be forgiven if we treat his opinions in general with some reserve. The truth is that Empson studied Eliot, and spun his finely drawn theories about Eliot's literary art, not from the relatively pure first or second editions, but from either the third or the fourth edition. By bad luck a printer's common transpositional error in the third edition exchanged the terminal punctuation of lines 10 and 11, making the end of the sentence come at line 10 instead of line 11, and wrongly beginning a new sentence with the final infinitive phrase of the correct old sentence: and the mistake was not caught up until the sixth edition. On the evidence of the periodical text of the poem, followed by its first two book editions, and the correction of the sixth edition, it was the faulty printer – and not the poet

[1] *The Printing and Proof-Reading of the First Folio of Shakespeare*, by Charlton Hinman (Clarendon Press, Oxford, 2 vols., 1963).

– who introduced the syntactical ambiguity that Empson so greatly admired and felt was the point of the whole poem. I should dearly like to know whether Eliot blushed, or laughed, when he read Empson on this poem and its non-existent point.[1]

The glee with which Professor Bowers caught out Professor Empson is a mild instance of the no-love-lost between scholars displayed weekly in the correspondence page of *The Times Literary Supplement*, which has been for half a century Britain's outstanding book-review journal. Future historians of the literary temper of authors and scholars in the twentieth century will find there a mass of evidence of the irascibility, the lack of philosophic calm, and (often) the discourteous quarrelsomeness pertaining to the literary profession – though this is perhaps only a sectional reflection of the widespread belief of the age that good manners are evidence of feebleness of character and are inferior to barbaric loutishness such as that exemplified by such 'anti-heroes' of the 1950s as Dixon in Kingsley Amis's *Lucky Jim* (1954) and Porter in John Osborne's *Look Back in Anger* (1956). A quarter of a century earlier Magnus was reminding Orinthia in Shaw's *The Apple Cart* that 'without good manners human society is intolerable and impossible'.

The Bloomsbury Group[2] who had an important place in the intellectual life of Britain during the second quarter of the century included Virginia Woolf, E. M. Forster, Lytton Strachey, J. M. (afterwards Lord) Keynes, Roger Fry, and others. That they constituted a 'group' was often denied, though the word is justified by the fact that they were a circle of friends who frequently met in the home of one or another in the Bloomsbury district of London, for the conversational hammering-out of ideas in which they had a common interest. The men of the company had been brilliant figures at Cambridge in their undergraduate stage, while Virginia Woolf (she married Leonard Woolf in 1912) had had the intellectual

[1] *Textual and Literary Criticism* by Fredson Bowers (Cambridge University Press, 1959), pp. 31–2.

[2] For a critical commentary on its 'members', see J. K. Johnstone, *The Bloomsbury Group* (1954).

advantage if also the psychological disadvantage of being the daughter of Leslie Stephen, an eminent Victorian scholar who was also a parent after the dominating Victorian pattern. G. E. Moore's *Principia Ethica* (1903), though mainly concerned to define the nature of goodness, had much to say also about the relationship between beauty and 'intrinsic value', and from this book, by paths too intricate to follow here, the young men of the future Bloomsbury set were led to attach great importance to art as a factor in civilized living.[1] Among their number, Roger Fry became a pioneer in converting British taste to the acceptance of Post-Impressionist art; Virginia Woolf's sister, Vanessa Stephen (later married to Clive Bell, art critic), was a painter, as also was another in the set, Duncan Grant. They were all intellectuals, but they valued good manners; they felt themselves to be of superior mentality, and they tended to be contemptuous of lesser minds, but since most of them had genuine creative ability they had some title to a sense of elevation. And they had firm contact with the world of actuality, though there may be ground for believing that Virginia Woolf tended to believe that the world was made in her own image. Amid this company of lovers of the arts, J. M. Keynes, though himself an art lover, stood out as also a man of affairs – an economist whose *General Theory of Employment, Interest and Money* (1936) and other works on related themes were destined to revolutionize British thinking and action in these fields. Perhaps more influential, though in a manner more difficult to demonstrate, was his *Economic Consequences of the Peace* (1919), a destructive commentary upon the reparations clauses of the Versailles Treaty in the course of which he brilliantly and with cruel wit demolished the Allied statesmen who conducted (or, as he believed, tragically misconducted) the Peace Conference. This book has been thought to have gone far towards encouraging the Germans in their view that the treaty was intolerably unjust. a humiliation that could only be wiped out by a war of revenge.

Certainly the economic consequences in Britain were disastrous,

[1] As might be supposed, the influence of *Principia Ethica* was not wholly aesthetic. Moore's observations on the Moral Law led them to the conclusion that their own individual judgement must be held superior to 'customary morals, conventions, and traditional wisdom'. See Keynes, *Two Memoirs* (1949).

though not fully apparent until the early 1930s, when mass unemployment accompanied the world financial collapse.

The most spectacular outcome of the war of 1914–18 was the establishment of the League of Nations, which intervened several times to prevent threatened outbreaks between minor Powers, and transacted with credit a vast amount of work making for international humanitarianism and social betterment. Yet, despite the Solemn Covenant and the subsequent treaties by which it was buttressed, the League failed to secure universal confidence. This was in part due to the use of the League less as an instrument of international justice than as a device for keeping the defeated in subjection. The League was fatally disrupted by the presence among its member-States of some who gave only temporary lip-service to its ideals and violated them as soon as national aspirations and the desire for territorial expansion appeared realizable. The League merely temporized when Japan attacked China, applied sanctions only half-heartedly and ineffectually when Italy invaded Abyssinia, tolerated a misnamed Non-Intervention Committee during the Spanish Civil War of 1936–8, and allowed itself the moral luxury of a valueless expulsion of Soviet Russia when the independence of Finland was violated in 1939, long after Japan, Germany, and Italy had withdrawn from membership.

Early in 1929 an avalanche of anti-war books had begun. The possibility of such a visitation was foreshadowed seven years earlier with the publication of C. E. Montague's *Disenchantment* (1922), read and admired as much for its distinction of style[1] as for its strong yet moderated protest – so well moderated as to seem scarcely more than good-mannered indignation. Later books by Montague – *Fiery Particles* (1923) and *Rough Justice* (1926) – were more definitely anti-war – the first ironically, the other tragically. But still his literary urbanity softened the attack. These were books for connoisseurs rather than for the multitude. What Montague had done for a few, Erich Maria Remarque's *All Quiet on the Western Front* (1929) did for millions throughout Europe and America and

[1] In the rougher mental atmosphere of the 1940s and after Montague's style seemed over-elegant and mannered.

beyond. Remarque's story and Richard Aldington's *Death of a Hero* (which came out late in 1929) proclaimed that the war had been fatal to a whole generation of youth by inflicting death either morally or spiritually, or both, even when it had spared the fighters' bodies.

There is no sure means of assessing the pacific value of these anti-war books, or of deciding whether their effect was not rather to habituate readers to horror and to pander to masochistic tendencies. But only a few of them were other than passionately sincere in intention. For those who desired a cooler statement of the soldiers' own view of war there was, besides C. E. Montague's books, Edmund Blunden's *Undertones of War* (1928); for those who preferred romantico-realistic heroics R. C. Sherriff's play, *Journey's End* (1928). By 1960 only Blunden's book had established itself as a prose classic of the war; and among the poems Wilfred Owen's 'Strange Meeting' and others by him were given new and wider currency through Benjamin Britten's musical setting of them in his *War Requiem*, composed for the new Coventry Cathedral in 1962.[1]

As the European scene darkened, and oppression, cruelty, murder, and the breaking of solemn engagements became common form, a long crescendo of protest and denunciation arose, not alone in political speeches and directly propagandist writings, but also in imaginative and creative literature. It became a conviction among the younger school of writers that, with liberty, truth and honour imperilled, no art could justify itself except as the handmaid of politics. This was a principle already firmly established by the totalitarian rulers of Russia, Italy, and Germany, where all artists were bound to use their talents to the sole end of exalting the State. The product of this creed, whether enforced – as in the countries named – or adopted voluntarily – as by many in England – was much dreary polemics. Young men and young women 'got politics', as their grandparents were accustomed to 'get religion'. In both cases the impulse was purely irrational. The same romantic idealism

[1] From 1945 onward there was an outpouring of war books of a different kind, mainly reminiscences. Some had historical value or direct human interest, but many appeared to be a morbid or commercially inspired raking over of the ashes of war.

which had led religiously converted Victorians to the foreign mission field led politically converted neo-Georgians to the battlefield in Spain and China. With the more stay-at-home kind, Victorian social slumming among 'the deserving poor' was displaced by intellectual slumming among 'the workers'. And whereas the grandparents had written pious tracts for unbelievers, the grandchildren wrote proletarian pamphlets for already converted comrades, since Socialist literature brought conviction almost exclusively to the already convinced.

A generation before, Bernard Shaw had eschewed art *qua* art, but his renunciation did little harm to his work considered as literature, for he kept firm hold on wit, humour, a sense of style (which implies a respect for words and their meanings), and independence of judgement. But numerous imaginative writers in the 1930s, out of a false sense of social service and in an illuded condition of mind, suppressed their creative abilities and turned to 'writings for the times' based on a set of assumptions usually incapable of proof and rarely supported by evidence.[1]

Most of those who wrote for the masses and professed to have simplified their way of saying things in the hope that poetry might thereby be brought back into popular favour, were actually employing a highly complex intellectualized language outside the mental range and unstirring to the emotions of most of the proletariat. Examining with sympathy the proletarian claim that the artist must sacrifice himself as an individual to the requirements of the community, E. M. Forster wrote:

> There are two chief reasons for Escapism. We may retire to our towers because we are afraid. . . . But there is another motive for retreat. Boredom: disgust: indignation against the herd, the community, and the world: the conviction that sometimes comes to the solitary individual that his solitude gives him something finer and greater than he gets when he merges in the multitude. . . . The community is selfish and, to further its own efficiency, is a traitor to the side of human nature which expresses itself in solitude. Considering all the harm the community does today, it is in no position to start a moral slanging match. . . . We are here on earth

[1] E.g. Christopher Caudwell's *Studies in a Dying Culture* (1938), one of the best of its class.

not to save ourselves and not to save the community, but to try to save both.[1]

The people of Britain faced the Second World War in a mood of stoical determination and endurance. In 1939 there could be no repetition of the spirit of 1914, when romantico-patriotic fervour and belligerent enthusiasm were not yet dimmed and ignorance not yet enlightened by experience of total war, and when stay-at-homes, still strangers to bombing, could be abused as shirkers. The Second World War could not produce a Rupert Brooke, a Siegfried Sassoon, or a Wilfred Owen. Whereas 1914–18 had borne a harvest of soldiers' verse that was stimulating and sometimes uplifting, 1939–45 produced little verse and that little was mostly in a minor key and often obscurely phrased.

The common view of the war as a vast crime imposed upon mankind by man, a crime to be combated by plodding endurance, was qualified by a minority who saw the war as a consequence of Sin against the Almighty. In both world wars religion recaptured popular attention, and the revival of interest in religious literature between 1939 and 1945 was no new phenomenon; nor was it unprecedented that some writers found it commercially profitable to exploit this interest.

Between the two wars the writings of Sören Kierkegaard (1813–55) found belatedly an English audience through American translations from the original Danish; and these, together with the poems and autobiographical prose of Rainer Maria Rilke[2] (1875–1926) and the novels of Franz Kafka (1883–1924), induced among English writers a pre-occupation with states of consciousness which, though they might be regarded unsympathetically as the product of spiritual morbidity or of mental sickness, were more commonly accepted as presentations, sometimes symbolic, of man's dire need of redemption. No previous generation had shown so close an

[1] 'The Ivory Tower', *London Mercury*, December 1938, pp. 119–30.

[2] Both Rilke and Kafka were born in Prague and wrote in German. Kafka was Jewish, Rilke of mixed Bohemian and Alsatian stock. Rilke, for a time secretary to the French sculptor Rodin, also had a marked influence on French writers. Jean Paul Sartre (whose Existentialist philosophy owed much to his reading of Kierkegaard and Kierkegaard's followers) was among those to whom English writers turned inquiringly in the 1940s.

interest in mental and spiritual disturbance as to create a growing assumption that most men and women are cases to be diagnosed, that the world is a vast clinic, and that nothing but abnormality is normal.

Simultaneously with the conduct of a desperate war, the British coalition government in the years from 1940 to 1945 laid plans to ensure that when the war ended there should be no repetition of the widespread unemployment that had dogged the nation in the 1920s and 1930s. 'Social security' became a familiar term denoting the various national services that were to usher in the Welfare State with its ideal of 'fair shares for all' – an ideal which in practice was found to be unrealized by the elderly and some other groups.

A sweeping victory at the general election in 1945 enabled the Labour Party to implement hurriedly its nationalization programme for the power-supply, transport and other industries, and to establish a National Health Service such as had been adumbrated by Bernard Shaw in the Preface to *The Doctor's Dilemma* more than thirty years before. Almost overnight, Britain found itself an affluent State in which full employment, high wages, family allowances and other public benefits appeared to promise a utopia for millions. It had been assumed that the removal of economic stresses would bring contentment if not positive happiness to the majority, but the experience of the following decades did not justify the expectation. The State was found as uncongenial and unsympathetic a master as many private employers had been, and the new master was permanent.

A mood of sullen discontent settled upon large numbers of those whom the new order had been designed to benefit, while crime and prostitution, hitherto believed to be by-products of poverty, flourished as never before. Those to whom much was now given desired more; increased educational opportunities up to university level bred a body of young men and women culturally severed from their families and socially rootless. Finding that a university degree did not of itself admit them to a well-rewarded profession, some tended to fall back upon the illusion that the world owed them an effortless living.

Perhaps the most disconcerting revelation was that social habits once condemned as 'conspicuous waste'[1] on the part of the 'idle rich' were in fact common to all classes when means permitted.[2] Advertisers were quick to recognize and take advantage of this, and the general desire to possess and display – to emulate and if possible to outdo one's neighbours – was accelerated by the rapid spread of the hire-purchase system which most prudent working people had shunned before the war when 'have only what you can afford' was a common principle. Though it was no new thing in the United States, the age of 'status symbols' and 'keeping up with the Joneses' was not fully born in Britain until after 1945.

During the war, and for several years after, the imperative need to buttress the national economy by maintaining export trade had ruthlessly denied many desired goods to the home market and imposed a drab austerity. The gradual loosening of government controls after the Labour Party had been displaced by the Conservatives in 1950 stimulated home demand, and though exports continued to be vital the dominant requirement was to prevent any severe lapse from full employment. A considerable part of the nation's productive sources was devoted to the manufacture of what would in the past have been stigmatized as 'luxury goods' – cars, domestic appliances, fashion wear, and such newer inventions as television sets – but had now come to be ranked as necessary adjuncts to a good life. 'Luxury' became an indispensable word in the vocabulary of advertising, which relied more and more upon language at once inflated and impoverished. Though old-style 'commercial English' had been both frowned and laughed out of currency, the new-style 'advertisers' English' was for more serious reasons undesirable. It was symptomatic of this trend towards inflation of language that those who before 1939 were content to describe themselves as 'advertising agents' now became 'Incorporated Practitioners in Advertising'. Before 1939, too, the industry com-

[1] This term was popularized through the writings of the American left-wing economist Thorstein Veblen (1857–1929), author of *The Theory of the Leisure Class* (1899), etc.

[2] British women were paying £100,000,000 a year to hairdressers by 1963. £1,500,000,000 per annum was said to be 'a conservative estimate' of the amount spent on betting and gambling. The amount spent on school books by education authorities was £8,000,000.

mitted itself to Truth in Advertising, a principle subsequently overlaid by conscious exaggeration sometimes bordering on misrepresentation. Growing concern about the social effects of advertisers' methods was reflected in the setting up of certain consumers' protection organizations[1] and of a government-appointed Advertising Commission. The Memorandum of Evidence[2] presented to the Commission by the National Union of Teachers expressed anxiety about 'the presentation of the advertised product in conjunction with ideas or images that are calculated to evoke an automatic emotional response . . . without reference to the merits of the articles or habits involved'. Examples of the emotional responses desired from the young were cited in connexion with 'advertising slanted to suggest that it is manly and grown-up to smoke and drink' and 'the type of advertising suggesting that a girl's sole purpose is to attract and keep a man'.

Hardly anyone would deny that advertising can serve a useful purpose and be interesting, amusing and genuinely informative. Numerous advertisements, however, had ceased to concern themselves with the quality or merit of the product. Professional advertising experts, indeed, would not (at least in private) claim interest in the nature of a product but only in selling it, utilizing such channels of subconscious influence as 'depth psychology' which subtly inculcate the belief that there is an intimate connexion between human love and (as examples taken from actual advertisements) beer, chocolates, gas stoves, refrigerators, corsets, face paint, footwear. The intended sexual link is seldom openly evident except in cinema advertising (where posters blatantly and cynically display in pictures suggestions of indecency often wholly absent from the actual films) and on the covers of much paperback fiction.

It cannot be claimed that the methods adopted in the advertising of books are always commendable. The high production cost of books can only be compensated by large total sales. If extravagant claims turn an indifferent novel or biography into a money-making best seller, the exaggeration might be defended on the ground that

[1] Such as the Consumers' Association (publishing *Which?*—a monthly guide) and the Consumers' Council set up by the government.

[2] *The Teacher Looks at Advertising* (National Union of Teachers, 1963).

it had produced a margin of profit that could help to subsidize better books with a more restricted appeal. Nevertheless the competitive shouting of publishers in literary papers often makes it impossible to distinguish between good and bad. Nor are readers helped when reviewer A gives unmeasured praise to what reviewer B dismisses with contempt. Readers are no better served, moreover, by reviewers C and D who exhibit themselves more often than they provide an exposition of the book in hand.

Current literature is inevitably influenced and conditioned by the mental and moral climate of the period in which it is produced, and especially so in the present century when literacy is no longer confined to a cultured minority. Since astronomical sales figures are claimed for fiction which exploits sex and sadism, the antidote (if it is agreed that some antidote is necessary) can only be found in the education of public taste.

In relation to literature, education of that kind could best be effected through the development of an instructed critical attitude towards words. Though it is sometimes alleged that a *well-written* 'immoral' book is more harmful than one badly written, the validity of the allegation remains much in doubt. Deliberate pornography, critically viewed, disgusts as much by its style as by its subject: the two are inseparable. A reader or potential reader whose literary taste has been trained will not tolerate a debased style and will thereby be protected if need be from debased subject-matter.

An appendix to the National Union of Teachers pamphlet mentioned above refers specifically to the language of advertisements and the need to urge school-children 'to ask about the meanings and uses of words'. This need extends far beyond any commercial relationship of language and beyond the vocabulary of the popular press, for literature as a whole and academic criticism in particular are in present danger of an illiterate hardening of the arteries as both become affected by clichés and by the jargon of psychiatry and pseudo-science which serve as substitutes for independent thought. Nor is it only the trade terms of psychiatry that have invaded literature. Freudianism in all its imperfectly understood manifestations and speculations has become rooted in the very substance of much contemporary fiction, drama and verse. Whatever light psychiatry may throw upon mental problems – as a new 'science' it seems often to be considered a panacea – it has led to as much disorder in imaginative literature as it has contributed to the disintegration of individual personality. No incontrovertible proof yet exists that sin and evil and devil-possession are only old outdated superstitions. The psychiatric vogue tends to postulate almost universal mental invalidism, with no guarantee that psychiatrists themselves are immune. A new trade has imposed itself on the community and is subserved by much modern literature that exploits abnormality.

The revolt of youth, an outstanding phenomenon of the 'affluent society' in the Welfare State, received more adult encouragement and approbation than it otherwise would, because the demand for adolescent labour endowed the young with unprecedented and mainly indiscriminating spending power. The consequent cult of immaturity was irrational and in the widest sense socially indefensible. Child welfare, better feeding and health care led to earlier physical maturity, but equivalent mental maturity can only be the slower outcome of experience.

The insurgent young of the late 1940s and the early 1950s were described as rebels without a cause. A cause was found when *The New Statesman* launched the Campaign for Nuclear Disarmament[1] and ban-the-bomb marches on government nuclear establishments and sit-down demonstrations in Whitehall and elsewhere became a form of organized protest, though as a public nuisance it antagonized many of those – virtually the whole nation – who sympathized with the cause. The presence among the marchers of the unkempt beatnik type of youths and girls became at length an embarrassment to the organizers, for beatniks were figures of fun to ribald observers.

Beatniks cannot, however, be altogether ignored in the contemporary scene, though in Britain they were scarcely more than a twisted reflection of the American prototypes who first appeared in

[1] See *The New Statesman: The History of the First Fifty Years 1913–63* by Edward Hyams (1963), p. 287.

California around 1946. These original beatniks, professing utter disgust with what they judged to be the incurably debased society of the United States, determined to contract-out and have no part in it, abandoning all its 'respectable' inhibitions and taboos, indulging such impulses as promiscuous sexuality and drug addiction, and living as homeless tramps. The beatnik books from across the Atlantic that became best known in Britain were *On the Road* and *The Dharma Bums*,[1] novels by Jack Kerouac. The American beatniks could be regarded by sympathizers as modern counterparts of the medieval *goliards* or wandering scholars or, in their indifference to personal hygiene, of the desert fathers. To non-sympathizers, on the other hand, they appeared as social parasites, since eating and drinking, acquiring clothes however shoddy and outlandish, and 'thumbing a ride' while hitch-hiking on the road, made them beneficiaries of the society they affected to despise. They did not beg in the name of God as their medieval predecessors had done, but flirted with Zen Buddhism as a refuge from Christianity.

The main nest of English beatniks was in Chelsea, London's resort of artists and multitudes of quasi-artists. There, numerous beatniks existed in high-principled squalor, perhaps only half-heartedly adopting the anti-respectable vices but wholly committed to decrepitude of person and dress. Youths and girls alike wore shoddy 'jeans' and baggy sweaters, making the sexes often indistinguishable[2] and encouraging the suspicion that shoddy garments are the index of shoddy minds. The ghost of Thomas Carlyle revisiting the streets of Chelsea could hardly have refrained from thundering in other-world Scots against the pervasion of shuffling bi-sexual 'forked radishes'.

The beatnik cult and other vagaries of nonconforming adolescents found defenders among reputable psychologists and devoted welfare workers who were disposed to attribute the rapid and statistically verified increase of crime among the young to environmental causes, though the non-professional public was less inclined to be complacent. Men in responsible posts were apt to express views

[1] Dharma bums = (approximately) spiritual tramps.

[2] 'The woman shall not wear that which pertaineth unto a man, . . . for all that do so are abomination unto the Lord.' (Deuteronomy 22:5.)

which condoned or even encouraged adolescent sexual experimentation on the ground that physical maturity now long precedes the economic security desirable as a basis for marriage. The rise in the illegitimate birthrate demonstrated the prevalence of pre-marital intercourse, and the further condonation of sexual irresponsibility seemed as ill-advised as commending intoxicants to infants. Neither from the ethical nor from the social angle could it be considered a gain that chastity became a by-word and to be chaste a matter for scorn and reproach in schools and colleges. Shakespeare had a phrase for it: 'The expense of spirit in a waste of shame is lust in action' (Sonnet 129). The current reaction against self-control can only be judged by its consequences.

A characteristic of the period was the prevalence of contempt for authority, shown (among other ways) in what can only be called bastard satire. Satire is perhaps the most valuable and potent social and political corrective, and as such it demands intelligence and understanding of what is satirized. Most of what was proffered as satire in the 1950s and after – on television, in places of entertainment, and in periodicals – did not rise above witless insolence, an infallible recipe for popularity with the many who delight in ridicule and derision. It is not so much that eminent men and women are traduced by 'the irresponsible malignancy of the contemporary satire industry'[1] as that a high and exacting literary art is cheapened and degraded. Satire is not a commodity to be delivered with a guffaw and a smirk by weekly instalments.

As the Victorian Age recedes in time and is seen in truer perspective, its so-called hypocrisies can be more fairly judged as commendable reticence and modesty, in favourable contrast with the later assumption that civilized manners and customs, virtues and restraints, are arbitrarily imposed by 'They', not the outcome of age-long traditional wisdom and social necessity. In the second half of the twentieth century many preferred to live their private lives in public, while the personality cult developed by television and other media created a passion for exhibitionism, not least among writers, scholars, and politicians. Literature and scholarship are not well

[1] *The Times Literary Supplement*, 26 July 1963, p. 536.

served when transacted under the public eye. The handicap imposed on writers hustled into premature brief fame by the importunities of journalistic reputation-makers is beyond estimation. In no previous generation had it been so easy to gain a reputation, or so easy to lose it.

CHAPTER II

NOVELISTS

1. H. G. WELLS

Without the Marshalsea prison and the blacking factory there would have been no Dickens. Without the underground kitchen, the broken boots, and 'the valley of the shadow of education', there would have been no H. G. Wells. There is little evidence in the history of literature to support the view current at the middle of the century that genius needs to be shielded from adverse circumstances. Lack of privilege and the experience of some measure of frustration have often served as a challenge to which determination and achievement have been the productive – and often a world-benefiting response. It might indeed be wondered whether the slackening of creative force in the literature of the mid-century could not be attributed to a general easing of economic conditions and to the tendency to coddle young writers whom literary agents and publishers hope to incubate as profitable investments.

Such questionings arise almost naturally from the case of H. G. Wells who, beginning with the barest minimum of social and educational capital, became in the eyes of the world one of the most impressive novelists and publicists of his generation.

Herbert George Wells (1866–1946) was the son of a professional cricketer in the Kent county team, who kept a small shop at Bromley in Kent, where H.G. was born. His mother, daughter of an innkeeper, served as a lady's maid and afterwards as housekeeper in a country mansion, Up Park, near Petersfield in Hampshire. The house, now a National Trust property, is still recognizable as Bladesover in the early chapters of *Tono-Bungay* which depict something of the life of servants of the upper classes in the days before the great houses of England dwindled, on their way to ultimate extinction.

H. G. Wells spent his childhood in a period when basement-rooms were a feature of suburban domestic architecture in England, and in a glimpse of his early life he is seen as a dweller in the underground:

> A very considerable part of my childhood was spent in an underground kitchen: the window opened upon a bricked-in space, surmounted by a grating before my father's shop window. So that, when I looked out of the window, instead of seeing – as children of a higher upbringing would do – the heads and bodies of people, I saw their underside. I got acquainted indeed with all sorts of social types as boots simply, indeed, as the soles of boots: and only subsequently and with care, have I fitted heads, bodies, and legs to these pediments.[1]

In the further course of this essay – which develops into a formidable socialist tract – the child H. G. Wells is shown suffering many of the disabilities that befall the family of a small tradesman whose business is drifting into bankruptcy. The author tells of sore feet due to over-darned socks; of the knots of broken laces; of over-trodden heels; of split and flapping soles. From this description of the state of young Wells's boots, it was safe to infer without other evidence that the rest of his circumstances were in similar disrepair. The English working-class parent at that time had a profound regard for the social implications of good boots, less general then than now, and broken footwear customarily followed and did not precede outworn clothing and inadequate food.

Mental clothing, however, is more important than a well-preserved suit, and the misery of boots was not the final blow. In the first chapter of *The History of Mr Polly* (1910), Polly suffers under the type of muddled and mind-deadening schooling that was the common lot of young people of Wells's class in the early days of State education. When Wells emerged at fourteen from what he calls 'the valley of the shadow of education', there followed the purgatory of 'the drapery'. He was apprenticed to a draper in Windsor and, later, to another in Southsea. From recollections of those years came several of Wells's best novels. When current problems of sociology, of international relationships and of religion

[1] *This Misery of Boots*, a Fabian Society tract (1905). Reprinted in *A Miscellany of Tracts and Pamphlets* (The World's Classics series), edited by A. C. Ward.

(discussed at length in Wells's later books) have become insignificant in the face of newer problems, there will remain the joyous misadventures of Mr Kipps, of Mr Polly, and of Mr Hoopdriver.[1] The 'little man' – later to be presented as the farcical hero of popular strip-cartoons in the national newspapers, and later still to multiply and degenerate into the mass-man – came amusingly, pathetically, and affectionately understood, into English fiction in these stories.

At sixteen, when Wells had sufficiently augmented his early schooling to obtain a teacher's post at Midhurst Grammar School, he broke his indentures and fled from the drapery for ever. In building up a composite picture of him as a young man, some characteristics of the hero of *Love and Mr Lewisham* (1900) are not without interest. Mr Lewisham is eighteen, an assistant schoolmaster in Sussex earning forty pounds a year, and 'called "Mr" to distinguish him from the bigger boys'.

> He wore ready-made clothes, his black jacket of rigid line was dusted about the front and sleeves with scholastic chalk, and his face was downy and his moustache incipient. He was a passable-looking youngster of eighteen, fair-haired, indifferently barbered, and with a quite unnecessary pair of glasses on his fairly prominent nose – he wore these to make himself look older, that discipline might be maintained.

Mr Lewisham was an ambitious young man. On his bedroom wall hung a time-table mapping out his intended progress through life, and among his aims was a London University degree with 'hons. in all subjects'. His creator did less well. After qualifying for a scholarship at the Normal School of Science (later the Imperial College of Science and Technology), South Kensington, Wells graduated as B.Sc. with first-class honours in zoology, and subsequently went as assistant-master to Henley House School, St John's Wood, in north-west London. There followed experience as tutor, lecturer, and demonstrator – with incursions into journalism – preceding a serious illness which ended his teaching career. In 1893 he turned wholly to journalism and authorship, and two years later published his first novel, *The Time Machine*, a strikingly original book, marked by unique inventive ability, prophetic vision, and a

[1] In *The Wheels of Chance* (1896).

command of clear and vigorous English. It was also a precursor of 'science fiction', which did not become an established genre until some half-century later.

In the following forty years Wells wrote scores of books. The list includes treatises on love and marriage, science and religion, peace and war; sociology, biology, politics; angels and mermaids, astronomy and world-history; the old world and new worlds to come; and even children's games. It is purposeless to lament Wells's prodigal dispersion of energy, though creative literature was certainly better served by the early imaginative Wells than by his later political self. *The History of Mr Polly* may still be read with pleasure and profit while *The World of William Clissold* (1926) and its successors have become hardly more than an anchorage for library cobwebs. Nevertheless, an annual duplication of Kipps or Polly would not have made Wells the significant figure that he was in early twentieth-century England. His eager, restless, inquiring mind unsettled him for orthodox fiction as the years went on. Though there is as much sound social criticism in the dyspepsia of Alfred Polly as in the diatribes of Clissold, the change in Wells's literary manner after 1910 was not wholly due to a decay of creative power. The change was at least in the first place a deliberate departure from methods that had previously satisfied him; a definite undertaking of the rigours of a crusade. Though the word 'commitment' did not become a cliché in Wells's lifetime, he was in the fullest sense a 'committed' writer, but not a narrowly partisan one.

Wells's manifesto of change (in his essay on 'The Contemporary Novel')[1] made plain his intention to abandon the 'Weary Giant theory' which posited that the novel was only a means of relaxation, a harmless opiate for vacant hours and vacant minds. He also dissented from the theory that the novel has an established form, in the sense in which a sonnet has form. The main principles laid down in this manifesto of the New Fiction were: (*a*) That the novel is in essence discursive, a tapestry of multifarious interests; (*b*) That it should be sufficiently elastic in form to take all life within its compass – 'business and finance and politics and precedence and pre-

[1] First printed in *The Fortnightly Review* (Nov. 1911); afterwards included in *An Englishman Looks at the World* (1914).

tentiousness and decorum and undecorum, until a thousand pretences and ten thousand impostures shrivel in the cold, clear air of our elucidations'; (*c*) That it should be, not a new sort of pulpit, but 'the home confessional, the initiator of knowledge, the seed of fruitful self-questioning', the great central platform for discussion and for the examination of human conduct.

What the nineteenth century thought about the novel is irrelevant. The kind of writing preferred by Wells after 1911 is not, indeed, 'THE NOVEL'; but it was *his* Idea of the Novel – and he claimed as the master of this discursive school Laurence Sterne, 'the subtlest and greatest *artist*,' he wrote, 'that Great Britain has ever produced in all that is essentially the novel'. It was a misfortune that in his pursuit of discursiveness Wells lost sight of artistry.

The essay on 'The Contemporary Novel' is illuminating for its indications of the change of outlook between the Victorians and the generation to which the younger Wells belonged. He instanced the passing away of the old 'feeling of certitude about moral values and standards of conduct', the old conviction that 'your sect, whichever sect you belonged to, knew the whole of truth and included all the nice people'. In place of these certitudes and convictions had come, he thought, 'a penetrating and pervading element of doubt and curiosity and charity', an assertion of initiative against organization, of freedom against discipline. Wells himself was to live on into a time when political certitude swept back with renewed and brutal energy, when partisan discipline became an article of faith, and freedom seemed a vanishing dream. His view of the future outlook for mankind (as expressed in, e.g., *The Fate of Homo Sapiens*, 1939) became empty of hope if the human race did not fundamentally change its ideals and habits.

Before any definite formulation of literary principles dominated H. G. Wells, he had for some years been reaching out towards a new method. His fiction (apart from short stories) may be divided into (*i*) *fantastic and imaginative romances*; (*ii*) *novels of character and humour*; (*iii*) *discussion novels*. Group (*i*) belongs mainly to the period between 1895 and 1908, and at that time it was usual to liken these imaginative romances to the stories of Jules Verne, though there is in fact little resemblance. Whereas fantastic adventurousness counted for everything in Jules Verne, in Wells it was not much more than a peg on which to hang speculation and social inquiry. He endeavoured, as it were, to step away from life and look at it from a distance which made possible a clear and proportionate view in perspective. He seemed to suggest in these books that we – being inside ourselves and all too close to our neighbours - are no more able to see the effect of life's whole picture than if we were to stand with our eyes only half an inch away from the surface of an Impressionist painting; and that the first step towards the cure of social muddles and disabilities is to see civilization in the mass and not in disjointed fragments. Equipped with an alert and rich imagination, he strove to see life from an appropriate distance. So, in the fantastic romances, he established his viewpoint (by turns) in the moon, in the past, in the future, in the air; he looked at life through the eyes of a mermaid, of an angel, of giants, of creatures from outer space: by these and similar devices labouring to prevail against common human limitations, and to see mankind and its works clearly in the round. *The Wonderful Visit* (1895) amounts to a comprehensive examination, through the lips of the wounded angel, of orthodox habits and observances so familiar to us as to seem beyond question—yet so fantastic to a citizen of heaven as to suggest incredible human madness. The angel demands to know the why and the wherefore of things as they are; but his host, the Vicar of Siddermorton, finds that there is no discoverable why or wherefore; that he and his people are obeying customs and conventions without reason, even without consciousness.

The process of asking *Why?* – and, in other connexions, *Why not?* – was the first step in Wells's crusade against 'emphatic, cocksure, and unteachable' people; and the fantastic romances form an integral part of the whole body of his work through their challenging spirit of inquiry and criticism. Though they did in some sense lay the foundations of 'science fiction', they did not aim at the sensationalism in which such fiction became saturated in the early years of 'the atomic age', i.e. from *c.* 1945. The atomic age was in a measure foreshadowed in Wells's *The World Set Free* (1914).

The second group – *novels of character and humour* – overlaps groups (*i*) and (*iii*) in point of time, and includes books which would of themselves have sufficed to make Wells notable in English literature. Polly, at least, is a memorable comic character who is also the embodiment of those bewildered and exasperated souls thrown up by modern civilization and stranded on the beach of life, though he belongs to a generation in which it had not yet become common form for social misfits to turn into political malcontents. He is an almost tragic civilization-crippled and frustrated genius; yet his pathetic and his tragic qualities merge into and increase his comic stature.

In 'The Contemporary Novel' Wells said: 'I find all the novels of Dickens, long as they are, too short for me'; and in a later passage commending Bumble, he adds, 'but it is not only caricature and satire I demand'. These references raise questions in regard to the methods of Wells and Dickens as social reformers. The effectiveness of Dickens lay in making iniquitous officialdom appear not only wicked but also ridiculous—and the conviction that they are ridiculous reforms wrongdoers more effectually than the conviction that they are wicked. Not only were caricature and satire Dickens's customary weapons, they were also the most powerful weapons he could possibly have chosen.

Under the laughter of Polly and Kipps there is the set face of Wells the reformer. In its own way, the humorous picture of Polly's education is as unforgettable as the Dotheboys Hall episodes; and the system indicted appears as unforgiveable. When he wrote *Joan and Peter* (1918), eight years after *The History of Mr Polly*, Wells questioned the English educational system more elaborately but less impressively. Throwing aside humour and satire, he became merely bad-tempered – though bad temper is ineffective equipment for a reformer. Oswald Sydenham (like Philip Rylands in *Meanwhile*, 1927) travels about England in a state of peevish indignation, producing his Catechism for Schoolmasters with an air that would exasperate any schoolmaster, and this tendency towards peevishness is the bane of several of Wells's novels from *Joan and Peter* onwards. When he laughed at abuses he was a second Dickens; when he grew fretful he became a second-rate edition of himself. He was perhaps the first of the host of propagandist writers who, particularly in the nineteen-thirties, endeavoured to hector rather than to persuade and convince.

The group of *discussion novels* began after *Tono-Bungay* (1909), which is the central point at which Wells's competing interests met and united. *Tono-Bungay* stands beside Galsworthy's *The Forsyte Saga* as a diagnosis (though from another angle) of the break-up of English society which began almost unnoticed in the later part of the nineteenth century. In these novels the authors surveyed the disintegration of the old-time strongholds of tradition and privilege – Galsworthy with a glance of regret; Wells with a glance of half-doubtful satisfaction – interrogative still; asking, by implication: 'Is Lichtenstein better than Lord Drew?' *Tono-Bungay*, a sprawling and shapeless narrative ('an agglomeration . . . without discipline', as the narrator confesses), stands with the later novels as an exercise in the discursive method, but its social diagnosis is inseparable from the engaging characters and the swift-moving story. The book is a forceful presentation of a significant historical spectacle: the outgoing of the aristocracy – 'the Quality' – and their replacement by moneyed charlatans and adventurers. 'The last sad squires ride slowly towards the sea' – and what comes? England's insufficiency in this process of social replacement is the substance of Wells's charge, and *Tono-Bungay* is itself a portent of 'the silent revolution' which was to invert the social order by the time the book was half a century old. Its merit as literature lies in the skill with which the characters themselves state and illustrate the social theme; the author is veiled in their personalities, and does not himself lecture as from a platform. Aunt Susan, 'round-eyed, button-nosed, pink-and-white Aunt Susan', with a faint ghost of a lisp and a nonsensically derisive attitude towards the world in general, is a fine piece of humorous portraiture; she is intensely real and likeable in her bewilderment as she bobbles from comparative poverty into affluence on a sea of patent medicine.

The theories set out in 'The Contemporary Novel' explain Wells's intention and achievement in most of his novels after 1911. Each successive volume marked a phase in his long inquiry concerning the aims and ideals of civilized man engaged in the Human Adventure. Everything that man does was, to Wells, a subject for ceaseless interrogation. He looked upon the civilization of his period as a system 'perpetually swaying and quivering and bending and sagging'. Would the whole vast accidental edifice come smashing down? 'Why shouldn't it?' he asked in 1909. By 1925 (after the First World War and the failure of the inter-wars reconstruction) he was occupied with the idea of mankind's progress towards the One World-State, which he then regarded as the next stage on the road of human development. Towards that One World-State he was urging men to work, saying:

> 'There was a time when men lived for a noble tomb and in order to leave sweet and great memories behind them: soon it will matter nothing to a man and his work to know that he will probably die in a ditch – misunderstood. So long as he gets the work done.'
>
> 'With no last judgement ever to vindicate him,' said Devizes.
>
> 'That will not matter in the least to him.'
>
> 'I agree. Some of us begin to feel like that even now.'[1]

It was a long pilgrimage from the little shop in Bromley Kent, to the One World-State; but the pilgrimage was continuous. Without the knowledge of what children in underground kitchens suffered from 'this misery of boots' the vision of the One World-State might have seemed less urgent. It was a vision too wide and comprehensive for the majority – an abstraction so vast as to be meaningless even to millions who shared Wells's desire to rid the world of miseries and hatreds and jealousies and wars. But if, in 1925, Mr Polly was closer to men's hearts than was the One World-State, the fault, if fault it was, may have been less that of H. G. Wells than of mankind in general, which then found it possible to love the least of its fellow-creatures more readily than it could love even the noblest of political ideas. In the nineteen-thirties, however, creeds loomed larger than men. Internationalism, of which Wells was a tireless advocate, was regarded by fanatical leaders of self-glorifying nations as a criminal heresy, not as a noble ideal. Amid this backward rush towards barbarism, the fervour and industry of Wells as a prophet never relaxed. Much of his work was merely ephemeral, journalism for a day. With *The Outline of History* (1920)

[1] *Christina Alberta's Father* (1925), Book III, Ch. IV, § 5.

he started a vogue for sweeping surveys of man's past and achievements; *The Work, Wealth, and Happiness of Mankind* (1932) and *The Shape of Things to Come* (1933) again showed his interest in perspectives. But he offered in these bulky works more than the popular mind could digest. His literary style gave no assistance, for he had lost his early verbal economy and now usually preferred to employ ten words to do the work of one.

In the middle part of his life Wells was in step with the general reforming trend of the age and was in an important degree a shaper of the minds of the growing generation. It is impossible, however, to determine the extent to which he impressed the age and the age impressed him: the two were closely interdependent until disillusion settled upon Wells and soured him almost to dementia in his last decade. He tragically outlived himself, coming in his final books – e.g. *The Outlook for Homo Sapiens* (1942) and *Mind at the End of Its Tether* (1945) – to a febrile despair. The lack of spiritual resilience thus displayed was not only a measure of his overstrained expectations of humanity but was also an exposure of the weak foundations of his own system of thought. Philosophically considered, he was no thinker: he was an imaginative artist gone astray. His great gifts of fantasy and humour enriched literature, but when in relation to practical politics his fantasies seemed a mirage, humour deserted him and he was left embittered and spiritually bankrupt. Nevertheless, the unrealized vision was not totally dissipated by his death. Though an age of fear swept the world under the threat of nuclear destruction, that fear bred the recognition that world-government must of necessity displace warring national governments. In the ultimately inevitable One World-State H. G. Wells will be vindicated and lastingly memorialized.

2. ARNOLD BENNETT

There is a class of novelists, rarer in England than in France, to whom the first principle in literary creation is that this world is nothing but a spectacle which it is the novelist's task to record with complete detachment – looking on, but making no sound of either approval or protest. It had never been H. G. Wells's purpose to report human affairs dispassionately. He ranks as an active and impassioned participant and protestant, not an observer merely. He was 'involved' in the dilemmas and problems of the contemporary community. Arnold Bennett's purpose was, as an artist, to stand aside. His masters in the early stages of his development were the French novelists Maupassant, Flaubert, and Balzac, and his aim was to record life – its delights, indignities, and distresses – without conscious intrusion of his own personality between the record and the reader. Like his French masters, he was a copyist of life, and only indirectly (if at all) a commentator, an interpreter, or an apologist.

The moral sense – and more especially the emotional sense – of the Victorian English novelists would have led them to shrink from the idea of 'detachment'. They would not have understood (nor thought it proper to attempt to understand) a writer who regarded a wife-beater and a nursing mother as equally interesting. But the wife-beater and the nursing mother are both part of the human spectacle; therefore, in a detached and dispassionate rendering of life in the novel, account has to be taken of both. A cinematograph camera does not register indignation over the wife-beater nor become lyrical over the nursing mother: it records both without passion or prejudice. The resulting pictures are a faithful representation of two aspects of life, and audiences are at liberty to adopt whatever attitude they choose; to find, it may be, the one distressing and the other ennobling. But with the distress as with the ennoblement the camera is unconcerned.

The purpose of the 'naturalistic' novelist, so-called, is to be as dispassionate and detached as a camera. It is often said that ugliness results from this method, though to a completely naturalistic novelist (if such a one could ever exist), there can be no ugliness as such – but only varying manifestations of life[1] to be recorded as they are seen. No 'naturalistic' novelist can record the whole of life; nor the whole of any one life; nor the whole, even, of any one extended period of

[1] 'Possibly no works have been more abused for ugliness than Huysmans',' which 'reproduced with exasperation what is generally regarded as the sordid ugliness of commonplace daily life. Yet . . . it is inconceivable that Huysmans . . . was not ravished by the secret beauty of his subjects and did not exult in it.' Arnold Bennett, *The Author's Craft* (1914), Part 2, II.

any one life. He is compelled himself to determine the nature of his picture of life, because (unable to include everything) he must select certain things as relevant and significant, rejecting others as irrelevant and without significance. And it is in the process of selection and rejection that naturalism breaks down. The naturalism of real life depends in part upon the empty interspaces between life's 'significant' periods. Neither the novelist nor the dramatist can afford to indicate these empty interspaces, since tedium is the essential characteristic of such periods in human experience, and tedium is fatal to art. The few instances on record where a complete and positive naturalism has been attempted have resulted in overwhelming dullness;[1] while, in other instances, novelists so feared to distort their picture by making life seem too pleasant that they tended to eliminate too much joy and too little misery.

Arnold Bennett's method was frequently described as naturalistic, though it was only partially so. It is true that in his outlook upon the world he was not obsessed by life's injustices; nor was he a tormented soul driven to attempt to build a new world or to evolve a new race of creatures to inhabit it. He was, apparently, a detached figure; but his detachment was not that of an 'unconcerned spectator' of life. He was merely detached, as an artist, from the habit of protest and the passion for utilizing creative literature as an instrument of moral and social reform.

Though he repudiated the naturalistic convention,[2] he nevertheless followed it in part. Another writer might be content to remark, 'Rachel lit the gas', but Arnold Bennett describes the simple act in minute detail in a passage five hundred words long.[3] While he was, intellectually, well qualified for the naturalistic method, temperamentally he was incapable of sustaining it. Life was not, for him, a spectacle merely. He became easily and delightedly conscious of it as a *wonderful* spectacle, a *thrilling* spectacle, a *fascinating* spectacle, an *awesome* spectacle. Trifles became charged with a tremendous, an apocalyptic, significance. Two boys spitting over a canal bridge on the day that one of them leaves school for the last time are made

[1] Cf. comments on James Joyce and Dorothy Richardson: below, pp. 67 ff.

[2] 'The notion that "naturalists" have at last lighted on a final formula which ensures truth to life is ridiculous.' *The Author's Craft*, Part 2, IV.

[3] *The Price of Love* (1914), Ch. I, i.

symbolic of the battle of youth against 'the leagued universe'.[1] Sophia Baines refuses to take a dose of castor oil ordered by her mother: 'It was an historic moment in the family life. Mrs Baines thought the last day had come. But still she held herself in dignity while the apocalypse roared in her ears.'[2] A girl holds out a lighted spill: 'The gesture with which she modestly offered the spill was angelic; it was divine; it was one of those phenomena which persist in a man's memory for decades. At the very instant of its happening he knew that he should never forget it.'[3] A slatternly servant-girl in the rain with an apron of sacking protecting her head, is presented as idealistically as if she were a celestial visitor wearing a bridal veil.[4] But, lest such passages as these should stamp him too definitely as the romantic he was by temperament, Arnold Bennett 'naturalized' his novels by a disproportionate attention to disease and physical decay. In a final analysis, however, it is not life as a drab and depressing spectacle, nor as a balanced spectacle of good and ill together, that is the dominant vision in his best books. It is, rather, life as a spectacle in which almost every sensation and every phenomenon is interpreted romantically: 'sweet, exquisite, blissful melancholy':[5] 'The incandescent gas-burner of the street-lamp outside had been turned down, as it was turned down every night! If it is possible to love such a phenomenon, she loved that phenomenon. That phenomenon was a portion of her life, dear to her.'[6]

Arnold Bennett's insistence upon the wonderment of life is partly the over-stressing of an obvious truth, supported by detail that is often irrelevant (and still more often inadequate to prove his case if it were in need of proof); and, partly, it is a relic of his provincialism. He strove with much success to become the sophisticated man of the world who knows all the ins-and-outs of life, and to reach that degree of knowingness when each sly dig and wink is comprehended. Yet he never became altogether urbanized, nor ceased to be one of literature's country cousins – a man to whom all things were astounding. Life never lost its glamour for him. He could not regret the passing of the glory and the grandeur of Greece and Rome,

[1] *Clayhanger*, Book I, Ch. I.
[2] *The Old Wives' Tale*, Book I, Ch. III.
[3] *The Price of Love*, Ch. IV, iii.
[4] *Riceyman Steps*, Part I, vii.
[5] *The Old Wives' Tale*, Book III, Ch. I, ii.
[6] Op. cit., Book IV, Ch. I, iv.

for he found recompense in the everyday life of the Five Towns, his native district, upon which he conferred an almost legendary impressiveness. Next to Hardy's Wessex, Bennett's Five Towns was the most notable addition to the atlas of topographical fiction since the Bröntes' Yorkshire and Trollope's Barsetshire.

Born at Shelton on the outskirts of Hanley, Staffordshire, in 1867, Enoch Arnold Bennett as a child lived behind a draper's shop ('Baines', in his novels). Educated at local schools, he matriculated at London University, and was a London solicitor's clerk at the age of twenty-one. Next, after receiving twenty guineas for a humorous story in *Tit-Bits*, he turned to free-lance journalism, contributed short stories to evening papers and to literary quarterlies, and became assistant-editor (afterwards editor) of *Woman*, for which he wrote 'smart society' paragraphs under the name 'Gwendolen'. In various ways, that paper enabled him to get the insight into the 'secret nature of women' which he afterwards turned to account in his novels. From 1900 Arnold Bennett lived in France for nearly eight years, steeping himself in French literature. He died in London in 1931. His naïve enjoyment of society and good living were misinterpreted by those who thought him smug and bloated with success.

He was in truth an abundant and generous creature who held out both hands to life. The best impression of his character is to be obtained from the posthumously published *Journals of Arnold Bennett* (1932–3).

His books were many and their quality unequal. Three novels, *The Old Wives' Tale* (1908), *Clayhanger* (1910),[1] and *Riceyman Steps* (1923), place him high among English novelists; *Buried Alive* (1908) and *The Card* (1911) are first-rate humorous character-novels; *The Grand Babylon Hotel* (1902) an entertaining and well-written extravaganza. His reputation was made and maintained by the first three books named above, but *Buried Alive* (later turned into a successful play, *The Great Adventure*) is a little masterpice that deserves more attention than it has received.

The Five Towns of Arnold Bennett's works are the Staffordshire

[1] *Clayhanger*, the first part of a trilogy, was followed by *Hilda Lessways* (1911), and completed with *These Twain* (1916); collected in one volume (1925) as *The Clayhanger Family*.

pottery towns later grouped as the federated borough of Stoke-*on*-Trent. Before 1908 there were five separate towns: Tunstall, Burslem, Hanley, Stoke-*upon*-Trent, and Longton (in Bennett's books named Turnhill, Bursley, Hanbridge, Knype, and Longshaw; while his Oldcastle is the town of Newcastle-under-Lyme). In this small area the people of *The Old Wives' Tale*, *The Clayhanger Family*, and other books spend most part of their lives. Readers become familiar not only with the principal streets and buildings and landmarks, but also with the men and women who walked the streets, inhabited the buildings, and looked admiringly upon the landmarks. The lifelike quality of Bennett's novels is contrived through the accumulation of carefully chosen detail. Some ugliness and coarseness are essential to his plan. He saw ugliness as part of the pattern of life; and the pattern of life without that element was too threadbare to interest him.

The Old Wives' Tale is a long panorama of the lives of two sisters, Constance and Sophia Baines, who – first seen in girlhood surging with hope and vigour and the fire of youth – have both died in advanced age before the end of the book, which combines humour and tragedy, pathos and indignity, beauty and ugliness. Excellent character-drawing abounds, and the trivial incidents are as compulsively interesting as the great events. Sophia and Constance did not realize, says the author on the first page, that they were living in a district pulsating with interest; and at no time were they fully awake to the tremendousness of their own sensations. Though Constance did on occasion discover wonder in her domestic affairs, Sophia, even in the turmoil of the 1870 Siege of Paris, was hardly conscious of living through strange and terrible days. But what *they* looked upon as commonplace, Arnold Bennett regarded as full of lively and romantic possibilities. To those who thought *The Old Wives' Tale* drab and prosy, he would have said: 'On the contrary, this is *life*; and life is always marvellous.'

There are few lovable characters in *The Old Wives' Tale*, but *Clayhanger* is populated by fine, friendly people. Edwin Clayhanger, the outwardly commonplace son of a Bursley printer, without loss of individuality embodies much general human experience. Most young Englishmen of a particular mentality experience the feelings which beset Edwin, who contributes largely to the convincingness of the book. In addition there are the attractive Orgreave family, fortunate in the harmony of its members, and good, solid, sensible Maggie (Edwin's sister) and the inimitable Auntie Hamps.

With the Clayhanger trilogy Arnold Bennett ended the Five Towns series. The novels which followed suggested that, in leaving his own people, he had sacrificed too much. He recovered much of his former skill, however, in *Riceyman Steps*, in which a decrepit district on the edge of the City of London is made as vivid as anything in the Five Towns sequence. *Riceyman Steps* is less substantial than Bennett's two masterpieces, and the characters are less intimately understood than the Baineses, the Clayhangers, and the Orgreaves. Yet Elsie – a slatternly servant-girl outwardly, but inwardly an angel of light – is beautifully drawn. There is also much merit in its descriptive passages, and nowhere else does Bennett succeed so well in communicating the exact atmosphere of a place as in his description of Riceyman Square 'frowsily supine in a needed Sunday indolence after the week's hard labour'.[1] Despite its drabness, the book is lit by that 'sense of beauty – indispensable to the creative artist',[2] which is the soul of Bennett's novels. He said that the foundation of the novelist's equipment is 'universal sympathy';[3] and his possession of some measure of this enabled him to see beauty almost everywhere and to transfigure commonplace people.

In *The Old Wives' Tale*, *The Clayhanger Family*, and other novels, Arnold Bennett sketches-in the historical and social background with considerable skill, and with a sounder appreciation of what is really significant than he showed elsewhere in his over-insistence upon the 'significance' of trifling objects. In *Clayhanger* the narrative is made forceful and convincing by allusions to contemporary events, allusions wide in their range, covering politics, religion, literature, and other interests.[4] Their effect is to give the story a 'livingness' that is absent from imaginative writing when the characters are

[1] *Riceyman Steps*, Part I, x. [2] *The Author's Craft*, Part I, II.
[3] Op. cit., Part II, V.
[4] The chapter (*Clayhanger*, Book I, Ch. IV) which describes Darius's experiences as a child in the grip of the factory system in early nineteenth-century industrial England, is an impressive piece of re-creation, though, being a digression, it could be considered an artistic fault.

suspended (historically) in a vacuum. Other writers have adopted this device of a panoramic background, with results not always happy.[1]

Arnold Bennett's last novel *Imperial Palace* (1930) was written to support his view that English novelists had given disproportionate attention to personal and emotional relationships and not enough to men and women in their daily work. *Imperial Palace* displays in detail the intricate organization of a vast hotel, but though the hotel is the central theme, there is also romantic human interest in the book, which is as abundant and generous and amoral as its creator.

In writing *The Author's Craft* Bennett gave emphasis to his belief that whatever aspiration a writer may have to be accepted as an artist, he must pre-eminently regard himself as a craftsman bound in honesty and honour to a steadily industrious life. While so pedestrian a concept is anathema to those who hold that Art bloweth where it listeth, it produced – from Anthony Trollope as well as from Bennett – a body of enduring work at variance with much brittle work from later hands.

3. JOHN GALSWORTHY

John Galsworthy, who came of a Devonshire family, was born at Combe in Surrey in 1867, educated at Harrow and Oxford, and called to the Bar in 1890. He practised little, but his legal knowledge is evident throughout his work, especially in *Justice* and in the court scene in *The Silver Spoon*. He travelled widely, but of this there is little sign in his books.

If no biographical facts were available about any one of the three, it could be deduced from their literary styles that Wells and Bennett were plebeians and Galsworthy, temperamentally, an aristocrat. For all his careful craftsmanship, Arnold Bennett's prose sometimes (and that of H. G. Wells frequently) shows traces of being 'puffy' and out of condition. There is some occasional fussiness

[1] The several effects of the use of this device can be seen in some of Rose Macaulay's novels, while in H. G. Wells's later books it is much more than a background—it is foreground and middle-distance as well—and he and other writers from the nineteen-thirties onward went far towards turning the novel into a journalistic running commentary on matters of the moment.

about the writing. But though it may be true that Galsworthy in his choice of subject was at times suggestive of a well-meaning but over-anxious aunt, his style has assurance and repose. His sentences are crisp, clear-cut, athletic, and free from the adiposity of a good deal of prose in his day. This is of advantage in his novels, but less so in his plays.[1] It clears his pages of what Pater called 'surplusage', and gives a sense of progression and narrative swiftness to books not especially rich in incident. Galsworthy occasionally produced passages of striking beauty, and created a curious sense of *abstract* beauty suspended in a clear, ethereal atmosphere. This effect is obtained in parts of *The Country House* (1907), *The Patrician* (1911), and *The Forsyte Saga* (1922), especially in the passage describing Old Jolyon's death.[2] Though Galsworthy's lucent prose was dismissed with contempt by less fine-drawn minds in the next generation, there can be no certainty that posterity will not applaud him rather than his detractors.

Galsworthy's purposes as a novelist were stated by himself in *The Inn of Tranquillity* (1912). 'A Novelist's Allegory' in that book introduces a figure, Cethru, whose function in the allegory is parallel to what Galsworthy thought the function of the novelist to be in the modern world. Cethru is charged by the Prince of Felicitas to go all his life up and down the dark street (Via Publica) bearing a lantern, so that wayfarers might see whither they are going and avoid danger in the darkness. The light shed by Cethru's lantern compels the citizens to act against evils previously unseen and unchecked. The man with the lantern is hated and persecuted because he disturbs the complacent. He does not himself observe the abuses he reveals to others, nor assist in quelling those abuses. He is the light-bearer, Cethru (*See-Through*) – the man whose ministry compels others to see. He is at length arraigned before the judges for disturbing 'good citizens by showing to them without provocation disagreeable sights' and endangering 'the laws by causing persons to desire to change them'. The defence of Cethru is that his lantern distorted nothing, it 'did but show that which was there, both fair and foul, no more, no less'. His advocate continues:

[1] For discussion of this point see below, p. 110.

[2] *The Forsyte Saga*, Interlude—'Indian Summer of a Forsyte'.

> Surely, reverend Judges, being just men, you would not have this lanthorn turn its light away from what is ragged and ugly because there are also fair things on which its light may fall. . . . And I would have you note, Sirs, that by this impartial discovery of the proportions of one thing to another, this lanthorn must indeed perpetually seem to cloud and sadden those things which are fair, because of the deep instincts of harmony and justice planted in the human breast.

Galsworthy's early readers were sharply divided on the question of whether he was an impartial or a biased writer. There is a parallel between Galsworthy and Cethru, between Galsworthy's novels and Cethru's lantern. Did Galsworthy write 'in cold blood, with his nerves at rest, and his brain and senses normal',[1] showing in a detached manner 'that which is there, both fair and foul, no more, no less'? Certainly he intended an impartial presentation. If he did not succeed, it was because of some personal factor he could not control. Readers might persuade themselves that they inclined towards the one side or the other 'because of the deep instincts of harmony and justice planted in the human breast', and that Galsworthy had not definitely prompted their inclination. But the *cult of the under-dog* was the ruling factor in his work, as in that of the Russian novelists by whom he was influenced. Galsworthy was an advocate who deluded himself into believing that he was a presiding judge perpetually engaged in a dispassionate summing-up. He weighed the evidence; he stated the case for each contestant; his intellect was on both sides at once; but his emotions disturbed the balance. On the one hand, a clear, cold, judicial statement; on the other, a presentation warmed and coloured by emotion. It is next to impossible to show by quotation Galsworthy's slanted championship; the evidence is submerged in the emotional current which engages sympathy for one party rather than for the other. Some idea of the working of this emotional element can be gathered from the argument between Stanley and Felix Freeland[2] about comparative conditions of life as enjoyed by the 'upper classes' and endured by the farm labourer. Felix, championing the under-dog, emphasizes that the wealthy Malloring is 'called with a cup of tea, at, say, seven o'clock, out of a

[1] *The Inn of Tranquillity*, 'The Windlestraw'.
[2] *The Freelands* (1915), Ch. VI.

nice, clean, warm bed; he gets into a bath that has been got ready for him, into clothes and boots that have been brushed for him'. Gaunt, the labourer, on the other hand, 'gets up summer and winter much earlier out of a bed that he cannot afford time or money to keep too clean or warm, in a small room that probably has not a large enough window; into clothes stiff with work, and boots stiff with clay'. The comparison is just, but Felix's statement is charged with sentiment and humanitarian feeling, whereas Stanley's contribution is a brief and stubborn defence of the system. Stanley is permitted to say far too little; Felix undertakes both prosecution and defence, with effects that destroy any superficial appearance of impartiality.

The Galsworthy world is peopled mainly by two classes – fugitives and pursuers. Love is closely related to pity, and hate was seen by Galsworthy as half-brother to fear.[1] The hunted creatures of the world, he felt, are hunted because of a blind insensate fear driving their pursuers. The hunters are therefore also to be pitied, for they are themselves hard-driven by the hag Fear, the 'black godmother' of all mankind. In 'The Black Godmother'[2] the hunted creature is a lost puppy who snapped at a farm labourer out of sheer fright when it was hungry and thirsty, and the farm labourer kicked it. Next, schoolboys stoned it. The puppy then fell in with a kindly man, but he drove it away out of fear that it might infect his own dog with disease. Later the half-maddened animal snapped at children who tried to stroke it, and was clouted on the head with a shovel by the children's father. An old stone-breaker was the next assailant:

> 'Well! you see,' the old man explained to me, 'the dog came smellin' round my stones an' it wouldn' come near an' it wouldn' go away: it was all froth and blood about the jaw, and its eyes glared green at me. I thought to meself, bein' the dog-days – I don't like the look o' you, you look funny! So I took a stone an' got it here, just on the ear; an' it fell over. And I thought to meself; "Well, you've got to finish it, or it'll go bitin' somebody, for sure!" But when I come to it with my hammer, the dog it got up – an' you know how it is when there's somethin' you've 'alf killed, and you feel sorry and yet you feel you must finish it, an' you hit at

[1] This view, at least, has been justified by subsequent world events.
[2] First collected in *The Inn of Tranquillity*; later republished in *Caravan* (1925).

it blind, you hit at it agen an' agen. The poor thing, it wriggled an' snapped, an' I was terrified it'd bite me, and some'ow it got away!'

A farmer afterwards wounded the puppy with a pitchfork because he was afraid it would bite his lambs. And in the middle of the night the wretched, hunted, harmless animal died in agony in the house of the kindly man who had at length taken it in and tended it – but too late. The little mealy-coloured mongrel was hunted to death, not by any vindictiveness of men (those who ill-used it were, at heart, kindly and protective), but by Fear, 'the black godmother of all damnable things', working through hag-ridden human beings.

Most of those who maltreated or drove off the puppy were goaded by fear to guard their own possessions. At the root of fear was the possessive instinct, an idea which led to Galsworthy's outstanding work, the sequence of novels and stories collectively named *The Forsyte Saga* beginning with *The Man of Property*. The central character, Soames Forsyte, obsessed by the lust of possession, cannot overcome his passion to acquire everything desirable within his reach. By marriage he acquired Irene Heron.[1] He over-persuaded her into marrying him, but the result was disastrous, and 'the profound, subtle aversion which he felt in his wife was a mystery to him and a source of the most terrible irritation'. But he was a 'man of property' and his wife was a property to be subjected to the exercise of full proprietary rights. Soames was at that time a selfish, acquisitive creature who could not endure beauty near him unless it was crushed and pinned in the specimen-case which was his house. Yet even here Galsworthy adduces the evidence for Soames – such as it is – through the thoughts of young Jolyon, who is less stultified by Forsyte prejudice and arrogance than most of his family. Young Jolyon meditates upon the deadlock in the Soames household:

Whence should a man like his cousin, saturated with all the prejudices and beliefs of his class, draw the insight or inspiration necessary to break up this life? It was a question of imagination, of projecting himself into the future beyond the unpleasant gossip, sneers, and tattle that followed on such separations, beyond the passing pangs that the lack of the sight of her would cause, beyond the grave disapproval of the worthy. But few men,

[1] The plight of Irene was linked in Galsworthy's mind with that of the woman he himself married. She had been the wife of his cousin.

> and especially few men of Soames's class, had imagination enough for that. A deal of mortals in this world, and not enough imagination to go round! . . . Most people would consider such a marriage as that of Soames and Irene quite fairly successful; he had money, she had beauty; it was a case for compromise. There was no reason why they should not jog along, even if they hated each other. . . . Half the marriages of the upper classes were conducted on these lines: Do not offend the susceptibilities of Society; do not offend the susceptibilities of the Church. To avoid offending these is worth the sacrifice of any private feelings. The advantages of the stable home are visible, tangible, so many pieces of property: there is no risk in the *status quo*. To break up the home is at the best a dangerous experiment, and selfish into the bargain.[1]

Such is the evidence in defence of Soames. Galsworthy delivers no judgement, but here again, in this earlier part of the *Saga*, the emotional current runs against Soames. As the long record proceeds, however, an interesting change is apparent. In the course of over twenty years in the bosom of the Forsyte family, Galsworthy's feelings mellowed in one respect and were exasperated afresh in another. For a long time Soames Forsyte the Victorian was metaphorically in the dock, with the Younger (Edwardian) Generation in the jury-box. The jury was determined to be fair and to weigh all the evidence, but it was nevertheless stern and implacable. In the second cycle of the *Saga*[2] a different figure stood in the dock: it was the Youngest Generation (the Neo-Georgian), Eton-cropped and rouged. The Edwardians were still in the jury-box, but now their faces were lined by perplexity and regret. Soames Forsyte the Victorian, grown into a benevolent old gentleman, is seen seated quietly in the well of the court. On the bench is Galsworthy, remarking sadly to the defendant, 'Young woman, in my earlier days it used to be said that your Victorian grandfather was an undesirable person. I am now being very reluctantly forced toward the conclusion that, compared with you, he was a perfect gentleman.'

But even if Galsworthy had become uneasy about the future of Fleur Forsyte, and indignant about the present of such as Marjorie Ferrar,[3] he was still able to understand and sympathize with young

[1] Book I, Part 2, Ch. X.
[2] Beginning with *The White Monkey* (1924).
[3] See *The Silver Spoon* (1926).

people of the restless early twentieth century. The mentality of that period has seldom been stated more lucidly than by Galsworthy in his analysis of Felix Freeland's young daughter, Nedda. He speaks of 'the ceaseless questioning that was always going on within her; the thirst to know why this was and that was not. . . . Why, when people wrote and talked of God, they seemed to know what He was, and she never did? Why people had to suffer; and the world be black to so many millions? Why one could not love more than one man at a time? Why – a thousand things? . . .'

The professional critics' almost total reaction against Galsworthy after his death is one of the minor curiosities of recent literary history. As has been said on an earlier page,[1] the reading public was unaffected by the critics' disfavour and it seems probable that *The Forsyte Saga* will become a classic by popular judgement. Even if its enjoyability as a narrative with an extensive sweep and an exceptionally large gallery of well-drawn characters failed to establish it, it could not be ignored as a social panorama presenting the final stages in a notable phase of English civilization – the Edwardian Age and its fading afterglow.

4. JOSEPH CONRAD

Joseph Conrad had clear advantages over his English contemporaries. Though England became his home and Englishmen his friends, he was not limited in outlook or sympathy by national or racial consciousness. Poland and England meant much to him, but his experiences on the sea and in many lands made him a man of no one country, though he retained a strong spiritual attachment to Poland, which he revisited in 1914.[2] It is almost literally true to say that Conrad was a citizen of the world. His Malays and Borneans, Swedes and Englishmen, Germans and Dutch were all, alike, children of the human family, with some superficial differences but more fundamental resemblances. H. G. Wells's endeavour to establish a world-outlook was a conscious and deliberate effort, and he did not cease to be, temperamentally, a twentieth-century Englishman. Conrad, as a writer, had no narrow allegiances from which to free

[1] See above, p. 8. [2] See his *Notes on Life and Letters* (1921).

himself: his interests were as wide as the world, and his outlook was, in that sense, universal. His Dain Maroola is no more 'foreign' than his Axel Heyst or Captain Anthony. And no *less* foreign. It would be true to say that Conrad's characters are all 'foreign', in a special sense. They move in a remote atmosphere, although actuated by the common passions of humanity. Their stature is heroic and therefore unlike the common stature. Captain MacWhirr in *Typhoon* (1903) is dull, unimaginative, a fool in the eyes of his subordinates. But his dullness and lack of imagination are the foundation of that magnificent tenacity which makes him unconquerable, a hero unawares. He is, miraculously, the immovable object withstanding the irresistible force: by temperament remote from his fellows and foreign to them; yet in his way as representative as Hamlet (though in a very different sense) of something universal in Man. This universality and this foreignness are distinguishing features of Conrad's men and women. They are universal in that Conrad's drawing of them is 'true' to certain general and basic experiences. They are 'foreign' in that he does not see them as they appear to be in the eyes of matter-of-fact neighbours, but through the diffusion lens of his own temperament.

To speak thus of the foreignness and the universality of Conrad's people is to express in another metaphor what is meant by those who refer to his 'romantic realism'. He was a realist because his creative genius, stabilized by experience, sought some central actuality as the starting-point for all his stories. He did not invent plots. He was almost incapable of such invention. His material was reality, subjected to the transmuting processes of a lively imagination. Seeds of fact planted in his mind germinated (sometimes through long periods) under the light of his imaginative temperament, until there grew the completed 'romantic-realistic' novel or tale. The change which facts underwent in transmission through Conrad's mind is evident. Describing how he first saw the original of Almayer, the chief character in his first novel, Conrad wrote:

> He was moving across a patch of burnt grass, a blurred shadowy shape with the blurred bulk of a house behind him.[1]

[1] *A Personal Record* (1912).

He wrote of another character:

> Nina fancied she could distinguish the graceful figure of the trader standing erect in the stern sheets, but in a little while all the outlines got blurred, confused, and disappeared in the folds of white vapour shrouding the middle of the river.[1]

And again in a letter concerning the first draft of *The Rescue*:

> The idea has the bluish tenuity of dry wood smoke. It is lost in the words as the smoke is lost in the air.[2]

The 'shadowy shape' of Almayer, the 'blurred outlines' of Dain Maroola the Malayan trader, and the bluish smoky tenuity of *The Rescue*, are equally typical of the romantic 'diffusing' tendency of Conrad's mind. And this softening of outlines, this modulation of the hard, glaring aspect of reality, is the essence of his romantic realism. His actualities and facts become clothed with romantic glamour and adventurous exaltation, more enduring than the excitement of romanticism of the common type because the imaginative treatment of truth is, in the long run, more satisfying than invention. Though the original fact comes to the reader with its outlines diffused, the diffusion does not pass into distortion. Conrad's aesthetic conscientiousness never relaxed after he had once determined his creed. His first two novels, *Almayer's Folly* (1895) and *An Outcast of the Islands* (1896), though vivid, powerful and original, are overpainted – the colours heavily laid on, the emotions crudely touched in. But by 1896 Conrad had become a sound self-critic. Writing to Edward Garnett, he says of *The Lagoon* (one of his earliest short stories), 'It's a tricky thing with the usual forests – rivers – stars – wind – sunrise, and so on - and lots of secondhand Conradese in it.' Yet though in the first two novels there was overmuch colour and insufficient drawing, he was even then capable of that pictorial exactitude which in so many instances gives his pages their astonishingly living quality. Much of his work is atmospheric and impressionistic, but he often paints-in detail with as much care as the seventeenth-century Dutch painters used, and without distracting

[1] *Almayer's Folly*.

[2] To Mrs Bontine, 22 Nov. 1898 (*Joseph Conrad: Life and Letters*, by G. Jean Aubry, 1927).

attention from his whole design. An example of this detail-painting is the description of Mrs Willems as she is seen by her husband:

> She trailed through life in that red dressing-gown, with its row of dirty blue bows down the front, stained and hooked on awry: a torn flounce at the bottom following her like a snake as she moved languidly about, with her hair negligently caught up, and a tangled wisp straggling untidily down her back. His gaze travelled upwards from bow to bow, noticing those that hung only by a thread, but it did not go beyond her chin. He looked at her lean throat, at the obtrusive collar-bone visible in the disarray of the upper part of her attire. He saw the thin arm and the bony hand clasping the child she carried.[1]

Whether he was describing splendour or squalor, Conrad's artistic integrity was unsleeping; the artist's delight in the process of creation governed all his work. Verloc's dismal shop,[2] Mrs Willems's disordered bedroom, glories of sunrise and sunset, the bowed form of a grief-stricken woman; upon these – as upon all his subjects, all his people, and all the incidentals of his books – he expended 'unremitting, never-discouraged care'. The last phrase comes from Conrad's original introduction to *The Nigger of the 'Narcissus'* (1897) (his 'beloved *Nigger*', he called it), an introduction that was, in fact, a declaration of method. Conrad regarded novel-writing as a definite art – 'like painting, like music' – and not only as a matter of story-telling. The 'story' element was secondary in his mind. He was aware of the paucity of events in his books, and remarked: 'As to lack of incident – well, it's life.' He maintained that the task of the worker in prose was not, primarily, to edify, console, amuse, improve, encourage, frighten, shock, or charm, but 'by the power of the written word, to make you hear, to make you feel . . . before all, to make you *see*'. The novelist has to strive for the perfect blending of form and substance, aspiring 'to the plasticity of sculpture, to the colour of painting, and to the magic suggestiveness of music', which Conrad believed might 'be brought to play for an evanescent instant over the commonplace surface of words; of the old, old words, worn thin, defaced by ages of careless use'.

To make his novels true works of art was, then, at least half of Conrad's purpose; the other half was addressed to the philosophical

[1] *An Outcast of the Islands*, I, III. [2] In *The Secret Agent*.

(almost mystical) purpose of awakening 'that feeling of unavoidable solidarity . . . which binds men to each other and all mankind to the visible world'. That unifying purpose is central in Conrad's writings, and he stressed again and again the need for fidelity in human relationships. 'Those who read me', he said, 'know my conviction that the world, the temporal world, rests on a few very simple ideas; so simple that they must be as old as the hills. It rests notably, amongst others, on the idea of Fidelity.'[1] Nothing stirred his admiration so profoundly as the keeping of faith between man and man. Who injured another (or, even, refrained from succouring another) was, in the terms of Conrad's philosophy, betraying the whole human brotherhood. The onus of judgement, of determining whether or not a fellow-creature is worthy of succour, does not rest upon us, Conrad would have said. Razumov, in *Under Western Eyes* (1911), betrays Haldin. Haldin is an assassin, and therefore (presumably) a fit subject to be handed over to justice. But under the law that governed Conrad's ideal universe the paramount fact was, in this case, that Razumov was a betrayer. His mentality is sympathetically explored with that power of intimate and subtle probing which gives to Conrad's books their intense psychological interest; but though Razumov may engage the reader's sense of pity and, possibly, arouse some degree of affectionate regard, he is a breaker of the solidarity of the human race, and, as such, must suffer as Haldin suffered before him. In 'The Secret Sharer',[2] a fugitive from justice is given refuge on the high seas by the narrator of the story, a ship's captain. The narrator acts instinctively upon the principle of Fidelity. He does not question whether the refugee is 'worthy'. He feels immediately that here is a fellow-creature bound inseparably to himself, and therefore to be protected from the Thing in pursuit – namely, man-made Justice. In this story, Conrad's idea of Fidelity is powerfully projected, not by statement but in action. The captain's sense of solidarity between himself and the 'sharer' is so acute that the two personalities become in a curious way almost unified. In his soliloquies the captain emphasizes his sense of the identity between himself and the

[1] *A Personal Record*, Preface.
[2] One of three stories in *'Twixt Land and Sea* (1912).

other, speaking of him as 'my double', 'my second self', 'part of me'; he experiences a sensation 'of being in two places at once', 'as though I had been faced by my own reflection in the depths of a sombre and immense mirror'.

The same sense of fidelity draws Captain Anthony to Flora de Barral (*Chance*, 1913) and Heyst to Lena (*Victory*, 1915); it dominates consciously or otherwise a score of characters whose creed is to keep faith. For these Conrad had an undying regard; his contempt was reserved for such as Donkin (in *The Nigger of the 'Narcissus'*), the creature who 'knows nothing of courage, of endurance, of the unexpressed faith, of the unspoken loyalty that knits together a ship's company. The independent offspring of the ignoble freedom of the slums, full of disdain and hate for the austere servitude of the sea.'

No mere accident of personal contact determined that the sea should occupy so important a place in Conrad's books. The sea and its 'austere servitude', its 'unconcerned immensity', the 'sleeping and terrible sea', the 'brotherhood of the sea', makes deeper demands upon fidelity than are made by life ashore, where men are more loosely knit together or altogether divided by indifference and diversity of interests. At sea, on the contrary, the solidarity of mankind is a primary condition for maintaining an unbroken front against the common enemy, the ocean. Conrad loved ships. He did not love the sea, though he was fascinated by it: 'Impenetrable and heartless, the sea has given nothing of itself to the suitors for its precarious favours . . . for all its fascination that has lured so many to a violent death.'[1]

The question arises: Why did the child Conrad, born in the heart of a coastless country, become possessed, even obsessed, by a passion for the sea, which (as he was afterwards to say) had 'never been friendly to man'?

Much of Joseph Conrad's life-story can be compiled in outline from his books, but as he was incapable of writing in the 'I-was-born' style, neither *A Personal Record* nor *The Mirror of the Sea* is

[1] *The Mirror of the Sea* (1906), section xxxv, which (with the preceding and following sections) gives a succinct statement of Conrad's attitude towards ships and the sea.

straightforwardly autobiographical. They are autobiography by lightning flashes.

His mother's family were Polish landowners named Bobrowski;[1] his father, Apollo Korzeniowski, was a temperamental member of an impoverished Lithuanian family. Teodor Josef Konrad Korzeniowski[2] (born in the Ukraine, southern Poland, 1857) had early memories of exile in company with his parents. Their house was a meeting-place for Polish insurrectionists, and when Russian officials discovered an impending plot the father and his wife and child were banished to Vologda in northern Russia. In consequence of hardships endured in exile, the mother died while Josef was still very young. The circumstances of his early days made him a lonely and brooding child without friends of his own age. He was driven in upon himself, and upon books 'which described countries where it was possible to breathe and act freely, to fight openly, if necessary, and to speak thoughts above a whisper'. When the father, in ill-health, was released from exile as being no longer dangerous, he and the boy settled (1869) at Cracow, where Josef attended a preparatory school.[3] As a youth labouring under many repressions, he began to 'desire to escape, cost what it might, into a freer world'. The fullest promise of freedom seemed to the boy to lie in a seafaring life, and especially in the life of a sailor in the British Merchant Service. This was the desire distinctly formulated in his mind (and maintained against the desperate opposition of his relatives): to become a sailor on an English vessel. Conrad's first sight of the sea was at Venice when he was sixteen, and in the next year (1874) he started for Marseilles, where he shipped as a member of the crew of a French vessel. In the intervals between voyages to the West Indies he spent some time in Marseilles, an important period of his life that remains obscure. Among his intimate friends was Dominique Cervoni, a middle-aged Corsican seaman, who afterwards appeared, in one guise or another, in several of Conrad's books. Cervoni was the original for Nostromo and for Captain Lingard (in *An Outcast of the Islands*, and *The Rescue*, 1920); and he appears under his own

[1] See the allusions to Mr Nicholas B. in *A Personal Record*.

[2] He took the name Joseph Conrad when naturalized in England in 1884.

[3] For reminiscences of his schooldays, see Conrad's *Notes on Life and Letters* (1921), Ch. IV, 'Poland Revisited'.

name in *The Mirror of the Sea* and *The Arrow of Gold* (1919). The last-named novel is largely autobiographical. Conrad was implicated in the Carlist conspiracy described therein, 'while in the character of Rita he drew the woman who first taught him to feel passionately'.[1] Conrad left Marseilles in April 1878 after recovering from a wound received in the duel with which his love-affair ended.[2]

His first landing in England was at Lowestoft on 18 June 1878, when he was twenty and knew only a few words of English. Six years later he obtained his Board of Trade certificate as a Master in the British Merchant Service, after voyages to Australia and the East which were to provide part of the central facts around which he afterwards built *The Nigger of the 'Narcissus'* and *Youth* (1902). The story of his first command is told in *The Shadow Line* (1927), while later experiences in Congo are outlined in *Heart of Darkness*.[3] Though at the time he had no intention of leaving the sea, what proved to be his last voyage ended on 14 January 1894 after nearly twenty years of sea life, chiefly on sailing vessels. In 1895 his first novel (*Almayer's Folly*) was published. If at first his manner of writing betrayed the foreigner, within a few years he was a master of English prose style. Yet his fame grew slowly, and when he died (August 1924) he had experienced only a few years of moderate popularity, though other writers recognized his mastery years before the public 'discovered' him on the appearance of *Chance*, one of his more difficult novels.

Conrad's usual deliberate method of indirect narration has been a cause of stumbling to some readers: 'he does not get on with the story'. This complaint is not unfounded, though it does not apply to more than half his books. When he does not 'get on with the story' it is because he had what he considered a more important task in hand: namely, to give as far as possible a clear revelation of the truth underlying the particular human problem engaging attention. So, in *Lord Jim* (1900) and elsewhere, he introduces Marlow as

[1] G. Jean Aubry, *Joseph Conrad: Life and Letters*.

[2] This was for long the accepted version, but Jocelyn Baines's biographical and critical study of Conrad (1959) offers evidence that the wound was self-inflicted in a suicide attempt, the circumstances remaining obscure.

[3] Included in the volume containing *Youth*, and other stories.

a receiver and sifter of evidence collected from several sources. Just as Browning in *The Ring and the Book* tells Pompilia's story again and again from different points of view, so Conrad introduces a number of characters for the purpose of considering the problem from their differing angles. Though the progress of the narrative may be slow, the final gain is considerable. At the close of *Lord Jim* many dark places in human personality have been explored and lighted up in a way that makes Jim's 'acute consciousness of lost honour' tremendously impressive. Jim deserted his ship, thus violating 'the solidarity of the craft' and offending against the immitigable law of Fidelity – an offence for which expiation had to be made. At the time of his desertion of an apparently sinking vessel he was young and untried; in essence a man of honour, but with a fatal tendency towards momentary panic. For the rest of his life he had the relentless ghost of lost honour ever pursuing him, and nothing could appease that spectre except the vow, 'I shall be faithful . . . I shall be faithful', which brought him after a dishonoured life to a brave and honourable death. Jim is an important figure in the Conrad universe since he is in himself so attractive that the temptation to make him more sympathetic than tragic must have been strong. But Conrad's moral integrity and artistic sincerity were always proof against the bribe of sentiment.

The high general level of Conrad's novels is remarkable. He wrote nothing that could without loss be dropped from the canon of his work, and he is one of the very few novelists of the century whose achievement does not appear smaller as time passes.

5. TRADITION AND EXPERIMENT

For nearly a century and a half – from Fielding to the last of the great Victorians – the English novel swept along on a tide of creative energy which reached full power in Dickens's careless vitality and exuberance. Dickens neglected form and style because his need for utterance was so urgent. Later novelists, George Meredith and Henry James among them, had less to say and could give time to saying it more elaborately; and when, after 1914, creative energy became still less abundant, disproportionate attention began to be given to theories of fiction.

But other phases of the twentieth-century novel intervened.

Round about 1910–12, when Wells, Bennett, Galsworthy, and Conrad were maintaining the prestige of the traditional type of English novel, a group of young writers began to produce able and promising work. After writing a warmly praised eighteenth-century story, *The Passionate Elopement* (1911), Compton Mackenzie turned to studies of contemporary young people. *Carnival* (1912), a novel of theatrical life, was followed by the two volumes of *Sinister Street* (1913, 1914), which set a fashion for long and detailed books dealing with childhood, adolescence, and undergraduate experience. This Oxford novel came to be for a time almost a charter of emancipated youth, and it retains a place amid the fiction of the period because it expresses so well the sensations of those who were young in the years immediately before the war of 1914–18, the springtime of the Rupert Brooke generation. Though Compton Mackenzie did not shirk ugliness, his prose style coloured the tale with a hazy golden light. In *Guy and Pauline* (1915) he wrote an idyllic love story, full of lyrical warmth and sunshine. By that time the war-storm had burst, and the young novelists soon seemed much less important than they had done two years earlier. The war ended, and though most of these writers survived, their reputations never fully recovered. Compton Mackenzie attained wide popularity, producing a long succession of readable novels, as well as volumes of memories of his war-time experiences as an Intelligence officer in the Aegean zone. In after years his most ambitious work was *The Four Winds of Love*, a novel in six volumes (1937–45), but it attracted less attention than the humorous novels, such as *The Monarch of the Glen* (1941) and *Whisky Galore* (1947) – suggested by the wreck of a ship with a cargo of liquor off the isle of Eriskay – in which he ventured to laugh loudly at foibles of his fellow-Scotsmen. He was knighted in 1952.

J. D. Beresford and Frank Swinnerton became established novelists after 1918, though none of their later works attracted as much critical attention as had been given to the former's *The House in Demetrius Road* (1914) and Swinnerton's short novel on the experiences of a few hours in the life of a group of Londoners, *Nocturne* (1917). Frank Swinnerton afterwards wrote a comprehensive survey of the writers of his generation, *The Georgian Literary Scene* (1935), and an autobiography, *Swinnerton* (1937).

Of all the novelists regarded as promising young men round about 1912, Hugh Walpole achieved the most solid success (he was knighted in 1937). As he matured, his competence as a producer of fiction was put monumentally beyond doubt. *The Herries Chronicle* (one-volume edition 1939), composed of four previously published long novels – *Rogue Herries, Judith Paris, The Fortress, Vanessa* – follows the experiences of members of the Herries family from the eighteenth century down to modern times. Its beginning as a robust narrative of the historical type set in the Lake District of north-western England gave a considerable impetus to the story at the outset, but was insufficient to sustain the book through its enormous length. The relative smallness (beside *The Herries Chronicle*) of Hugh Walpole's *Mr Perrin and Mr Traill* (1911) does not prevent its being a more significant and impressive achievement – one of the author's best books – dating from days before he became a figure in the contemporary social scene and before he was spoken of, with little discretion, in the same breath as Trollope and Scott. Yet, except for a few stories with a sadistic trend, Walpole as a novelist kept to the traditional path, though the break-up of smooth tradition, and dissatisfaction with competence alone in fiction, had begun as early as 1913 in the second half of D. H. Lawrence's *Sons and Lovers*. A deeper and never-satisfied need in Walpole's character kept him from coming to terms with the wealth and popularity earned by his too facile pen. He strove with a naïvely pathetic desperation to be an important novelist, but succeeded in being only a competent and popular one. His attractive and generous disposition was enfeebled by an under-developed personality, and his longing to ingratiate himself with the intellectualists confused his mental sense of direction.

Francis Brett Young (1884–1954), a beginner about 1914, served as a medical officer attached to the Rhodesia regiment campaigning in East Africa during 1914–18 and that experience produced an account of his doings, *Marching on Tanga* (1917), and provided the setting for a novel of character, atmosphere, and adventure, *The Crescent Moon* (1918). As that novel indirectly suggested, Brett Young's native place was Worcestershire, the locality he chose for several novels. *Portrait of Clare* (1927) and *My Brother Jonathan* (1928) are representative examples of the solid and honest English novels of his second period; but there followed the more immediately attractive books in which the history of modern South Africa was assimilated to the purposes of fiction, successfully blending story and fact: e.g. *They Seek a Country* (1937), *The City of Gold* (1939).

In the early years of the century, writers of historical novels were still mainly concerned with the sword-and-cloak and fancy-costume type of narrative (see the work of Stanley Weyman, Henry Seton Merriman, Maurice Hewlett, and Marjorie Bowen; the last-named also wrote as 'George Preedy'), but different standards were set by Naomi Mitchison and Robert Graves. Both dealt at first with remote times – the former with Greeks and Barbarians, the latter with Roman times in *I Claudius* and *Claudius the God.* Using a documentary convention and avoiding 'literary' airs and graces, Robert Graves produced in these novels two of the most original books of his generation. Claudius, physically hideous, is made to tell his own story, with very subtle effect, against the background of splendour and horror, of majesty and misery and murder, in Imperial Rome. The sustained greyness of much of *I Claudius* (1934) increases the vividness of the lurid passages, which are charged with a mounting terror, up to the last fantastic scene where Claudius, after the murder of Caligula, is thrust into the imperial seat by the soldiery. Naomi Mitchison also mitigated none of the cruelty of the ancients. She tried the interesting experiment of making her characters talk in a modern colloquial style, even introducing modern slang. This radical departure from the nineteenth-century practice of attempting to suggest period-atmosphere by the use of archaisms induced in the reader a direct feeling of intimacy with the past, which thus was made to seem close and real instead of unreal and distant. Robert Graves's later historical novels were less distant in time and place: they include *Wife to Mr Milton* (1943), a story of the poet's first wife, Mary Powell. A growing concern with political affairs of her day tended to draw Naomi Mitchison away from her earlier interests, and she failed to recapture the strength and timeless interest of *The Conquered* (1923,) *Cloud Cuckoo Land* (1925), and *The Corn King and the Spring Queen* (1931).

By the nineteen-thirties, after having for many years been either despised or ignored by intellectuals, Somerset Maugham had moved unobtrusively to a high place both as a dramatist and as a writer of fiction. In his case, popular favour preceded critical acclaim, and his satirical mind must have found a wry satisfaction in the spectacle of the experts belatedly hastening to catch up with independent public approval. Somerset Maugham told of his transition from medicine to literature in *The Summing-Up* (1938), which is less an autobiography than a statement of his purposes as a writer, and a recital of his mental and moral attitude. His early novel *Liza of Lambeth* (1897) belongs to the period when tales of Cockney life were in fashion, and Maugham's obstetrical experiences among the poor of south London brought him into close touch with the human material he treated understandingly in that book. For some years after, narrative fiction was of only minor interest to him, while he was becoming a celebrity in the theatre. In 1916, however, he published an excellent long novel, *Of Human Bondage*, some part of which is recollective of phases of his own life. This is a fine achievement, but work of a more distinctively personal kind was to come. *Cakes and Ale* (1930) has incisiveness, brilliance, genuine pathos, and beauty. It is his best novel, for, here, sardonic wit and satire do not drive out human sympathy and understanding. Novels about novelists are usually meat chiefly for the literary, but this story of Driffield – whose attraction to common things and common people in bar parlours and the like makes him faintly derisive of his own fame as an author – has a much wider appeal. The character or Rosie, the barmaid who becomes Driffield's first wife, is Somerset Maugham's masterpiece and one of the great creations in English fiction. In *Cakes and Ale* the main characteristic of the mature

Maugham – absence of romantic illusion – is less productive of what often seems in his short stories to be a cynically sterile view of life. Rosie is warm and abundant, the generous-breasted ministrant. The author laughs and feels with her; he is not aloof or contemptuously amused, and she is safe from the cracking and cutting lash of his wit. In the illuminating preface to a single-volume collection of his short stories, *Altogether* (1934), Somerset Maugham acknowledged a debt to Maupassant, though he himself contributed far more than he borrowed from the Frenchman. The short stories are often dazzling, though occasionally only glittering. The impish audacity of his wit and his disrespect for self-righteousness are breathtaking in *The Vessel of Wrath*, the perfect story of its kind. The tragic note is not outside his range (see *Red*), but his celebrated story, *Rain* – of a prostitute, Sadie Thompson, converted by a missionary who then succumbs to lust, solicits her, and commits suicide – misses tragedy and achieves only a painful sordidness. Tragedy is, indeed, a will-o'-the-wisp to Somerset Maugham. It led, in the novel, *A Christmas Holiday* (1939), to his one major failure.

Maugham's output of novels and short stories[1] during the nineteen-forties showed little diminution of his sharp-focused curiosity concerning the behaviour and motives of men and women. If he then wrote nothing that increased his reputation, he nevertheless indulged certain wider personal interests by taking up semi-historical themes in *Then and Now* (1946) and *Catalina* (1948), and a quasi-mystical one in *The Razor's Edge* (1944), without sacrificing his ironical scepticism and incisive humour. The cynicism with which it became a lazy cliché to charge him was in truth and in the main a humorous appreciation of human oddity and incalculability, though he was never unaware of nor unresponsive to the pathos and pain which human relationships may generate.

Following a limited success with *The White Peacock* (1911) and *The Trespasser* (1912), D. H. Lawrence stepped into the front rank of contemporary novelists with *Sons and Lovers* (1913). The earlier part of that novel is largely a circumstantial record of the author's own early life and environment, and indicates the source of the

[1] See the chapter on Playwrights for comments on Somerset Maugham's plays.

emotional fixation between himself and his mother which was subsequently to make him a man divided against himself and unable to adjust himself in a fully integrated love experience. Almost to the end of his life (1885–1930) Lawrence regarded a woman in love as a harpy set on tearing asunder the man she loves, destroying his personality, and absorbing his being into her own. Lawrence's men, therefore, display a Laurentian tendency to be the bitter enemies as well as the lovers of their wives and mistresses. Sexual warfare in a limited degree is not uncommon, but D. H. Lawrence enlarged it to the measure of the whole, and fabricated a *mystique* of frustrate passions employing its own turgid terminology – 'mystic . . . suave loins of darkness, dark-clad and suave', 'the immemorial magnificence of mystic, palpable, real otherness'[1] – phrases which, taken alone, appear incredible, but which are yet a part of the very texture of Lawrence's books and served to create strong prejudice against them.

After his death too many of his disciples wrote about him in a manner seldom illuminating and often misleading, before Aldous Huxley's long introduction to *The Letters of D. H. Lawrence* (1932) and the letters themselves portrayed him more accurately.

By the beginning of the 1960s an extensive Lawrence literature had piled up. His wandering life (which in Mexico yielded material for *The Plumed Serpent*, 1926, as well as *Mornings in Mexico*, 1927; as Australia had done for *Kangaroo*, 1923), the devotion and adulation, the importunities and absurdities of his female flatterers and other disciples, and his tantrums and spongings and spasms of self-pity are all chronicled with particularity in *The Intelligent Heart* by Professor Harry T. Moore of the University of Delaware, the most minutely informative of the numerous books on Lawrence. It has been his posthumous misfortune to be memorialized often in terms that fail in their purpose of intensifying admiration and are sometimes productive of nausea. Until he ceases to be a controversial figure, harmed as much by overpraise as by undervaluation, there is little prospect of a balanced assessment of his true rank in literature. He has been too long a whipping-boy for moralists, and for amoralists an Ajax defying the lightning of convention and

[1] *Women in Love* (1921), Ch. XXIII.

authority. His astral body appeared in both roles at the Central Criminal Court in London in 1960 when an obscenity charge against the publishers of an unabridged cheap edition of *Lady Chatterley's Lover* was dismissed after a long procession of witnesses had testified to the literary merit and the moral and even spiritual value of the novel.[1] The practical outcome of this misconceived Old Bailey fantasy was that the sales of the indicted paperback edition soared to 3,500,000 copies in three years.

His main and persistent purpose – to revolutionize the modern English attitude towards sex – became stronger towards the end, and in *Lady Chatterley's Lover* (1928) he threw off such restraints of convention as had hitherto kept that purpose in leash. He wished to rid mankind of the shame complex which associates sex activity with indecency: 'I want men and women', he wrote,[2] 'to be able to think sex, fully, completely, honestly and cleanly.' He wanted sex to be the source through which comes the pure central fire of life. He deplored the modern dualism – the setting up of dividing barriers between mind and body, between brain and blood – and protested against the grey misanthropy which seeks to make the body the prisoner of the mind: 'I have always inferred that sex meant blood-sympathy and blood-contact. Technically this is so. But as a matter of fact, nearly all modern sex is a pure matter of nerves, cold and bloodless.'[3]

By 1960 the consensus of critical opinion appeared to have settled on *The Rainbow* (1915) as Lawrence's best novel. The banning of it when it was first published aroused fury as well as distress in the author and his friends, and a generation later its alleged obscenity had come to seem innocuous in the much changed moral climate. Even the most stubborn of Lawrence's admirers would find it difficult to deny that *The Rainbow* contains some of his worst writing, if also some of his best. An anthology of fine nature descriptions could be compiled from the book, but this simple and more normally pleasing aspect of Lawrence's work has been given less attention and less commendation than the autobiographically-

[1] *The Trial of Lady Chatterley: Regina* v. *Penguin Books Limited*, edited by C. H. Rolph (1961).

[2] *Apropos of 'Lady Chatterley's Lover'* (1930).

[3] Ibid.

rooted tortuosities of the love-hate relationships that torment the Brangwen family and their sexual mates through two or three generations. In the exploration of such relationships Lawrence fell into a kind of verbal frenzy and hysteria in which he abandoned the language of reason and became obsessed by terms originating below the diaphragm. In four consecutive not untypical pages of *The Rainbow* (chapter XV), 'dark' or 'darkness' appears forty-five times, and in two of the same four pages 'fecund' or 'fecundity' make eight appearances: 'the hot, fecund darkness'; 'A turgid, teeming night, heavy with fecundity'; 'secretly urgent with fecund desire'; 'the relentless softness of fecundity'; 'the warm, fecund flow of his kiss'; 'one dark fecundity'; 'one fecund nucleus of the fluid darkness'; 'the nucleolating of the fecund darkness'.

Discussion of the stylistic quality of Lawrence's writing is far from easy, since he detested every appearance of professionalism and, as a writer, endeavoured to retain the mark of the amateur. 'He despised fine writing even where it would best suit his purpose',[1] and preferred a crudely dynamic style. Yet almost in spite of himself a good deal of his prose has beauty. He said somewhere that 'if you write about anything you should write about it *hot*', and much that he wrote is furious with a convulsive energy and fire, though his debating style sometimes suggested the peevish shrillness of intellectual immaturity. But mostly he was a good hater, hating principally the lust for money and the 'modern' way of living, which seemed to him to bring the splendid freedoms of the body into bondage to the mind. He was not an advocate of animalism, he did not (as was alleged) idealize 'the morals of the farmyard'; his aim was to return to the primal energy of Eden, before the human consciousness became besmirched by the sense of sin, and before man became womanized.

Reference has already been made to the repeated emphasis in Lawrence's books on the conflict between Man and Woman, a conflict he believed to arise from civilized woman's having become the desperate antagonist of man, drawing from him his greatest possession – his manhood, his masculinity – and in time feminizing him and bringing him under the control of her will. In

[1] Bonamy Dobrée, *The Lamp and the Lute* (1929).

Aaron's Rod he makes one of the characters say, speaking of Woman in general:

> I hate her, when she knows, and when she *wills*. I hate her when she will make of me that which serves her desire. She may love me, she may be soft and kind to me, she may give her life to me. But why? Only because I am *hers*.

And again:

> Women are the very hottest hell once they get the start of you. There's *nothing* they won't do to you, once they've got you. Nothing they won't do to you. Especially if they love you.

There is much more of this anti-feminine frenzy in *Aaron's Rod* and other of Lawrence's books. Yet at the heart of it there is a terrible clear-sightedness – a revelation of the closeness of love and hate, of creation and destruction. Lawrence was especially interested in birds and beasts, with whom creation and death are sometimes almost simultaneous. Birth – love – the new creation – death. It was in this sequence that Lawrence saw the universe moving. Of this sequence, he seemed to feel, man is the victim: all things moving towards creation and re-creation, with, amid this process, man the instrument of creation – to be devitalized when he has served his immediate end.

D. H. Lawrence was a lop-sided genius – over-sensitive to attack, and so tormented by the necessity of rousing men and women to a full consciousness of the importance of creative energy expressed through sex, that he under-estimated the love-value of playful and pure delight. He was a neo-Puritan mislabelled as a libertine. *Lady Chatterley's Lover*, a sexual purgative, was received either as pornography or as an unassailable masterpiece. Both judgements were distorted. His ultimate masterpiece, *The Man Who Died* (1930), was little noticed, though that fable is a perfect and final reconciliation of the elements that warred within him, a discovery of atonement on the threshold of death, a vision of apocalyptic harmony between Osiris and Christ.

The spectacle of a society withering in a desert of make-believe and joyless gaiety, served novelists and dramatists in the 1920s and

1930s with material they turned to gruesome use. The most prominent of this group was Aldous Huxley (1894–1963), grandson of the eminent Victorian, Thomas Henry Huxley. As a writer of fiction (he wrote, also, a variety of other prose works as well as plays, and some verse) he had the useful gift of being, at least in his earlier works, irresistibly readable. He was well equipped as a humorist and wit, mainly sardonic and often savage enough to lead to his being regarded as a modern Swift. The inclination to consider him also as a follower of D. H. Lawrence had little foundation, for Huxley wrote, not as Lawrence did with the fervour of the blood, but in the deadly chill of a cerebral contempt which distilled vitriol. The contemporary Dance of Death had for him its moments of ludicrous humour, recorded in such books as *Crome Yellow* (1921), *Mortal Coils* (1922), and the more acerb *Antic Hay* (1923) in which the human being becomes something of a Gothic grotesque. As the political atmosphere grew more and more saturated with intolerance and hatred, Aldous Huxley's novels became more darkly charged with antagonism towards these tendencies. *Point Counter Point* (1928) is corrosive with detestations, so generously distributed as to leave few unscathed. *Brave New World* (1932)[1] pictured horribly a possible future in which laboratory-produced creatures would be mechanistically conditioned to serve the will of their masters in a world where everyone performs the motions of life without, in any acceptable sense, living. The measure in which this 'brave new world' was already existing for the radio and newspaper and otherwise 'capitalistically-conditioned' masses, gave Aldous Huxley's vision a more immediately sobering significance than any mere story of an inverted Utopia could have had. But as he became more immersed in the fearful contemplation of a threatening cosmic catastrophe, Huxley sacrificed his creative talent and therefore much of his readability, as was apparent in *Eyeless in Gaza* (1936), though some of his original verve was recovered in *After Many a Summer* (1939).

From that point Aldous Huxley as a novelist was a spent force and his *Time Must Have a Stop* (1944) and *Ape and Essence* (1949)

[1] In *Brave New World Revisited* (1958) Huxley commented upon aspects of current English life which led to the conclusion that some at least of his pessimistic forecasts in the earlier book had come to fulfilment considerably faster than he had anticipated.

stirred a more limited interest. His disgust with the world seemed to be less the repulsion of a superior intellect by the follies and enormities of common humanity than the outcome of protracted adolescence, an aspect of arrested development frequently found among twentieth-century intellectuals whose abnormal mental growth had been at the expense of emotional comprehension and human understanding. Some part of Huxley's later fiction was more vomitous than satirical.

After 1937 he lived in California, combating the eye trouble that had seriously handicapped him from early years and studying the mystical Eastern religions. His non-fictional writings comprise several volumes of miscellaneous essays (brought together in *Collected Essays*, 1960), *Grey Eminence* (1941; a biography of Father Joseph, Cardinal Richelieu's political intriguing favourite and backstairs adviser), *The Devils of Loudon* (1952; an account of the particularly fiendish witch-hunt which made that French town notorious in the seventeenth century), and books on mysticism, mescalin (*The Doors of Perception*, 1954; a record of experiments with a distillation from a Mexican plant which 'produces hallucinations when administered, and is useful in experimental psychiatry'), and other subjects. Huxley's experience of high acclaim in the 1920s and 1930s followed by relative neglect and semi-obscurity in the succeeding decades might be taken as a cautionary tale for young writers dazzled by early fame. In Aldous Huxley's case, however, it is probable that he will survive the vagaries and fluctuations of critical opinion and be remembered in the future by the best of his short stories and essays and possibly by those novels which have a period interest for social historians.

The argument between traditionalists and experimentalists in the modern novel has been in some measure an argument about Time. Traditionalists keep their eyes upon the calendar and the clock: hours pass, the years go on – and proportion is kept between time and action.[1] Dorothy Richardson, James Joyce, and other modern-

[1] 'Traditional' novelists, of course, have sometimes ignored the time-factor. Conrad was challenged by traditionalist critics because Marlow's narratives could seldom have been spoken within the time assigned. And Samuel Richardson's Pamela could have had little time for domestic duties in the intervals between her letters.

ists set themselves to annihilate the time-factor. They did not accept as a fixed formula that the morning and the evening are one day; evening or morning – or any part of either – might represent eternity or (on the other hand) less than a single pulse-beat. Time, in that connexion, ceases to be a positive factor; its value and duration are relative to other fluctuating factors; one person's whole life-story may have no greater time-value than twenty-four hours in the life of another.

This destruction of the tyranny of Time in fiction brought other changes. Old forms and old idioms suffice for novelists who accept the time-convention and the correlative conventions of plot, action, and character. But since action *qua* action is firmly delineated and fixed in Time, action was almost entirely eliminated from the novels of Dorothy Richardson and James Joyce, and thought *qua* thought was also eschewed, as being susceptible of a certain fixity. Action and thought abandoned, consciousness remained – without beginning and without end – able to effect infinite reduction of Time and infinite extension also. In the sequence of novels by Dorothy Richardson about Miriam Henderson, and in James Joyce's *Ulysses* (1922) and *Finnegans Wake* (1939), plot, action, character, and thought are merged and lost in the 'stream of consciousness', down which a mass of mental flotsam and jetsam drifts endlessly without cohesion. *Ulysses* is a phantasmagoria. The 'stream of consciousness' running through carries everything, including mental sewage, since that cannot be excluded except by social and moral influence exercising censorship in the mind. In consciousness, *per se*, moral (or other) censorship is inoperative; distinctions between fantasy and fact, between 'the decent' and 'the indecent' are not made. It is irrelevant, therefore, to dwell upon or even to refer to 'indecencies' in parts of *Ulysses*; to do so is as unprofitable as to feel shocked by 'indecent' dreams. *Ulysses*, like the later *Finnegans Wake* (which as *Work in Progress* took seventeen years to bring to birth), is a repository of the author's rare erudition and linguistic attainments. *Finnegans Wake* is written throughout in a virtually new language, much of it unintelligible to the average mind. Distorted sound-echoes of sense-making phrases can be caught from time to time, while the whole may perhaps be better considered as a kind of musical notation for the communication of profundities incommunicable in standard language. In these later works of James Joyce, so it is declared by his disciples, all knowledge is synthesized. The majority of readers may, however, turn with relief to his earlier books written in normal language (e.g. *Dubliners*, 1914, and *Portrait of the Artist as a Young Man*, 1916).

Joyce is regarded by some, including other writers, as the great genius of his time and, in prose, the paramount literary force. *Portrait of the Artist* has passages of shattering power which suggest that Joyce might have developed into a great traditional novelist if he had not preferred to engage in prolonged psychological and linguistic games. 'Games' is the appropriate word, for a sane approach to his two major volumes demands that the common reader need not adopt the solemn and awesome bearing of the totally enraptured Joyceans. Much that has been accepted without scepticism as proof of genius is more accurately regarded as no more than evidence of ingenuity: the construction of *Ulysses* in conformity with the basic pattern of Homer's *Odyssey*, and the symbolic correspondences with its episodes; the containing of the whole narrative within a period of twenty-four hours; Molly Bloom's entirely unpunctuated 'interior monologue'[1] which fills some sixty pages without a break at the end of the book; the circularity and endless punning and word-making and echoic language effects in *Finnegans Wake* – these constitute an elaborate verbal game. If it all builds up to a philosophy, if *Finnegans Wake* is a compendium of all knowledge, as the disciples assert, the seven years spent on the writing of *Ulysses* and the seventeen years on *Finnegans Wake* may find justification, but only outside the bounds of imaginative literature.[2]

Dorothy Richardson, James Joyce, Virginia Woolf, and others who have followed them, may be thought to give insufficient

[1] The 'interior monologue' was a device used by the 'stream of consciousness' novelists to represent the dissociated fragments of 'thought' which pass involuntarily through the human 'mind'. The originator of the device was Edouard Dujardin (1861–1949), from whose novel *Les Lauriers sont coupés* (1888) Joyce learned its possibilities.

[2] *James Joyce's 'Ulysses'* by Stuart Gilbert, *James Joyce: A Critical Introduction* by Harry Levin, and *A Skeleton Key to Finnegans Wake* by J. Campbell and H. M. Robinson should be consulted for detailed explication.

weight to the truth that the time-factor is governed by the *varying intensity* of human experience. The many hundreds of pages of *Ulysses* cover only one day in the lives of three Dublin people, whose sensations are flattened out, like a desert unbroken by any sandhill or oasis. So also, Dorothy Richardson's books amble onward, as Miriam goes through a life which has few emotional contours.

Pages might be filled by giving the names, only, of other authors who, between 1901 and 1960, wrote distinctive novels. One of the most interesting and influential was E. M. Forster. The thin, dry atmosphere of Forster's books is bracing, yet too rarefied for the characters to live healthy and fully physical lives; they are sometimes so overstrung, emotionally and intellectually, that their crises seem to be rooted in hysteria. Miss Quested's charge against Dr Aziz[1] is a tragic consequence of hysteria; Lucy Honeychurch's reaction to George Emerson's kiss,[2] a semi-comedy of hysteria. E. M. Forster's style is luminous and sensitive, and his books have many beautiful passages; his satire is sharp and penetrating as he deals with conventions and incidentals; and there is profound (sometimes bitter) irony in the poising of massive effects upon tiny causes, like a monstrous inverted pyramid. Nevertheless, when admiration has been fully expressed, the feeling returns that the characters are caged in the author's mind, unable to escape into actuality. There is in the manner of his novels, too, a quality that falls just short of austerity by being a trifle over-close to frigidity. This chill is less apparent in his essays on a variety of subjects in *Abinger Harvest* (1936), a companionable and often a wise book, which is supplemented by the further collection in *Two Cheers for Democracy* (1952).

With his small output of five novels E. M. Forster obtained a unique repute with a select audience including a large number of fellow-novelists of both sexes. His key phrase, 'only connect', is indicative of his sense of the essential loneliness of the modern civilized human, a theme taken up more ponderously by other writers who surprisingly overlook its familiarity in general experience, and treat as a harrowing semi-tragedy what is in fact a

[1] *A Passage to India* (1924). [2] *A Room with a View* (1908).

universal commonplace. In Forster's novels, however, the theme is handled with austere grace and distinction of language by a humanist and liberal thinker.

George Moore (1853–1933), though belonging to the older generation, takes a place among the experimenters. Born in Ireland, he went to Paris in the 'seventies to study painting, but realizing that he could make no headway in graphic art he turned to literature. After attempting verse in the manner of Baudelaire, Moore found his way at length to fiction, and three Zolaesque novels were followed in 1894 by *Esther Waters* (a landmark among English realistic novels) written in London. In 1901 he went back to Ireland for several years, producing short stories and a novel of Irish peasant life (*The Untilled Field*, 1903; *The Lake*, 1905), and his superb masterpiece of indiscreet memories, *Hail and Farewell* (1911–14). But Moore's chief claim to remembrance rests upon *The Brooke Kerith* (1916), in which his later phase of unremitting devotion to a prose style distinguished by unornamented clarity and lucidity is carried to perfection in a story of Jesus and Paul among the Essenes. Moore continued his experiments in austere and crystalline English prose until he died, writing and rewriting to the end. His later novels include *Heloïse and Abelard* (1921) – with which Helen Waddell's *Peter Abelard* (1933) can be illuminatingly compared – and *Aphrodite in Aulis* (1930), as well as *A Storyteller's Holiday* (1928), which shows the sensual element that flushed his somewhat spinsterish nature.

Many novels arising out of the experiences of soldiers in the war of 1914–18 appeared in 1929 and 1930. Among these Frederic Manning's *Her Privates We*[1] (issued in 1930 as by 'Private 19022' and first recognized as in Manning's style by T. E. Lawrence – 'Lawrence of Arabia') and Richard Aldington's *Death of a Hero* (1929) were prominent. Manning (1882–1935) was a scholar and a stylist already valued by a few for his essays and poems. The anger against war in *Death of a Hero* was only palely reflected in the spleen of some

[1] The original unexpurgated version was issued in a limited edition as *The Middle Parts of Fortune* (1929).

later books by Richard Aldington (1892–1962), but he rose to his best again in *All Men are Enemies* (1933). In addition, Aldington was a poet and translator, and as biographer he produced *Portrait of a Genius but . . .* (1950), an attempt to correct impressions of D. H. Lawrence given by earlier writers, and *Lawrence of Arabia: a Biographical Enquiry* (1955) which was indignantly attacked for its assault on the Lawrence legend.

David Garnett (son of Edward Garnett, who, as publisher's reader, was the guide, comforter, and stimulator of many writers including Joseph Conrad; and grandson of Richard Garnett of the British Museum, the author of a book of short stories, *The Twilight of the Gods*, 1888, cherished by literary connoisseurs) became famous overnight with his short fantasy *Lady into Fox* (1922), followed by *A Man in the Zoo* (1924), and two books inspired by aviation, *The Grasshoppers Come* (1931) and *A Rabbit in the Air* (1932). David Garnett also wrote full-length novels of a more usual kind, and edited *The Letters of T. E. Lawrence* (1938). Fantasy has a place in the rural novels of T. F. Powys, brother of J. C. Powys and Llewellyn Powys. T. F. Powys's *Mr Weston's Good Wine* (1927) is an impressive parable, beautifully written and less repellently coloured than were most of his other books by a Puritan horror of (but detailed dwelling upon) lustful doings among villagers.

J. B. Priestley's *The Good Companions* (1929) recaptured, in motoring days, the spirit of the English roads which had been destroyed when the railways took the traffic and the life that had meant so much to the novels of Dickens, Fielding, and others. *The Good Companions* was an honest piece of work that deserved its popular success, though the capers of a small concert party were subjected to a great strain in supporting so large a book. Considered technically, *The Good Companions* is a clumsy affair, but so, for the most part, were Dickens's novels; and Priestley's book, like all Dickens's, has gusto, a flair for comic characterization, and a general warm-heartedness. With this novel Priestley became suddenly a leading figure in contemporary fiction and, shortly after, a respected playwright.[1] None of his later novels surpassed

[1] See below, pp. 132 ff.

The Good Companions and by 1950 his stature as a novelist had dwindled.

The eminence of John Masefield and Walter de la Mare as poets drew attention away from their achievements as writers of fiction. The former's early novel, set mainly in tropical Africa, *Multitude and Solitude* (1909), was too soon forgotten; while there is much attractive and vigorous narrative writing and adventure in *Odtaa* (1926), *Dead Ned*, (1938), and *Alive and Kicking Ned* (1939). De la Mare's *Memoirs of a Midget* (1921) and his several volumes of short stories have the same elusive grace and strangeness as his poems. Charles Williams, another poet turned novelist, was the inventor of 'the metaphysical thriller', a kind of novel combining various strains – religion, philosophy, poetry, and mystery. *War in Heaven* (1930) was the first of these, *The Place of the Lion* (1931) perhaps the best. They require an instructed, even an initiated, audience, for Charles Williams played esoterically with myths and legends, ideas and images.

L. H. Myers's *The Near and the Far* (1943; a sequence of four novels published individually in 1929, 1931, 1935, and 1940) is an exquisitely written meditative story in an Indian setting and dated in the time of Akbar, but it is outside time and place and is one of the major productions of the period. Though wider attention was given to Charles Morgan (1894–1958) than to L. H. Myers (1881–1944), the latter was a finer artist and a more profound thinker. Charles Morgan's *The Fountain* (1932) flattered its admirers' intelligence by appearing to make philosophical ideas easy to comprehend. But the well-bred immaculate manner of Charles Morgan's writings is possibly – time will tell – a deceptive piece of literary tailoring, like a perfect Savile Row suit on a lay figure. Though the satisfactions of perfect tailoring are not to be underestimated, a novel, like a suit, needs a body with guts. In Charles Morgan's works there appeared early what afterwards became a persistent mood of frustration, as though the characters lacked the courage to come to terms with life on the basis of its own robust actualities, and shrank into a state of mental, moral, and spiritual elegant invalidism that led to the death complex of *Sparkenbroke* (1936). This disquieting characteristic was less obtrusive in *The Judge's Story* (1947) and *The River Line* (1949), which maintained the standard of high-bred writing without adding notably to the author's total achievement.

Eric Linklater had the well-compensated misfortune to write in *Juan in America* (1931) so popular and amusing a book that he was thereafter expected to produce others in the same genre. *Juan in China* (1937) did not satisfy those expectations, but among his earlier novels the very different *White Maa's Saga* (1929) should be noted. *Private Angelo* (1946), a product of the late stages in the Italian phase of the Second World War, may well remain Linklater's best novel, for its effective union of humour and humanness, laughter and irony, rascality and pathos.

6. WOMEN NOVELISTS

Women had already written fine novels in the early years of the twentieth century, and as masculine force and creative energy died down among men writers women seemed to take over those qualities. Elizabeth Robins (1862–1962), who began to publish in the 'nineties, continued to produce novels marked by a combination of feminine insight and masculine vigour. In *The Magnetic North* (1904), one of several books in which she dealt with the Arctic region, she displays an astounding knowledge of men's minds. Whether for incident, atmosphere, or psychology, *The Magnetic North* is a very remarkable novel.

May Sinclair (1879–1946), a restless genius, did not settle to any one type or style. Her sixth book, *The Divine Fire* (1904), is a long and detailed study of a poetic genius, in which character and discussion are of equal interest. The difficulty of creating a literary genius in a fictional work is evident, and May Sinclair never succeeds in making Savage Keith Rickman the Keats-like person he seems intended to be. Though he talks perfect Greek he is tortured by an imperfect control of English; he has 'the soul of a young Sophocles battling with that of a junior journalist in the body of a dissipated young Cockney' . . . the child of 'Ellas and of 'Olywell Street'. But even if the whole extensive plan is not realized with uniform success, *The Divine Fire* is nevertheless a book of uncommon merit. Both in this novel and in *The Combined Maze* (1913) the author showed much ability in portraying drab and mean lives, with their jumbled pathos, kindliness, and folly. Subsequently May Sinclair came under the influence of Freud's psycho-analytical theories and of Dorothy Richardson's literary methods. *Mary Olivier* (1919) dabbles with the 'Oedipus complex', spiritual inhibitions, fears of insanity, and thwarted desires.

Rose Macaulay (1881–1958) entered upon fiction as an acute social critic and her brilliance was almost insolent. In a succession of satirical novels she demolished the follies and pretences of several generations. *Orphan Island* (1924) was little more than a satirical paraphrase of Victorian history – too easy game for her keen and glittering weapons. *Potterism* (1920) – the first of the novels to show fully Rose Macaulay's spirit of lively satire – was dedicated to the 'unsentimental precisians in thought, who have, on this confused, inaccurate, and emotional planet, no fit habitation'. 'Potterism' is a synonym for the discarded term 'philistinism' – the worship of commercial success, 'the booming of the second-rate', the admiration of popular things. Mrs Potter is a 'best-selling' novelist; Mr Potter a flourishing Press magnate; the young Potters (Johnny and Jane, university bred) are members of the Anti-Potter League, a youthful group who 'talked and discussed and played . . . and thought they had found things out'. Then came 1914, and the war to stop their talk; then the armistice of 1918. The war period briefly, and the post-war period at greater length, provided Rose Macaulay with opportunities for that dispersed irony which she used half-maliciously, half-contemptuously. Neither Potters nor Anti-Potters escaped the lash. She saw humanity as a horde of 'minds crowded together, making a dense atmosphere, impervious to the piercing of truth. All this mass of stupid, muddled, huddled minds . . . Greedy minds, ignorant minds, sentimental, truthless minds. . . .' Clear-minded, witty, and immensely diverting, Rose Macaulay nevertheless exposed too much. *Potterism*, *Dangerous Ages* (1921), and (the best of these books) *Told by an Idiot* (1923) leave mankind stripped naked of the rags of illusion without which human souls cannot in decency walk abroad. By the time she wrote *Staying with Relations* (1930) Rose Macaulay had exhausted the satiric vein. But in 1932 she produced a novel of a different kind and one that at last worthily exercised her full talent. *They Were Defeated*, an historical novel of the seventeenth century, introduces the great poets of the time – Herrick, Marvell, Milton, Lovelace – and the Cambridge Platonists. Herrick is depicted at length, both as pastor and as poet, and Rose Macaulay communicates a feeling of excitement to the reader, as though he were actually meeting these people. The novel is wise and witty, moving and tragic – a book to engage fully both mind and heart. *The World My Wilderness* (1950), an affecting and penetrating novel depicting the influence of the war-time 'resistance' mentality upon the after-war lives of a young woman and a youth, was obtusely under-praised. The characters of Barbary and Raoul are drawn by Rose Macaulay with sympathy and understanding, and the wilderness of the bomb-desolated area around St Paul's Cathedral is so accurately and vividly projected that future social historians may well find in this novel something more than a word-portrait of the City in ruins.

The Towers of Trebizond (1956), though ranked by critics as Rose Macaulay's best novel, is neither her best nor wholly a novel. The posthumous publication five years later of the first volume of her *Letters to a Friend* 1950–2 showed that this 'novel' was in part autobiographical in so far as the heroine's quest of a lost faith was analogous to Rose Macaulay's own, and that the death of Vere at the end of the book was a desolation such as she had herself experienced in the loss of the man whom she had loved for many years, though the deep joy of that relationship had never fully compensated her disturbed conscience. In *The Towers of Trebizond* these personal strands are interwoven with threads of irony and civilized satire in a narrative that is part fiction and part travel book. Its record of the experiences of Aunt Dot and her camel, travelling with her niece the narrator and the Rev. Father Chantry-Pigg on a misconceived religious mission in Turkey, is supplemented by the niece's journey into Israel after Dot and Chantry-Pigg have ventured across the Russian frontier on an escapade which permitted Rose Macaulay to expose the basic absurdity of espionage psychosis. Wise, affecting, and amusing as *The Towers of Trebizond* is, it is nevertheless too discursive and loosely constructed to compete with *They Were Defeated* as Rose Macaulay's finest novel.

As the youngest daughter of Sir Leslie Stephen, Virginia Woolf lived in early years amid a scholarly circle such as that glimpsed in her first and simplest novel, *The Voyage Out* (1915), which presents no difficulty to those who enjoy good talk and are satisfied with action on the mental plane alone. *The Voyage Out* is to some extent reminiscent of Meredith's style, but in atmosphere it has little of the sharpness, the astringency, the hard clear outlines of Meredith. On the contrary, it has a golden radiance; its outlines are tremulous, like a landscape seen through a heat-haze; and the whole book is touched by an extraordinary sensitiveness, both emotionally and intellectually. If *The Voyage Out* has an affinity with the work of any other writer, it is with E. M. Forster's novels. There is the same sense of life so delicately poised, of people so sensitively balanced in thought and feeling, that the harsh breath of common life would cause the very structure of their culture to topple. A reader of *The Voyage Out* feels that it is essential to tread softly and to breathe lightly. Beginners will find this the most satisfactory of Virginia Woolf's novels, for the narrative has more continuity than is to be found in her later stories, where she adopted a fragmentary method of presentation.

About the middle of the nineteen-twenties, in a pamphlet called *Mr Bennett and Mrs Brown*,[1] Virginia Woolf prophesied that we were on the verge of a new great age in English literature. She pleaded, however, that for the present we must 'tolerate the spasmodic, the obscure, the fragmentary, the failure', because (she thought) the younger writers were feeling their way towards a new method of portraying character in fiction. She was herself one of the important

[1] First delivered as an address to a Cambridge society (The Heretics) in 1924. Reprinted in *The Captain's Death Bed and Other Essays*, collected by Leonard Woolf (1950).

experimenters, and though, considered purely as fiction, her novels are unsatisfying to those schooled in the traditional mode of the English novelists from Fielding and Smollett to Dickens and on to Wells and Priestley, she undoubtedly extended the boundaries of the novel. For her literary ancestry we should look back to Laurence Sterne rather than to the robust stylists.

Virginia Woolf made her prose almost as sensitive an instrument as poetry. She might, indeed, be regarded as a poet who had the misfortune to be born into an age of prose. The improbabilities over which many readers stumbled in her *Orlando* (1928) would be accepted without a moment's surprise if presented in verse. She composed numerous enchanting passages which never lack the clarity of good prose, even when they incite to the mood of exaltation produced by poetry. Virginia Woolf's work is also notable for the demands made upon *all* our senses. Her books cannot receive an adequate reception from the intellect unaided; they invite the active co-operation of the reader's faculties of sight, hearing, touch, taste, and smell. In her story of Elizabeth Barrett Browning's dog, *Flush* (1933), she introduces a world of sensation in which smell is the liveliest sense, as it evidently is to a dog; and invariably, in reading Virginia Woolf's books, it is essential that all channels of perception should be open and unobstructed. Reason must sometimes be held in check, as in the case of *Orlando* (called a biography, but partly a novel, partly a fantasy, partly a satire), which requires the initial concession that, in the world of the imagination, centuries and sexes may blend and blurr. That concession once made, *Orlando* is easy to read and often beautiful in its descriptions and style. Attempts have been made to interpret *Orlando* as allegory, though its concluding sentences might have led 'interpreters' to suspect that they were conducting a wild-goose chase.

Virginia Woolf charged Arnold Bennett and others with encumbering their characters with too much material litter, yet Edwin Clayhanger, Soames Forsyte, Alfred Polly, do somehow convince us of their existence in an actual world. Her own major weakness was that all her characters talk alike – with their creator's voice – and rarely seem to live outside her own mind, a limitation shared with some of E. M. Forster's people.

Katherine Mansfield (born in New Zealand) became famous first as a writer of short stories (assembled in *The Collected Stories of Katherine Mansfield*, 1945) which in some respects naturalized in English the manner of Tchekov. She was especially happy in her studies of children, whom she made charming and touching without sentimentalizing them or abating the natural realism which is interwoven with fantasy in the child's life. Katherine Mansfield married John Middleton Murry (critic and writer on philosophical subjects), who edited her journal and letters after she died. These (with *The Scrapbook of Katherine Mansfield*, 1939) deservedly increased her fame, for there are few finer expressions of a sensitive spirit and an exquisite mind.

Dorothy Sayers broke new ground for the 'serious' woman novelist by specializing in detective fiction. She was frequently more ingenious in spinning a plot than convincing or interesting in unspinning it, and the character of her amateur investigator of crime, Lord Peter Wimsey, usually counted for more than the mysteries he solved. Wimsey is an intellectual aristocrat with a nice taste in wine and rare books and a gift of abstruse quotation born of Dorothy Sayers' own intimate knowledge of the lesser as well as the principal English and other authors, a gift too resolutely and habitually displayed. The Wimsey books are for the most part better as novels than as detective novels; they have wit, humour, good character-drawing, and a quality of high seriousness imparted to them by the author's religious sense. Murder is seen as a mortal sin – as a spiritual outrage – not simply as the starting-point of a puzzle for readers. G. K. Chesterton's stories of Father Brown were the first of the kind to propound spiritual issues, and Dorothy Sayers made a long step forward in the same direction. Her ingenuity can be judged from *The Nine Tailors* (1934), her rank as a novelist proper from *Gaudy Night* (1935) – a novel in which the detective element seems intrusive – and her humour and common sense from *Murder Must Advertise* (1933). Dorothy Sayers abandoned detective fiction for religious writings and radio drama before the end of the nineteen-thirties, but other women were among the chief providers of crime novels for the rest of the half-century. The pioneer of them all,

Agatha Christie, wrote purely as an entertainer, and her ingenuity persisted through more than fifty detective novels from *The Mysterious Affair at Styles* (1920), while she improved greatly as a writer in later books. Though they did not equal her in massive output, Agatha Christie's books were in certain respects equalled and sometimes bettered by Marjorie Allingham's and Ngaio Marsh's detective novels.

The conditions of the developing twentieth century made it inevitable that, among the increasing number of highly educated women, fineness of perception and sharpened sensibility would be accompanied by emotional tension. Of the novelists whose work reflects these states Elizabeth Bowen and Rosamond Lehmann were possibly the most distinguished. The transition from the ferment of youthful ecstasy to the far from untroubled depths of mature experience can be tracked in Rosamond Lehmann's novels from *Dusty Answer* (1927) to *The Ballad and the Source* (1944). Elizabeth Bowen's work, wider in emotional range, reached its best in *Death of the Heart* (1938), a movingly perceptive study of the disrupting effects of accelerated emotional development in a young girl whose mental development proceeds at the normal slower pace.

If expert contemporary judgements were faultless, the supreme place among women novelists of the second quarter of the century would be given to Ivy Compton Burnett. But the enthusiasm she excited among other novelists and the professional critics did not gain for her books a corresponding large body of readers. It would be rash to hail as evidence of genius certain literary idiosyncrasies which may subsequently be classed as products of talented oddity. The Compton Burnett formula combines a Victorian stuffiness of atmosphere and a Victorian appetite for melodrama with a twentieth-century ruthlessness in stripping off conventional veils of pretence in order to expose make-believers, hypocrites, and petty tyrants naked to their souls. Written in a prim style with dialogue in which vocabulary and syntax above and below stairs, in nursery and in drawing-room, are scarcely differentiated, the Compton Burnett novels appealed mainly to connoisseurs of mordant irony.

Iris Murdoch, a sometime Oxford lecturer in philosophy, is better known as a talented and original novelist. Starting in 1953 with a small but enlightening study of the French existentialist, Sartre, she launched into fiction with *Under the Net* (1954), a semi-ribald semi-picaresque account of masculine racketing in London, robust and vigorous, though with some incoherences of plot. Her second novel, *The Flight from the Enchanter* (1956), is more substantial, with a rich texture in striking contrast with the threadbare fabric of much contemporary fiction. It can be described as a tragi-comedy of obsessions and emotional entanglements, for each of the characters is caught in the net of one or other of these spiritually confining influences. The author's command of uproarious humour appears in hearty laughter-rousing form in the chapter dealing with the annual meeting of the eccentric shareholders of *Artemis*, a once healthy but now decrepit periodical originally started as a feminist organ; and her sense of pathos and tragedy appears movingly in the life and death of Nina the refugee dressmaker. Over all is the shadow of the enigmatic Mischa Fox, a sinister enchanter who is never fully explained and is therefore never reduced to common stature. The latent dramatic quality in Iris Murdoch's books was brought out in J. B. Priestley's stage adaptation of her later book, *A Severed Head* (1961). In that novel, one of the characters remarks of another '*she* certainly has power in her'. That can also be said of Iris Murdoch, in whose writing there is a compelling element of power, though there were signs in her later novels that it might become dissipated in a quaking bog of symbolism.

7. DETECTIVE STORIES

Reference has been made above to detective novels by women, but a footnote is required on some general aspects of this branch of imaginative prose, which flourished for a long time as one of the uncultivated wildings of inventive minds, but was subsequently drawn into the arcana of the intellectualists. A pattern for the short detective story was supplied in certain of the *Tales of Mystery and Imagination* by the American Edgar Allan Poe (1809–49), while Wilkie Collins's *The Moonstone* (1868) is an admirable early full-length detective novel. But the wider popularity of this class of fiction began in 1891 with the first of the Sherlock Holmes short stories and novels of Conan Doyle (1859–1930). Though when considered purely as a literary product these may seem sometimes contemptible – jejune in style and elementary in contrivance – the character of Sherlock Holmes is a memorable creation,[1] and his 'cases' supplied thrills and a certain degree of mental exercise in days before more ambitious writers brought into service a considerable amount of expert and pseudo-expert knowledge of criminology, forensic medicine, and cognate matters. And even when expertise became the mode, Sherlock Holmes retained much of his original fascination – so much so, that learned men amused themseves and others by writing treatises on various aspects of the life and labours of the detective, whose non-existent rooms in Baker Street were also frequently sought by pilgrims. Conan Doyle, himself a doctor of medicine, was far from deficient in specialized knowledge, but an entertaining gusto was his most attractive quality as a writer. The Sherlock Holmes series was intended by the author to end with *The Hound of the Baskervilles* (1902), and although the popular demand for more produced the short stories in *The Return of Sherlock Holmes* in 1905 and several other volumes up to 1927, the genuine impulse may be said to have been exhausted after the 1902 novel, one of Conan Doyle's best pieces. Between that date and the first of G. K. Chesterton's Father Brown volumes the detective story had no literary standing. The revival begun by *The Innocence of Father Brown* (1911) brought a new element into crime fiction – religion; for as a Roman Catholic priest (Chesterton himself finally embraced that faith in 1922) Brown – like Dorothy Sayers later[2] – viewed crime as a sin, not chiefly as a medium for more or less ingenious detection. Though the several other Father Brown volumes were as well received as the original, they are all a side-product of the detective genre rather than a main contribution.

Two years after Chesterton's initial stories came out, his friend

[1] He is understood to have been based by Conan Doyle upon the eminent Edinburgh surgeon, Joseph Bell, some of whose characteristics are suggested in the likeable mannerisms and eccentricities of the detective.

[2] See above, p. 78.

E. C. Bentley,[1] with *Trent's Last Case* (1913), not only started the popular vogue that the detective novel retained for the next half-century or so, but also gave it new literary respectability. The vogue has been deplored as one fragment of evidence of what has been called in another connexion, a 'collapse of public taste'. The truth is, however, that the detective novel came to be the only surviving form of unsentimental fiction in which inventive skill – the ability to frame a plot and tell a story – was kept alive.

The output of detective novels in the fifty years from 1913 is beyond counting. Poets and academics, such as C. Day Lewis (under the pseudonym Nicholas Blake) and J. I. M. Stewart (as Michael Innes) brought a scholastic touch into the commission and elucidation of crime, Robert Bruce Montgomery (as Edmund Crispin) combined humour intelligently with murder, while (to return to the detection-minded women) Elizabeth Mackintosh[2] (as Josephine Tey) wrote, among several others in the kind, *The Franchise Affair* (1948), an outstanding piece of mystification suggested by an actual occurrence.

8. SURVIVORS AND NEWCOMERS

By 1950 all the novelists who at the beginning of the century were either adding to the prestige of English fiction or were soon to do so were dead: Conrad, Bennett, George Moore, Galsworthy, Wells. The principal innovators in a younger generation – James Joyce and Virginia Woolf – were also dead. Among the survivors none was of assured major rank, and among the new writers who first came into prominence in the closing decade only one – Joyce Cary – was established; while of none could it be said that his name was a household word as Wells's and Galsworthy's had been. More people were reading than at any time before (television had encroached little until after 1950), but there was an almost total cleavage between 'popular reading' and 'literature'. Public

[1] An account of the genesis of *Trent's Last Case* is given in its author's autobiography, *Those Days* (1940). Bentley was best known as the inventor of the four-line comic verse 'biographies' he called Clerihews, after his own middle name.

[2] Under another pseudonym (Gordon Daviot), she was the author of the extremely popular historical *Richard of Bordeaux* (1933) and other plays.

librarians were aware of the extent to which 'thrillers', 'Westerns', and 'love romances' monopolized the reading time of a vast proportion of borrowers, and these classes of fiction were even more nearly the exclusive mental food at the 'commercial' lending libraries which multiplied in the nineteen-thirties and nineteen-forties.

For many years up to 1940 there had been one living writer (in addition to several crime novelists) whose fiction pleased all classes. P. G. Wodehouse's humorous stories brought him a fortune and, from Oxford, an honorary doctorate; and though he lost favour with a large part of his public during the Second World War his post-war books were found hard to cold-shoulder, and his popularity, and the favour of the critics, had been recovered by 1960.

Although Wodehouse's stories are by no means lacking in literary merit, they belong to the low comedy tradition and their author is akin to a music-hall 'comic'. His kind is rare and no one has yet replaced him as a provider of fun. While it might be possible to concoct a thesis on the social content of Wodehouse's stories, any inclination towards satire is subordinated to the claims of happy nonsense. At the opposite extreme, Evelyn Waugh's *Decline and Fall* (1928) and *Vile Bodies* (1930) and the rest of his satirical novels have a taste of mental and moral superiority. Contemporary humour and satire are in many cases held in duress by a pervasive undergraduate jocosity. The imprint of an unadult mind is upon Waugh's *The Loved One* (1948), devised as a satire upon the repulsively sentimental and grossly sanctimonious commercialized burial customs of the modern Americans. The theme is in reality so grotesque and nauseating that an exceptional degree of literary discipline and tact is required to treat it. Waugh exhausts the theme in the first dozen or so pages and the book thereafter becomes contaminated by prolonged gnawing at its own material. It must be noted, however, that reviewers gave *The Loved One* unmeasured praise. Waugh committed himself to a more ambitious theme in *Brideshead Revisited* (1945), a family chronicle which may well become his longest-remembered book, for its sense of period, the firmness of its character-drawing, and its convincing record of a Roman

Catholic family whose religious foundations are shaken by a dipsomaniac son and an adulterous daughter. Amid the tragedy there are flashes of comedy, notably through the detached sardonic humour of the narrator's father. As a novel, though not as a demonstration of divine grace in terms of Catholic theology, *Brideshead Revisited* is weakened by an over-determined final contrivance of Faith Triumphant.

There is little, superficially, to link Evelyn Waugh and Graham Greene, but as Catholic converts they have inevitably been inclined to employ the novel as an instrument of social and spiritual purgation. Sympathy with Greene's extra-literary purposes has no doub, been responsible for some exaggerated commendation of his workt and his endeavour to pivot novels upon the tardy awareness in the leading characters of the saving need of a Sense of Sin is not conducive either to artistic unity or to spiritual integration. The brutal violence of razor gangsterdom in *Brighton Rock* (1938) makes an impression unlikely to be effaced by the confessional scene in the final chapter: there is no genuine purgation. The unreconciled though undeclared antagonism between Greene the fictional narrator and Greene the Catholic apologist produces both the tension and the over-strain of *The Power and the Glory* (1940); while the display of grubby human second-rateness in *The Heart of the Matter* (1948) could be mistaken for a discarded early Somerset Maugham subject worked over by an earnest and anxious missionary. When his natural talent for entertainment is freed, as in his film scripts, from the burden of inexpert sermonizing, Graham Greene is an excellent teller of exciting tales.

Joyce Cary (1888–1957) was the most original and versatile novelist of his generation, and, alone among his contemporaries, in the main stream of English fiction. Cary shared with Browning the ability to get into the skin of a great diversity of characters and to think with their minds so completely that he *becomes* each character in turn. No writer less thoroughly identified with his creation could have drawn Gully Jimson in *The Horse's Mouth* (1944) so convincingly as rogue and genius; and what applies to Jimson applies to a score of other Joyce Cary characters entirely different in type; all, men and women equally, are imagined so intensely and so thoroughly that they live with the substance and spirit of their creator, not simply as shadows from his mind. His later novels, *Prisoner of Grace* (1952) and *Except the Lord* (1953), were of a political character, though still predominantly concerned with individual human relationships. Not the least remarkable of his books is *Charley is my Darling* (1940), a penetratingly tragic story of evacuated London children in the Second World War.

George Orwell (1903–50) has an uncertain place in literature, for the critical as well as the popular view of his writings became clouded by politics and propaganda. Born in India, educated at Eton, and for five years (1922–7) in the imperial police service in Burma, he then conceived an intense hatred of his class and upbringing, and cultivated a sincere but self-righteous poverty which led him into menial employments and social contacts with the depressed, and provided him with material for *Down and Out in Paris and London* (1933), *Keep the Aspidistra Flying* (1936), and *The Road to Wigan Pier* (1937) – all documentary novels of the Great Depression of the 1930s. Orwell went to Spain in 1936 to fight on the republican side in the civil war (see his *Homage to Catalonia*, 1938), only to develop a detestation of the side he had joined. *Animal Farm* (1945), an anti-Communist fable, gave him a long-deferred experience of fame, reinforced in the last year of his life by the bitter forecast of a totalitarian Britain (under the pseudonym Oceania) in *Nineteen Eighty-Four* (1949). The high praise given to these two books was divorced from any assessment of their literary quality, for although Orwell had said that he aimed to make political writing into an art, he died too soon to consolidate his aim. *Animal Farm* received unmeasured praise, but as satire it is naïve and laboured. Its immediate fame may indeed be said to have hung upon one phrase – easily remembered, and doomed to end as a cliché too easily quotable – 'all animals are equal but some are more equal than others'. Orwell was handicapped not only by ill-health (he died of tuberculosis) but also by an inborn passion for non-conformity which made him an instinctive and fanatically sincere defecter. He defected from his social class, from his first employment, from his communistic sympathies. Would there have been other and less commendable defections if he had lived longer? Sincerity is not enough when it is accompanied by instability arising from an egotistical assurance that yesterday's errors are annulled by today's revelation and acceptance of a changed creed. Orwell was subject to political hysteria which reached its culmination in *Nineteen Eighty-Four*, where the 'chief symbol, Big Brother, resembles the bogy-man of a rather inartistic nursery tale'. This comment by a one-time colleague and astute political historian is reinforced by the same writer's judgement that 'Orwell lacks the richness and subtlety of thought and philosophical detachment of the great satirist'.[1]

The mood of repudiation, dominant in Orwell, was prevalent also in the works of the younger writers after 1945. Their experiences during the war and dismay at the exploding of the first nuclear bomb convinced them that the standards and values of their elders were false and disastrous and must be rejected. But the rejection of past and present by youth intent on a better future, inevitably allied with the raw arrogance of inexperience, did nothing to commend an excellent purpose. It is only in a state of political innocence that blame is laid on a single generation or a single class for faults and crimes common and seemingly natural to all mankind.

What came to be regarded as the 'type' novels of the 1950s – John Wain's *Hurry on Down* (1953), Kingsley Amis's *Lucky Jim* (1954), and John Braine's *Room at the Top* (1957) – were all studies in the repudiation of traditional values. Although a novel is not to be taken as a statement of a personal attitude – and may indeed represent its opposite – there was a perhaps illogical tendency to assume that Charles Lumley, Jim Dixon, and Joe Lampton spoke for their authors. Lumley, finished with university, rejects 'the sacred law of self-effacing, mute compliance' which is the formula for getting-on in life and having a career. He becomes a window cleaner and revisits his old school only to ask the Head for the window-cleaning job. He afterwards runs through other 'low' occupations before ending as a radio script writer.

[1] Quoted from Isaac Deutscher's essay on Orwell in *Heretics and Renegades* (1955)

> So far, he had set himself target after target that had proved out of reach; economically, the quest for self-sufficient poverty: socially, for unmolested obscurity: emotionally, first for a grand passion and then for a limited and defined contentment. And now he valued his niche simply because it gave him the means, through his new wealth, to put himself beyond the struggle . . . (Ch. X).

In a period when earnest young writers were dedicating themselves to 'commitment'[1] *Hurry on Down* presented a hero dedicated to social 'neutrality'.

The irritation which it seemed that *Lucky Jim* set up in many readers no doubt arose from the air of smug 'knowingness' that encases Dixon, and the assumption of superiority that leads him as by second nature to outrage good manners and the common decencies of civilized behaviour. This was part of the shock treatment Amis's generation proposed to administer to the complacent, a campaign in which *Lucky Jim* preceded by two years John Osborne's play, *Look Back in Anger*.[2]

The success, in terms of sales, of *Room at the Top* cannot easily be separated from the contemporary public's liking for erotic scenes and the current disposition to admire a young man 'on the make' who does not set up scruples as a barrier on his way to material prosperity.

It appeared by 1960 that, so far as popular acclaim was to be distributed, Wain, Amis, and Braine were looked upon as 'one book' authors, for their following books attracted much less notice.

Even those novelists who have already produced a more substantial body of work cannot be 'placed' in literature while still in mid-career. C. P. Snow – scientist and civil service commissioner – embarked in 1940 on a sequence of novels (intended to run to eleven books), each self-contained but linked by the presence in each of the character named Lewis Eliot. The first, *Strangers and Brothers* (also to be the group title of the series when completed), was, relatively to later volumes, clumsily written, and Lewis Eliot tends to become a boring presence in more than one of the novels.

[1] See below, p. 138 ff. [2] See below, p. 140.

Snow is not a continuously enlivening writer and when, as in *The Masters* (1951), he delves into university politics the effect is one of enclosed parochialism. Yet, while in the same *milieu*, *The Affair* (1960) is tense and exciting, though sympathy is strained for the boorish but brilliant young scientist accused of faking, and wrongfully deprived of his college fellowship, until he is reluctantly vindicated. This volume and *The New Men* (1954) can be related to the theme of Sir Charles Snow's[1] controversial Rede Lecture, *The Two Cultures and the Scientific Revolution*, at Cambridge in 1959, where he speaks of 'a gulf of mutual incomprehension' existing between scientists and 'literary intellectuals'. His animadversions on these latter stung their apologist, F. R. Leavis, to a rare display of invective in his Richmond Lecture, delivered in Cambridge in 1962.[2]

The multi-volume novel also occupied Anthony Powell, whose *Music of Time* sequence, begun with *A Question of Upbringing* (1951), is a more lighthearted and entertaining undertaking than either Snow's or the Alexandria Quartet of Lawrence Durrell (*Justine*, 1957; *Balthazar*, 1958; *Mountolive*, 1958; *Clea*, 1960). There is much fine descriptive writing in the Quartet, as well as much complex bed-going; while Pursewarden – comic, eloquently witty, vividly scurrilous, and finally tragic – is a grand creation: speaking of a married couple, he says: 'The Errols are . . . *both* economists. . . . They make love to two places of decimals only. Their children have all the air of vulgar fractions.'

Angus Wilson's reputation was founded by his short stories (*The Wrong Set*, 1949, and other volumes), 'all horrid' in theme but all told with compelling power. His novels – *Anglo-Saxon Attitudes* (1956), *The Middle Age of Mrs Eliot* (1958), etc. – maintained his reputation but do not carry conviction that the more extensive form is an equally appropriate medium for his individual talent.

William Golding's *The Lord of the Flies* (1954) brilliantly but horrifically carried several stages further the disturbing view of children given by Richard Hughes a quarter of a century earlier in *A High Wind in Jamaica* (1929).

Science fiction has so far produced little, after H. G. Wells, that

[1] He was knighted in 1957.

[2] Printed in *The Spectator*, 9 March 1962.

can be ranked as literature. The one sure exception is John Wyndham: *The Kraken Wakes* (1953), *The Midwich Cuckoos* (1957), and *The Day of the Triffids* (1960) are irresistible masterpieces in their kind.

CHAPTER III

PLAYWRIGHTS

1. THE TWILIGHT OF THE DRAMA

After the death of Shakespeare and his contemporaries the drama in England was in decline for upwards of two centuries. Occasionally, during that long sickness, it seemed that the English theatre might again become a place to which writers would turn as naturally as the Elizabethans had turned. But the hope was delusive; and neither Congreve in the seventeenth century, nor Sheridan and Goldsmith in the eighteenth, restored the drama to prolonged good health.

The closing of the theatres by the Puritans in 1642 was less harmful than the order of release some twenty years later, after the accession of Charles II. Although the Restoration gave a strong impetus to the stage, the profligacy of the Stuart Court was reflected in the Restoration drama. Intellectual brilliance fought a rear-guard battle with cynical indecency, and others besides religious fanatics regarded the theatre with disgust. Moreover, the drama was handicapped by the grant of an exclusive Royal Patent to the Covent Garden and Drury Lane theatres in 1662, making these the only houses at which classical drama could legally be performed; for this purpose, 'classical drama' was considered to be the plays of Shakespeare, Beaumont and Fletcher, Congreve, Otway, and some others. In 1766 the Royal Patent was extended (in a modified form) to the Haymarket Theatre, but other theatres were still restricted to plays of poor quality with musical accompaniment – whence the term *melo-drama*, later to become a byword for extravagant theatricalism.

The 'minor theatres' (as the non-Patent houses were called) found means to evade the royal imposition, and it was at the theatre in Goodman's Fields, Whitechapel, that David Garrick made his name as a great Shakespearian actor. But only by subterfuge could these houses produce 'classical' plays. At Garrick's first theatre, the audience paid for a brief musical entertainment, after which a play from the restricted categories was performed without further charge. This method of evasion had obvious disadvantages, and it certainly was not a condition of affairs in which a healthy national drama could flourish. Nor was the Royal Patent lightly to be ignored. In 1819 and 1820 Junius Brutus Booth gave Shakespearian performances at the newly opened Coburg Theatre (later known as the 'Old Vic') in Waterloo Bridge Road. As a consequence the manager of the Coburg was prosecuted at the instigation of the management of Drury Lane and heavily fined.

Not until 1843 were these disabilities lifted from the non-Patented London theatres. In that year 'An Act for regulating Theatres' was passed by Parliament, and all theatres placed on an equal footing. Every theatre (except those already 'licensed' by the Royal Patent) had to be licensed by the Lord Chamberlain or by the local Justices; and every new play or new addition to an old play had to be submitted to the Lord Chamberlain's department for approval.[1] But, subject to those provisions, any theatre could put on any play: Clause XXIII stated 'That in this Act the word "Stage-Play" shall be taken to include every Tragedy, Comedy, Farce, Opera, Burletta, Interlude, Melodrama, Pantomime, or other Entertainment of the Stage. . . .' Instead of three protected theatres with traditions and reputations to uphold and a scattering of negligible smaller places, there now sprang up an oddly assorted collection of playhouses all with equal rights. The old protected companies broke up and became distributed piecemeal elsewhere. Supernumeraries of Covent Garden, who might with training have developed into accomplished performers, hurried to small local

[1] This was the origin of the still-existing censorship of stage plays, which has from time to time aroused the fury of playwrights who claim that it has been exercised against the discussion of serious subjects in drama while permitting salacious triviality. In 1909 as a consequence of protests against the suppression of plays by Bernard Shaw, Granville Barker, and others, Parliament set up a Joint Committee to inquire into the working of the censorship. The Preface to Shaw's *The Shewing-up of Blanco Posnet* gives a detailed account of the Committee's rejection of the statement he prepared as part of the evidence he proposed to offer. The Preface prints the Rejected Statement in full, thus preserving a valuable document.

theatres where their immature talents failed to sustain them in exacting parts.

For twenty years and more a period of chaos ensued. During that time the theatre had no intellectual or social standing, and playgoers had perforce to leave their brains at home when setting out for the theatre.

The name of Thomas William Robertson (1828–71) is inseparably associated with the beginning of the modern revival of English drama. Like other forerunners, he passed and became almost forgotten, and his plays now seem crude and commonplace. But he was a pioneer in bringing back life and intelligence to the theatre, and the production of Robertson's comedy, *Society*, by Marie Wilton and Squire Bancroft, at the Prince of Wales's Theatre in November 1865, was a more important occasion than either the dramatist or the players realized.

In the Bancrofts' company at a later date (1881–2), when they had moved to the Haymarket Theatre, was a young actor, Arthur Wing Pinero, who had previously been with Irving and the Wyndhams. He was the son of a lawyer and was intended for his father's profession, but at nineteen he took to the stage. In 1882 Pinero abandoned acting for writing. Plays by him had already been performed by Irving, John Hare, and Mr and Mrs Kendal (Madge Robertson, T. W. Robertson's youngest sister). Pinero's first notable work, *The Money Spinner*, produced in 1881, was followed by other original plays and adaptations, before he established a reputation with what became known as the Court Theatre farces: *The Magistrate* (1885), *The Schoolmistress* (1886), and *Dandy Dick* (1887). Thereafter, he turned from farce to comedy, to more serious drama, and even to tragedy. In *Sweet Lavender* (1888) the influence of Robertson is seen; while *Trelawny of the 'Wells'* (1898) is a delicate picture of the life of an earlier generation of actors, the character of Tom Wrench being a sketch-portrait of Robertson. *The Second Mrs Tanqueray* (1893) was one of the first-fruits in England of the influence of Ibsen, though Pinero was far from expressing in this and subsequent plays the unorthodox individualism of the Norwegian dramatist. Pinero did something towards transporting to the English stage the husk of Ibsen; but the substance of Ibsen's message provoked in England an outburst of rage that only a Bernard Shaw could face with self-possession. Pinero had an effective sense of stage situation; his plays are well constructed and his characters nearer to lifelikeness than characters in English drama had been for generations before he began to write, though by the time of his own death in 1934 most of his plays appeared naïve and artificial to a generation more sophisticated and better informed. Yet in later revivals several of the Pinero plays showed a surprising ability – through stagecraft, humour, and suspense – to override their lack of a valid 'criticism of life'.

While Pinero was addressing himself to stagecraft and the narrative aspects of drama, Henry Arthur Jones was promoting the development of social drama. He began with melodramatic pieces – the best known was *The Silver King* (1882) – but later conducted extensive propaganda designed to give the theatre a more important place in the social life of the time. He insisted that the drama should provide an uncompromising criticism of manners and institutions, though in practice he was disinclined to pursue his flirtations with unorthodoxy to any unorthodox end.

Oscar Wilde (1856–1900) brought into the theatre an acute and brilliant wit, while his care for style helped to clear the drama of verbiage and to make its dialogue keen-edged and clean-cut. His epigrams quickly lose their surprising and attractive impertinence, however; his characters are wooden, and his sentiments almost wantonly insincere. Yet he did much to improve the literary standing of the modern drama, and his own notoriously brilliant talk echoes in the dialogue. When, as in his last play, *The Importance of Being Earnest* (1895), the theme is entirely fantastic, his weaknesses become less obvious. This play has no purpose except to be gay; it is a brilliant piece of inconsequent extravagance; while as a contribution to English comedy it equals the plays of Sheridan. It ran in London even during the deepest disgrace of its author (whose name was meanwhile removed from the playbills!) and has taken a sure place in the repertory of English stage classics.

The career of Stephen Phillips (1868–1915) was a curious episode in contemporary theatrical history. The advertisement pages at the end of early editions of his plays quote reputable critics whose praises could not have been warmer if Shakespeare had been under review. Stephen Phillips's poetic dramas show a smooth facility in versifying and some knowledge of stage technique, but they contain little true poetry or true drama. Yet the interest they aroused probably encouraged other writers and led to further experiments in poetic drama. Even if they did nothing else, Phillips's plays at least exposed the limitations of pseudo-Elizabethan blank verse, and led poets to seek another medium.

2. BERNARD SHAW

There came to London from Dublin in 1876 a young Protestant Irishman belonging to a family that prided itself upon being connected with 'the gentility'. His father, a feckless and impecunious gentleman, was related to a baronet; and his mother, grown weary of her husband's shiftless ways, had preceded her son to England. This obscure youth – George Bernard Shaw – had little money, no prospects, and no hope of settled employment; yet he was able to say, twenty years later, 'My destiny was to educate London.'

He was born in Dublin in 1856, began his education under an uncle, the Rev. William George Carroll, and went on to the Wesleyan Connexional School in Dublin, where (he said) he learnt little – mainly because he himself did little and relied upon the help of two more brilliant boys, whom he repaid by reciting stories from Homer.

Mrs George Carr Shaw, his mother, was the 'New Woman' before the New Woman had properly arrived. Independent and self-reliant, she cared nothing for the frowns of the orthodox. Music was her great passion, and the Shaws' home became a rehearsal centre for the amateur operatic society of which she and her singing master, George John Vandeleur Lee, were the leaders: Lee as producer and conductor, Mrs Shaw as *prima donna*. By the age of fifteen, her son had memorized operas and oratorios by Mozart, Handel, Beethoven, Rossini, Mendelssohn, Bellini, Donizetti, Verdi, Gounod. He whistled these as London street-boys whistled music-hall songs; and when, not long afterwards, he was working as a cashier in a Dublin land office, he taught the articled pupils there to sing (in office hours) Italian operatic arias. In March 1876, he walked out of the office and crossed St George's Channel.

Shaw spent over sixteen years in London before his first play was produced, and in the nine years between 1876 and 1885 he earned only £6 by spasmodic literary efforts – £5 being for a patent-medicine advertisement. He wrote five novels which were refused by publishers, though two or three of the stories ran serially in small magazines, and all have since been published in book form, the first, *Immaturity*, not until 1930, when Shaw added a valuable autobiographical preface. In 1882 he heard a speech on land nationalization by Henry George, the American author of *Progress and Poverty*, which fired him to enlist in 'the liberative war of humanity'. At that time, also, he came under the influence of Shelley's humanitarian and vegetarian doctrines. Shaw's circle of friends included Sidney Webb (afterwards a Labour peer, Lord Passfield) and other socialistic thinkers, and he became a member of the Fabian Society, which turned from current extremism to 'gradualism', through the propagation of Socialist principles by methods of investigation, education, and general penetration. Some of Shaw's earliest writings were done for the Fabian Society's economic and political tracts.

During those years of political agitation and ferment he determined to become an effective public speaker, and took every opportunity that offered for addressing public meetings, becoming a familiar figure at street-corners and in the rooms of debating societies. By 1885 he was reduced to 'quite straitened financial circumstances', and with the help of introductions from William Archer[1] began his career as a journalist, writing for the *Pall Mall Gazette* and *The World*. He was appointed music critic to *The Star* in 1888; in 1895 dramatic critic of the *Saturday Review*, at that time entering a new phase of brilliance with Frank Harris as editor. The two volumes of *Dramatic Opinions and Essays* gathered from Shaw's contributions to the *Saturday Review* were over-shadowed by his later works; but the essays still delight by their freshness and

[1] Archer (1856–1924) was a leading dramatic critic, the first translator of most of Ibsen's works, and the author of *The Green Goddess* (1921) an extremely popular play, deserving its success, though its wild improbabilities were at variance with its author's earlier enthusiasm for drama with a realistic social purpose.

originality, their sound and well-informed standards of judgement, and their lively wit and Shavian audacity. They were collected, complete, in *Our Theatres in the 'Nineties* (1931).

At that time the 'New Journalism' was being born in England. Compulsory elementary education was in its first decade at the time Shaw reached London, and by 1895 a new reading public was growing up. The settled dignity of the Press began to be shaken by new methods and by new periodicals in which liveliness was considered more important than authority. One of the liveliest new journalists was Bernard Shaw. Whatever he said or wrote was governed by the determination to make himself heard and to keep his hearers alert. 'In order to get a hearing', he said, 'it was necessary for me to attain the footing of a privileged lunatic, with the licence of a jester. . . . My method is to take the utmost trouble to find the right thing to say, and then to say it with the utmost levity. And all the time the real joke is that I am in earnest.' Already he had impressed himself upon public notice. His quick, eager, destructive questioning of social institutions provided the mental stimulant for which the younger generation was ready. Though he aroused hatred, he also gathered by degrees an enthusiastic following. As a matter of considered policy he lived in the limelight and used the paraphernalia of the circus to attract and hold his audience. He behaved, consciously, as a mountebank, employing the weapons of laughter and ridicule to attack bad housing, bad education, bad conditions of labour, bad morals, and other social evils which troubled him so deeply that he would have paraded London with a barrel-organ and in a clown's attire if he could have got a hearing upon no other condition; for, he held, 'it is only the man who has no message who is too fastidious to beat the drum at the door of his booth'.[1] Nevertheless, his circus-tricks were not simply a cloak for flippancy or self-posturing. Unlike the inaccurately-called 'satirists' of the 1950s and 1960s, he founded his satire upon well-digested knowledge, not upon the verbal smartness which substitutes derision for understanding.

After trying many devices and using many platforms, Shaw concluded that the stage was the finest platform in the world. He

[1] Preface to *Three Plays by Brieux* (1911).

taught himself the dramatist's job, and in addition to being a great controversialist became an incomparable playwright. Some of his characters are lively marionettes, rather than human beings standing on their own feet and using their own tongues; he had lapses from good taste; his humour is sometimes laboriously contrived. Yet when all deductions are made, and when Shakespeare has been put at the head of the roll of English dramatists, who is to be placed second if not Shaw? Ben Jonson, Marlowe, Congreve, Webster, Tourneur, Sheridan? The failings of any of these are no fewer than those of Shaw, though they may be different failings; their achievements seem less than his. Not one of them directed and dominated the thought of the seventeenth or eighteenth century as Shaw directed and dominated the thought of the early twentieth century – in England and beyond. Not one of them was moved by a blaze of moral passion, as Shaw was. Not one of them had a greater command of rhetoric or a more brilliant wit. Some of them were great poets – as Shaw was not; yet which of them commanded a better-sustained prose style than Shaw at his best?

Whatever Bernard Shaw's actual stature as a dramatist, his potential stature was still greater, for he consciously subordinated his literary talent to moral purpose. He became the Knight of the Burning Pencil, a crusader whose appointed lifework was the endeavour to restore colour and light and joy to England's once green and pleasant land. The 1890s, the period of his beginnings, was a period of 'art for art's sake'. Bernard Shaw, however, could find no justification for art that was not controlled by moral passion; his watchword was 'art for life's sake'; ' "for art's sake" alone I would not face the toil of writing a single sentence'.[1] He was a natural literary artist fettered by reforming zeal, and his plays are a continuous record of the long struggle between artist and moralist. Whenever he found himself writing as an artist, as a master of prose, he was possessed by the dread of being *merely* an artist, a dilettante. He realized his great command of majestic rhetoric, and feared lest it should become a mental drug, tending to make audiences dull and solemn. When he suspected any such danger, his method of correction was (he said) to 'introduce a joke and knock the solemn

[1] *Man and Superman:* Epistle Dedicatory.

people off their perch'. Perhaps he underrated the good sense of his audiences. Whatever the motive, it does not appear that any benefit – moral, psychological, or literary – came (for example) from following the sublime rhetoric of Caesar's address to the Sphinx with the childish prattle of Cleopatra,[1] and it is fortunate that his distrust of the aesthetic element did not prevent such things as Joan's speeches before her judges (*Saint Joan*), the litany at the end of that play, the last speech of Lilith (*Back to Methuselah*), or the opening scene and the interlude to *The Apple Cart*.

Shaw's first play appeared in 1892, three years after Ibsen's *The Doll's House* reached the London stage. There is a tendency to overemphasize the extent of Ibsen's influence upon Shaw, strong though it was. The unorthodox trend of his mind had been evident before he left Dublin, and before he knew anything of Ibsen. Contact with Ibsen's ideas did not bring about a revolutionary change of mental attitude in Shaw, it only confirmed an attitude previously adopted. He was impressed by the 'technical novelty' of Ibsen's plays: by his judgements upon ideals and idealists; and by his anti-romantic impatience of 'the womanly woman'. Ibsen's conviction that the real slavery of his day was 'slavery to ideals of goodness' was heartily approved by Shaw, for he, too, believed that unrestrained idealism was unintelligent idealism, without thought or reasoning, and therefore dangerous, destructive, and pernicious.[2] Shaw claimed and exercised the right of private judgement on all questions of conduct, as against the conventional habit of allegiance to 'accepted' institutions: 'conduct must justify itself by its effect upon happiness and not by its conformity to any rule or ideal'.[3]

To Shaw, the practice of questioning orthodox and 'accepted' standards of belief was at once the beginning of wisdom and the beginning of goodness. Anything popular (in the sense of being automatically accepted as the best thing possible) should, he believed, be looked upon with suspicion – whether it be vaccination, an educational system, the family, or a religion. One of his first propositions was that good institutions and bad institutions alike were

[1] *Caesar and Cleopatra* (1901), Act I.
[2] See *Brand* for Ibsen's most massive presentation of this theme.
[3] *The Quintessence of Ibsenism* (1891).

regarded with confidence by the multitude only because the whole mass of accepted institutions had hardened into *custom*; so that what is *customary* is likely to be confused with what is virtuous and what is right. His career was one long incitement to insistent questioning of *What is*, with the purpose of establishing a rightful conception of *What should be*: 'Progress is not achieved by panicstricken rushes back and forward between one folly and another, but by sifting all movements and adding what survives the sifting to the fabric of our morality.'[1]

Widowers' Houses, the first of Shaw's plays, was started in collaboration with William Archer, but, on Archer's withdrawal, the manuscript lay untouched for nearly seven years. It was at length completed by Shaw alone, and produced at the Independent Theatre by J. T. Grein towards the end of 1892. In 1898 the first collection of Bernard Shaw's plays appeared: *Plays: Pleasant and Unpleasant*, in two volumes.

Historically considered, *Widowers' Houses* was a dramatic essay in 'social realism' long before the term had been coined in Russia or elsewhere. Dealing with the social disgrace of ruthless oppression of the poor by financier slum-landlords, it dealt no less with an apparently ineradicable human vice, for as long afterwards as 1963 the evils it exposed were still active in London and elsewhere, despite much social legislation. But though *Widowers' Houses* can be described as an economic tract in dramatic form, it is none the less to be considered, in its merits and its faults, as a stage play. The characters are mostly (and intentionally) shown as hypocrites and humbugs: Trench is an ignorant sentimentalist, Blanche Sartorius a designing minx with a touch of insane unrestraint. It is, however, lively and humorous: the opposing groups of characters are permitted to state their own case fairly; but there is little dramatic objectivity. Here, in his first play, Shaw's stock-character – the obtuse, thick-skinned, unimaginative, humorless Englishman – already appears. This character, the Cokane of 1892, is brother to a dozen others down to the de Stogumber of 1924 (in *Saint Joan*). These absurd Englishmen of Bernard Shaw's have been much abused by critics; but a more dispassionate consideration might

[1] Preface to *Three Plays by Brieux*.

suggest that they have a long and interesting ancestry. In respect of themselves they are Shaw's own creation; yet in respect of their dramatic function in the plays, they might be compared with the buffoons of an earlier tradition: the Vice of the medieval drama, and the Fool of the Elizabethan – before the Fool had been transformed by Shakespeare from a buffoon into a philosophic and poetic genius.

The stage situations in *Widowers' Houses* are contrived with less dramatic power than those in *Mrs Warren's Profession*, yet in each of the three *Unpleasant Plays* the characters are for the most part controlled by the hand of a puppet-master. In *Pleasant Plays*, for the first time, the ideas become less important than the persons who state them – but the ideas lose none of their force. *Arms and the Man* is a success not because of its ideas – impressive though these are – but because Bluntschli picks up the play and walks off with it. The artist in Shaw had already begun to play pranks with the moralist. William the butler, in *You Never Can Tell*, is another fully individualized creation, as also are the majority of the people in *Candida*.

These two volumes, then, as well as the *Three Plays for Puritans* (1901) which followed, show the preacher struggling in the embraces of the siren, Art. The sole desire of the preacher was to communicate his ideas and convictions. The dramatic artist had other purposes. Though the preacher succeeded in keeping his feet, he had to fight constantly against the pull and lure of 'mere litera-ure'.

By 1903, when *Man and Superman* appeared, Bernard Shaw was a well-equipped playwright. His apprentice days were over, and he was equal to whatever demands the theatre and the dramatic form could make. The later plays do not, however, show him going uninterruptedly forward from strength to strength. It is now pull devil, now pull baker, as reforming zeal or literary power gets the upper hand. In *Man and Superman* the ideas may be found more memorable than the characters, and there is little reliance upon stage situation; but the tremendous stirring of moral and intellectual passion is compensation enough, and even if the characters appear subsidiary to this, there is nevertheless a good deal of life in John Tanner and 'Enery Straker. Described by the author as 'A Comedy and a Philosophy', *Man and Superman* was Bernard Shaw's earliest full statement of his conception of the way of salvation for the human race, through obedience to the Life Force,[1] the term he used to indicate a power continually seeking to work in the hearts of men and endeavouring to impel them towards a better and fuller life. In later plays the Life Force seemed to become more and more closely identified with what most people mean when they speak of the Will of God and the Holy Ghost.[2] Though Shaw's Life Force is not anthropomorphic, in its functions it is not vastly different from the Christian idea of the function of the Holy Ghost. It might be described as the Holy Ghost denuded of personality – IT, not *He*. If in future times the medieval habit of posthumously Christianizing the works of non-Christian writers should be resumed, the editing of Bernard Shaw on such lines would be a comparatively simple task, demanding only a few suppressions here and there, and the substitution of some Christian term for the words Life Force. Shaw himself led the way by writing, in his essay on Parents and Children, 'the child feels the drive of the Life Force (often called the Will of God)'.[3] But even if 'the Will of God' had exactly defined Shaw's idea of a universal directing power, he would not have used the familiar words, for he was convinced that over-familiarity with current phrases is the great obstacle to clear thought and positive action. If he had spoken about 'the Will of God', only the already converted would have listened. He chose, instead, to commend an apparently new discovery, the Life Force. But the Life Force was no newer than God. If the religion of Bernard Shaw was, to many twentieth-century ears, more attractive than any orthodox faith, this was largely because of the invigorating call put into Barbara's mouth: 'I have got rid of the bribe of heaven. Let God's work be done for its own sake: the work he had to create us to do because it cannot be done except by living men and women.'[4] The idea of working for the world's good without thought of personal reward,

[1] The contemporary French philosopher Henry Bergson (1859–1941) strongly influenced Shaw through his theories of *l'élan vital* and *L'Evolution Créatrice* (developed in Shaw's *Back to Methuselah*).

[2] 'The man who was scientific enough to see that the Holy Ghost is the most interesting of all the hard facts of life got easily in front of the blockheads who could only sin against it.'—*Back to Methuselah*, Preface.

[3] Preface to *Misalliance* (1910).

[4] *Major Barbara* (1905), Act III.

here or hereafter, was in selfless contrast with the familiar Christian desire for eternal personal felicity.

The philosophy (or the religion) of the Life Force, introduced in *Man and Superman*, ran through most of the later plays. Unlike Hardy's Immanent Will, Shaw's Life Force is represented as a power making consciously towards a state of existence far more abundantly vital than anything yet experienced by mankind. But the Life Force does not purpose to work unaided: men and women are required to act as willing and eager agents for the furtherance of its great work. The existing race of men, however (so Shaw thought in 1903), was too mean-spirited and too self-centred to serve the Life Force, which would consequently be compelled to supersede Man by a more effective instrument of its will – the Superman. The means likely to be adopted for the production of that higher type were suggested in *Man and Superman*, where Woman is indicated as 'Nature's contrivance for perpetuating its achievement', and Man as 'Woman's contrivance for fulfilling Nature's behest' that the Superman should be born to replace the existing 'feverish, selfish little clod of ailments and grievances'.[1] In *The Revolutionist's Handbook* (appended to *Man and Superman* as a work by John Tanner) Shaw turned back to scriptural language to express his convictions: there he speaks of Man as the Temple of the Holy Ghost; and urges, ' "ye must be born again" and "born different" '.

The crux of the whole problem, in Shaw's interpretation, is whether Man will or will not address himself to 'the work of helping Life in its struggle upward'.[2] If Man will not undertake this work, if he will not help towards getting himself born again and born different – if, indeed, he sets obstacles in the way, or becomes, himself, a passive obstacle – what is to happen? Will the Life Force permit its purposes to be thwarted in order that Man may enjoy the prerogative of 'free will'? The latter question was answered by Shaw with emphatic negatives in more than one of the plays that followed *Man and Superman*;[3] until, at length, the unregarded warning of those negatives blazed up into prophetic denunciation of 'cultured, leisured Europe'. *Heartbreak House* was begun in 1913,

[1] *Man and Superman*, Epistle Dedicatory. [2] Ibid.
[3] Particularly in *The Shewing-up of Blanco Posnet* (1909).

and even while Shaw was writing to remind men and women that Nature's patience was not inexhaustible, the judgement fell; and a generation that did not know how to live was forced back upon demonstrating, in a world war, that it knew how to die. Nature 'demoralizes us with long credits and reckless overdrafts, and then . . . suddenly Nature takes her revenge'.[1] When Mazzini Dunn remarks that there is much to be said for the theory of an over-ruling Providence, Captain Shotover replies: 'every drunken skipper trusts to Providence. But one of the ways of Providence with drunken skippers is to run them on the rocks.'[2] To Shaw, a generation that gave no heed to the purposes of the Life Force was like the drunken skipper to whom there comes – late, perhaps, but surely – 'the smash of the ship on the rocks, the splintering of her rotten timbers, the tearing of her rusty plates, the drowning of the crew like rats in a trap'. That was his vision of Europe in *Heartbreak House* (1919). There followed *Back to Methuselah* (1921), in which Shaw considered further the causes of the smash of the ship of Europe on the rocks, and contemplated the outlook for the future. Once again the purposes and claims of the Life Force were stressed; once again, and in plainer terms than before, he spoke his warning: that if Man did not come up to the mark, Man would be replaced (perhaps catastrophically) by a less tragically futile creature. Shaw proclaimed that the effect of modern civilization had been to store up 'the social disease and corruption which explode from time to time in gigantic boils that have to be lanced by a million bayonets'; and he went on to say:

> This situation has occurred so often before, always with the same result of a collapse of civilization. . . . This does not mean that if Man cannot find the remedy no remedy will be found. The power that produced Man when the monkey was not up to the mark, can produce a higher creature than Man if Man does not come up to the mark. What it means is that if Man is to be saved, Man must save himself.[3]

He laid the heaviest blame for the alleged failure of civilization upon Darwin and the theory of Natural Selection, which had (Shaw believed) 'banished mind from the universe' and created a stultifying

[1] *Heartbreak House*, Preface. [2] Ibid., Act III.
[3] *Back to Methuselah*, Preface.

conviction that life was 'a chapter of accidents' not capable of being modified or controlled by human action. He pleaded for the substitution of Creative Evolution – his 'religion of the twentieth century' – which teaches not only that Man is the potential Superman, but also that Man can himself hasten the evolutionary process by 'willing' his own upward development: 'If the giraffe can develop his neck by wanting and trying, a man can develop his character in the same way. . . . Indifference will not guide nations through civilization to the establishment of the perfect city of God.'[1] The Life Force is not named as frequently in *Back to Methuselah* as in *Man and Superman*, but it remains the power behind the idea of Creative Evolution. The ultimate desire of the Life Force is to establish the city of God on earth. The intention at the back of the idea of Creative Evolution is that Man should work intentionally (*creatively*) towards the evolution of a human type that will be strong enough to establish and worthy enough to maintain the earthly paradise. Creative Evolution was the doctrine commended by Shaw as a means through which the desire of Man and the purpose of the Life Force might be made identical.

Bernard Shaw's ideas may long continue to overshadow the literary aspect of his work. But in one mature play now quite out of date in its subject-matter (*John Bull's Other Island*, 1904) it is possible to see the dramatic strength behind the fabric of topical interests. This play remains one of his most effective pieces, displaying his dramatic power – mastery of rhetoric and exalted prose, effective handling of stage situation, skill in depicting character, and sense of comedy. Elsewhere, also, these merits are unmistakable, particularly in *Saint Joan* (1924), where, as in previous plays,[2] the Discussion Scene is employed with triumphant effect. One of the most thrilling experiences that could come to a theatregoer was to be present at an early performance of *Saint Joan*, as a unit of a great theatre-audience held spellbound – motionless and silent for some half an hour – while three men sat at a table on the stage and did nothing but talk, *talk*, TALK.[3] In 1903, Shaw wrote, 'I wanted a pit of philosophers'. Twenty years later he had a theatreful night after

[1] *Back to Methuselah*, Preface.
[2] E.g. *The Doctor's Dilemma* (1906), Act I.
[3] *Saint Joan*, Scene IV.

night. Some were not profound philosophers, perhaps; but at least they had brought their brains to the theatre – what is more, they were using their brains – and they were thrilled, as perhaps they had rarely been thrilled before, by the power of words and the excitement of ideas.

But the fact that Shaw was always a *laughing* philosopher made him suspect to the Solemn Old of the nineteen-tens and caused him to be rejected by the Solemn Young of succeeding decades. To the former he was morally a menace, to the latter politically and sociologically a trifler. Yet he did far more for sane moral and political education than his detractors had the power or the wit to do. He was the master of words and notions, not their slave; he was sure enough in his own faith to continue to be heartily good-tempered about it, even when he found himself in the midst of an insurgent generation that identified aggressive bad manners with strength of mind and force of argument.

Shaw's mental agility continued into his eighties, and, only a few years before, he wrote, in *Saint Joan* (1924), what is probably his best all-round play, though he had had greater moments of genius. *The Apple Cart* (1930) is one of his wisest and most genial pieces, wise not so much because of the political acumen of King Magnus as for the dicta on the art of self-sufficingness in the opening dialogue and on the art of human relationships in the Interlude, which is also a passage of sparkling comedy rarely equalled in the modern English theatre. Shaw's plays from *The Apple Cart* to the end of the nineteen-thirties were mostly topical commentaries upon the European nightmare: *Too True to Be Good* (1931), *On the Rocks* (1933), and *Geneva* (1939) have flashes of Shavian fire, though, like *In Good King Charles's Golden Days* (1939), they suggest that the playwright was tiring of his medium. By the time of his death in 1950 at the age of ninety-four he had added nothing further of importance to his nearly fifty works for the stage, but always, when he chose to be so, Shaw was a master of the spoken word (a gift he acquired in his early days of public speaking) even as in his prefaces he was a master of the written word in the tradition of Bunyan and Defoe and Swift, though he had no trace of Swift's sick horror of the human race.

3. JOHN GALSWORTHY

In his essays, John Galsworthy wrote of 'naturalistic technique' in relation to both the novel and the drama not as the ideal technique but as a method offering definite advantages. Naturalistic art, he said, 'is like a steady lamp, held up from time to time, in whose light things will be seen for a space clearly and in due proportion, freed from the mists of prejudice and partisanship'.[1] The parallelism between these words and the allegory of Cethru[2] is sufficiently close to make it evident that Galsworthy desired to reproduce, both upon the stage and in his books, the natural spectacle of life, presented with detachment. The influences operating against this desire have been referred to on a previous page.[3] Those delicate sympathies which made him so gently persuasive a partisan in the novels are active in the plays also, and since dramatic technique demands a form of treatment less expansive than that natural to the novel, stage plays gave Galsworthy little scope for concealing the direction of his own sympathies. He was drawn into the mists of partisanship, sometimes by his choice of incident at the climax of a play; sometimes by an alienating strain of blatancy in a particular character; sometimes by the emotional weight of a 'third party' commentator.

In *Strife* (1909) the case for both sides *is* seen, 'for a space, clearly and in due proportion'. When the play begins, old John Anthony is presiding with adamant absolutism over a meeting of the directors of the Trenartha Tin Plate Works on the Welsh border. A strike has been going on for four months, through a hard winter, and tentative movements on both sides towards a settlement are prevented from making progress only by the persistent 'No compromise!' cry of John Anthony for the owners, and the equally unyielding 'No surrender!' of David Roberts, the men's leader. But at a critical moment, when the men are wavering, Roberts's wife dies. Both sides yield simultaneously, and, throwing over their leaders, accept the precise terms they had rejected four months earlier. In the interval there has been suffering, privation and death on the side of the men, and heavy financial loss by the owners. In the earlier part of

[1] 'Some Platitudes Concerning Drama' (in *The Inn of Tranquillity*).
[2] See above, pp. 42 f. [3] See above, pp. 43 ff.

the play the scales are held dispassionately by the dramatist, and the audience feels only the desperate futility of the tragic pride and prejudice on both sides. But then, by his choice of incident at the climax of the play, Galsworthy dispels in a moment the illusion of objectivity. The death of Mrs Roberts is not an appeal to human instincts of harmony and justice; it is an appeal to humanitarian sentiment which, fundamentally, has no bearing upon the real problem of *Strife*.

The Skin Game (1920) presents the conflict between Hillcrist, one of the better type of old-established aristocratic landed proprietor, and the loud, pushful, uncultured, new-rich manufacturer, Hornblower. Dissension has arisen between the two families because the Hillcrists will not accord social recognition to Hornblower's family. In his resentment, Hornblower buys a beautiful estate, The Centry, which provides the Hillcrists with one of their finest views; and on The Centry he purposes to build a factory – unless the Hillcrists admit the Hornblowers' right to a place in the social sun. Mrs Hillcrist, discovering that Chloe (Hornblower's daughter-in-law) has a questionable past, proposes – in opposition to the wishes of her husband and her daughter – to use this information as a weapon of protection against Hornblower's scheme of aggression. Chloe, in dread of the threatened revelation, attempts suicide, and at the end of the play (in the printed version) she is carried in, just breathing: a victim hunted between two forces – neither having any direct grievance against her. The motto of the play is 'Who touches pitch shall be defiled'; and a question repeatedly on the lips of Hillcrist and his delightful daughter Jill is: 'What's gentility worth if it can't stand fire?' A case is stated (and well stated) for both sides, but Hornblower's case is weakened by the blatancy of the man himself. It is the same phase in the problem of social replacement as H. G. Wells comments upon in *Tono-Bungay*, and it is fair to say that (although he makes no claim to impartiality) Wells there 'directs' the sympathies of his audience less definitely than Galsworthy does in *The Skin Game*. When Hornblower concludes a discussion by shouting 'I'm going on with as little consideration as if ye were a family of blackbeetles', it is difficult for any audience to retain a balanced sense of justice.

Justice (1910) is a commentary upon the prison administration of that period.[1] Falder, a young unstable-minded solicitor's clerk, alters a cheque, with the idea of getting money to help Ruth Honeywell to escape from a brutal husband, and is sent to penal servitude. Cokeson, the managing clerk of the office where Falder was employed, visits him in the prison a month before his term of solitary confinement expires. In a subsequent interview with the prison chaplain, Cokeson says:

> I can't help thinking that to shut him up there by himself'll turn him silly. And nobody wants that, I s'pose. I *don't* like to see a man cry.
>
> *The Chaplain.* It's a very rare thing for them to give way like that.
>
> *Cokeson (looking at him – in a tone of sudden dogged hostility).* I keep dogs.
>
> *The Chaplain.* Indeed?
>
> *Cokeson.* Ye-es. And I say this: I wouldn't shut one of them up all by himself, month after month, not if he'd bit me all over. . . . If you treat 'em with kindness they'll do anything for you; but to shut 'em up alone, it only makes 'em savage.

The soundness or otherwise of Cokeson's view is not in question; the point is that the effect of his remarks upon an average audience is that of an emotional bludgeoning; and such emotional reactions as follow from this are a hindrance to impartiality and justice.

Disproportionate attention was given to the social and ethical problems in Galsworthy's novels and plays, and there was a consequent tendency to overlook his technical efficiency as a dramatist. William Archer was among those who pointed out the fullness of effect by the utmost economy of means in the opening scene of *The Silver Box* (1909). The curtain goes up on an empty, well-furnished dining-room; the electric light is burning; the clock shows that the time is after midnight. The door is opened fumblingly by a young man in evening dress, benevolently drunk. He is carrying a lady's velvet bag. In the first speech, which consists of only fifty-nine broken words, incoherently spoken, the audience learns:

(1) That the house is the young man's home.

(2) That he has had to have assistance from a stranger in order to get into the house.

[1] It was reported that certain prison reforms introduced shortly after this date were due to *Justice*.

(3) That the velvet bag is the property of a temporary lady companion who has annoyed him.

(4) That he has purloined her bag in order to 'pay her out'.

(5) That he has forgotten to 'tip' Jones, the man who helped him in.

(6) That he has in his pocket only one shilling (which he drops and loses among the furniture).

Six facts, several of them important in the development of the play, are thus conveyed in fifty-nine broken words: and each fact excites interest and stimulates curiosity. But that is not the whole of the dramatic content of those few minutes. The young man has taken a cigarette out of a silver box lying on the table – thus drawing attention to the mainspring of the play. And the apparently unimportant action of dropping his last shilling sets that mainspring in motion. The dropping of the shilling is the most important factor in the play, for if the young man had kept hold of his shilling, or if he had had other money in his pocket, he would have been able to tip the man who helped him into the house; the man, being paid, would have gone away; and there would have been no consequent series of events. Therefore, in addition to providing an important body of information about the characters, the words and actions of those opening moments also contain the nucleus of the ensuing tragi-comedy. When the young man has dropped his last shilling, he goes out to tell his guide that he has no money to give to him, and then returns with him to give him a drink in lieu of cash. This second man is seen to be fairly young but shabbily dressed, haggard and shady-looking, with a suspicious air. It is learnt, in a few further words, that Borthwick's father is a Liberal Member of Parliament, and that Jones's wife is the Borthwicks' charwoman. In the course of a further short rambling speech, more light is thrown upon the velvet bag and its owner, before young Borthwick falls asleep on the sofa. Jones is then free to get drunk on the whisky. Partly as a result of his natural predatory instinct, and partly because of whisky-inspired malevolence, he steals the cigarette box, and also the crimson silk purse from the lady's handbag, before (without waking Borthwick) he leaves the house; and the scene closes. What is conveyed to the audience in that short passage shows that already, in his first play, Galsworthy was an able dramatist who delighted in his craft. The economy of construction noted in *The Silver Box* is also a characteristic of other plays by him. There is here, moreover, an effective economy of style and characterization, which in the later plays run to extremes. In *A Bit o' Love* (1915) and in *Loyalties* (1922), the treatment and the language are so denuded of superfluity as to be almost threadbare. Dialogue in a play, though it must be free from cloudiness and tautology, cannot afford to be meagre and bare. The illusion of life upon the stage depends largely upon the quality of the dialogue, which must have warmth and a certain richness, and, even, what might be called a fine excess.[1] Simplicity of aim and singleness of purpose are merits in literature, but when these are carried too far the result is bloodlessness and absence of human warmth. *Loyalties* is saved from bloodlessness only by the character of Jacob Twisden the old solicitor, but neither he nor any other character in Galsworthy's later plays can compare with Mrs Jones, the charwoman, in *The Silver Box*, or John Anthony in *Strife*. The latter, though a monument of human stubbornness, is cast in a tremendously impressive mould; and of the memorable episodes in Galsworthy's plays probably the finest is John Anthony's cry when, after half a century of work, he is flung overboard by his fellow-directors: 'Fifty years! You have disgraced me, gentlemen.'

4. THE IRISH THEATRE

From the middle of the eighteenth century down to the beginning of the twentieth the chief additions to English drama were the work of Irishmen. Until the end of the nineteenth century, however, there was no genuinely Irish drama. Sheridan and Goldsmith, Wilde and Shaw, were not engaged with Irish themes. Bernard Shaw's *John Bull's Other Island*, an Irish play, is an isolated example. Shaw, like his predecessors, was an English *dramatist* though he was an Irish *man*. In the Victorian period there were lesser Irish playwrights who took Irish subjects, but such plays as Dion Boucicault's *Colleen Bawn* and *Arrah-na-Pogue* do not belong either to literature or to life. They

[1] Cf. comments upon Granville Barker, p. 120.

helped to perpetuate the 'stage Irishman' – a travesty which the new drama set itself to destroy.

William Butler Yeats (1865–1939), who led the new Irish literary movement, was born in Dublin, and spent some years of his early life in Sligo, the background to much of his work. His father was Jack B. Yeats the painter, and the family were in London for some time while W. B. Yeats was still a boy; he was educated first at Hammersmith and afterwards in Dublin. When about twenty-two years old he returned to London, and became acquainted with W. E. Henley, William Morris, Oscar Wilde, Bernard Shaw, among others. Yeats went back to Dublin in 1891, having established in London an Irish Literary Society in which he enrolled all the Irish authors and journalists in the metropolis. He founded a similar Literary Society in Ireland in 1892, regarding it as a preliminary to his great hope of establishing an Irish National Theatre. That hope was realized in 1899. Much had previously been done by the Gaelic League to revive popular interest in the old fairy stories and folk-lore of the Irish people. Yeats himself had been inspired by the Gaelic movement, and he was convinced that through a wide dissemination of these Celtic myths, not alone Ireland but the whole world might be stimulated. No form of literary art then moved so large an audience as the acted drama, and drama was the medium to which Yeats looked. Yet the only means then available for producing plays was the commercial theatre, representing all that he detested: stage-conventions were anathema to him; stage-realism the very antithesis of the symbolism which moved him strongly. When, therefore, the Irish Literary Theatre gave its first performance at the Antient Concert Rooms in Dublin on 8 May 1899, the *play* was the main thing, and stage-setting comparatively unimportant.

A beginning was made with the help of Lady Gregory and the backing of a group of guarantors, upon whom it never became necessary to make any call. At first, English actors and an English producer were engaged, though (at least in intention) the scheme was thoroughly Irish. The plays chosen for the first performance were Yeats's *The Countess Cathleen*, and *The Heather Field*, a modern play by Edward Martyn. The opening season was so promising that, in the next year, the promoters were able to accept an invitation to give their performances at the Gaiety Theatre, Dublin.

The Irish Literary Theatre, with professional English actors performing Irish plays under an English producer, lasted only three seasons. In 1902, an Irish amateur company of players under W. G. Fay – in co-operation with Yeats and Lady Gregory – produced *Deirdre*, by A. E.,[1] and *Cathleen ni Houlihan*, by W. B. Yeats, at St Teresa's Hall, Dublin; and out of that performance grew the Irish National Theatre Society and the world-renowned Irish Players. In 1904 Miss A. E. F. Horniman[2] provided money to enable the company to acquire and reconstruct the Abbey Theatre, Dublin, which became the permanent home of the Society. The opportunities afforded by the Irish National Theatre Society made it possible for young Irish dramatists to get a hearing. Although reasonable financial success was secured by the Irish Players, they took risks that commercial managers would not have taken; artistic sincerity and literary promise were regarded as more important than immediate profit.

The first prominent figure among the dramatists of the Irish literary theatre movement was, of course, W. B. Yeats himself. His *The Countess Cathleen* (1892) and *The Land of Heart's Desire* (1894) became widely known, but their popularity depended more upon poetic charm and strangeness than upon dramatic power. In such an exacting medium as poetic drama exceptional skill is required to ensure a balance between poetry, action, and characterization. Yeats's plays are defective in organic construction. They do not create the illusion of possible people behaving credibly and using an appropriate speech-medium. Though the characterization is more effective in *The Land of Heart's Desire* than in *The Countess Cathleen*, poetry is obtrusive in both plays. When the characters speak extended passages of verse they belong as obviously to an artificial convention as a *prima donna* who persistently takes the centre of the stage.

Yeats was, in the beginning, essentially a romantic lyrical poet, and he did not move with ease in the dramatic form. Every playwright has, of necessity, to use artificial conventions; but a true

[1] The pseudonym of George Russell. [2] See below, p. 118.

dramatist uses these conventions so skilfully that the audience is not conscious of assisting at an artificial display: the illusion is complete. A revival of interest in Yeats's plays around the middle of this century was inspired mainly by the current attraction to symbolism, a leading factor in his later poetry and plays alike. But it still seems improbable that Yeats can be established as a playwright for the living stage.

In 1903 two new names appeared in the Irish National Theatre Society's list of authors: Lady Gregory and J. M. Synge.

John Millington Synge (1871–1909) was born near Dublin, of a family of landowners. He graduated at Trinity College, Dublin, afterwards wandering through France, Germany, and Italy for several years, separated from Irish life and interests until W. B. Yeats met him in Paris in 1899 and advised him to get away from the Continent altogether and go back to Ireland to live among the peasants on the Aran Islands in Galway Bay. Synge took this advice, dwelling as a peasant among peasants, steeping himself in their language, storing his mind with their tales, and observing closely their customs and character.

The great merit of Synge's plays is at the same time their chief fault. His material is reduced to the utmost degree of concentration, until his humour becomes bitingly grim and sardonic, and his tragedy bitter pain. He rarely admits a superfluous word; indeed he uses the pruning-knife too ruthlessly. Some part of Shakespeare's greatness lies in his generous superfluity – corresponding with the super-abundance of life itself. Synge's plays never quite 'live' outside the mind, for he failed to recognize that there is a point beyond which the virtue of economy passes into the fault of deficiency.

Riders to the Sea (1904) is nevertheless one of the few twentieth-century examples of true tragedy, and it comes short of being a great tragedy only by being excessively harrowing and ruthless. Jack B. Yeats said that Synge's plays were 'poetry in unlimited sadness'. There is austere beauty in the unlimited sadness of old Maurya (in this play) who loses all her men-folk one by one. But the beauty fades out, and only the shadow of death remains as the curtain falls upon Maurya kneeling by the body of the last of her sons. Yet, though *Riders to the Sea* presents Life as all darkness and winter, it is the true winter of Life, not merely a gloomy artificial obscuring of the light which some writers of near-tragedy mistake for the authentic darkness of Nature.

Synge's bleak comedy *The Shadow of the Glen* aroused much protest when it was first produced in Dublin in 1903. It was a tradition among Nationalists that Irish women were more virtuous than English women. When Synge made Nora Burke unfaithful to her husband it was felt that he was maligning Ireland, and there was uproar in the theatre. These demonstrations, however, were a storm in a teacup compared with the tornado that fell upon the Abbey Theatre when Synge's *The Playboy of the Western World* was first acted at the beginning of 1907. Each night for a week the performances were violently interrupted, but the players stood firm, and this became the most popular of Synge's plays. An old man in the Aran Islands told Synge a story which began: 'If any gentleman has done a crime we'll hide him. There was a gentleman that killed his father, and I had him in my house for six weeks till he got away to America.' *The Playboy of the Western World* was based upon that story, and the suggestion that Irishmen were capable of glorifying a murderer provoked the riots. *The Playboy* gives an impressive representation of Irish peasant life and character, and is full of 'striking and beautiful phrases' heard by the author on the roads from Kerry to Mayo or among beggar-women and ballad-singers around Dublin. What Synge desired in drama (he wrote in the preface to *The Playboy*) were reality and joy, and speeches 'as fully flavoured as a nut or apple'. He felt that in Ireland

> . . . for a few years more, we have a popular imagination that is fiery and magnificent and tender; so that those of us who wish to write, start with a chance that is not given to writers in places where the spring-time of the local life has been forgotten, and the harvest is a memory only, and the straw has been turned into bricks.

Deirdre of the Sorrows, left uncompleted, was Synge's only departure from the treatment of modern themes; but he worked upon the legendary story of Deirdre in his own austere way, and endowed it with the gaunt granite-like beauty that is characteristic of most of his work.

Lady Gregory (1852–1932) experimented extensively in her dramatic works, which ranged from Irish historical plays to versions of Molière in Irish dialect. In addition, she did much to preserve the folk-lore of her country. Her best-known pieces are the *Seven Short Plays* (1909). Her characters are more genially human than those of Synge; and she approached nearer than Synge himself to the joy he speaks of in the introduction to *The Playboy*. Though her dialogue may not be as remarkable as Synge's it has a savour all its own, and there is no 'baldness' about the language of her peasants.

Yeats, Synge, and Lady Gregory were the leading figures of the older generation of dramatists in the modern Irish theatre. In the next generation three names again stood out: St John Ervine, Lennox Robinson, and Sean O'Casey.

As a vigorous and controversy-loving dramatic critic in the nineteen-twenties, St John Ervine did much useful service for the theatre. Like Lennox Robinson, he was for a time manager of the Abbey Theatre, and his two Irish domestic tragedies, *Mixed Marriage* (1911) and *John Ferguson* (1915), had fair success, particularly in America. Both these plays, powerful and moving, contain excellent examples of character-drawing, though a strain of hopelessness runs through their picture of the invincible and devastating stubbornness of men in the grip of religious and political 'convictions'. St John Ervine afterwards had a notable run of success in the commercial theatres of London and elsewhere with such competent and agreeable comedies as *The First Mrs Fraser* (1929), *Anthony and Anna* (1925), and *Robert's Wife* (1937). He was then an exponent of the settled views of middle age, opposing its stable standards of conduct to the raw enthusiasms and predatory instincts of the young. The clash was always entertaining and the issue gratifying to middle age; it might have carried more conviction if it had been made clearer that Youth, even when most self-seeking, has a point of view that should in fairness be ably and fully expressed in any play in which Youth is a chief protagonist.

Lennox Robinson dealt impressively in *The Lost Leader* (1919) with the legend that Parnell did not die at the time his death was announced, but lived in hiding. *The Whiteheaded Boy* (1920), an extremely laughable comedy, contains a gallery of human portraits that are not the less delightful because they verge upon caricature. In later experimental plays, such as *The Round Table* (1924), Robinson seemed to lose himself in a metaphysical mist.

When W. B. Yeats began his work for the Irish National Theatre, he proposed to found the new drama upon ancient Irish folk-lore. He wanted the new literature to be undated; or, when it was dated at all, to be set in a remote period, as in the vaguely indicated age of his own *Countess Cathleen*. The actual course of literary history in Ireland after 1900, however, was away from folk-story, and towards the peasant life and town life of modern times. The most remarkable of the 'town' dramatists was Sean O'Casey, whose *Juno and the Paycock* (1925) at once caused him to be acclaimed as a great dramatist. Brought up in the Dublin tenements which serve as a setting for his plays, he found ripe comedy as well as intense tragedy in those grim slum dwellings. Out of the recent history of Ireland O'Casey created tragi-comedy on the grand scale; and considering the partisan passions aroused by the Easter rebellion of 1916 and the subsequent Civil War, his objectivity was astonishing. The promise shown in O'Casey's early work was sufficient to place him, with Synge, at the head of the Abbey Theatre dramatists. His faults were those of undisciplined power and exuberance, rather than of inadequacy. *Juno and the Paycock* might have been a better play if the comic material in the first half had been kept under firmer control: the plunge into overwhelming tragic intensity after the appearance of Mrs Tancred near the end of the second act is too sharp a transition. In *The Plough and the Stars* (1926) there is again a disturbing juxtaposition of comedy and tragedy, but the proportions are more skilfully kept. What inward disturbance an audience may feel on account of the close and incongruous relationship between comedy and tragedy in the later play, is a disturbance due rather to life itself than to the dramatist. Sean O'Casey's first plays are much more than tragedies of the individual person or of particular groups of persons; they suggest, in symbolic form, the tragedy of Ireland itself, where heroism and cupidity, idealism and vainglory, vision and vice, beauty and foulness, poetry and profanity were inextricably mingled. The language of these plays is distinguished: though it is the language of the slums, it is full of beauty. The humorous characters are almost Falstaffian in stature, abundantly comic, though without the wit and subtlety of Falstaff; and the portraits of women are, in general, extremely well drawn.

There appeared to be few qualifications necessary to a fine dramatist that Sean O'Casey did not possess, and it seemed, in principle, all to the good when he was found to be reaching out to a different kind of play in *The Silver Tassie* (1928) and *Within the Gates* (1933). These were received as masterpieces by those to whom propaganda is the breath of life, though to others they seemed inferior as plays. O'Casey was here flirting with Expressionism, which requires a tendentious and subjective interpretation of the political and social order and the use of symbolic types instead of individual men and women. These requirements, in turn, demand a method of non-realistic (or semi-realistic) presentation upon which the playwright, or the producer, must impose his own mechanistic pattern in place of the less obvious but more rhythmic pattern of life. *Within the Gates* is a deeply felt product of the author's social conscience, admirable in intention as an indictment of society, ludicrous in its heavy solemnity, and, in its effect upon the unconverted, hotly null. Though at long intervals other plays by O'Casey came out, his later works were mainly a retreat from the stage into the printed book, and the praise of critics did not bring him new successes in the theatre.

5. THE REPERTORY MOVEMENT

The Irish theatre movement and the repertory theatres in England brought about that decentralization of the drama which became the most important development in English theatrical history since the sixteenth century. From the time of Shakespeare onward, 'English drama' meant, almost entirely, the plays produced in the London theatres. Dramatists had come to accept the London monopoly as one of the natural conditions of their craft, and grew accustomed to working within the limits imposed by that monopoly. The theatre was a place existing mainly for one of two purposes: (*a*) the exploitation of the personality of an actor-manager; (*b*) the provision of financial profit for a commercial manager who 'kept' a theatre as other men might keep a betting-shop.

The first confident challenge to the London monopoly came from the Irish theatre in Dublin; but meanwhile, in London itself, there had been the beginnings of revolt. J. T. Grein's Independent Theatre experiment introduced Bernard Shaw as a dramatist, and there were other sporadic efforts of a similar kind in the middle of the 'nineties.

One name stands out from the list of pioneers – that of Miss A. E. F. Horniman (1860–1937). Miss Horniman (a Londoner, born at Forest Hill) studied art under Professor Legros at the Slade School, and horrified her Victorian parents by interesting herself in woman's suffrage and in theatrical affairs. In 1894 she provided money for a season at the Avenue Theatre, London, which helped forward the Ibsen–Shaw movement. The season was 'a fruitful failure'. Ten years later Miss Horniman put the Abbey Theatre in Dublin firmly on its feet; and in 1907 she established the first modern repertory theatre in Great Britain at the Midland Theatre, Manchester. Next year she took the Gaiety Theatre in Manchester, and for over twelve years 'Miss Horniman's Company' set a standard for the rest of the theatrical world. When she retired in 1921, the Manchester Gaiety fell from grace and became a cinema. By that time, however, Miss Horniman's work had had substantial and lasting results elsewhere. Other provincial towns had instituted successful repertory theatres. Sybil Thorndike and her husband, Lewis Casson, having done excellent work at the Manchester Gaiety, helped Lilian Baylis to give London a permanent Shakespeare theatre at the Old Vic in Waterloo Bridge Road; after which, on their own account, they proceeded to popularize Greek tragedy throughout the country in the intervals of much other work.

The repertory movement was not only an attempt to free the theatre from the dictatorship of the financier and the actor-manager; it was also inspired by definite theories of dramatic art. (1) The 'long-run' system was regarded as injurious to both the play and the players, since it led to a mechanical style of acting that deadened the mind of the player and made him a machine instead of a sensitive instrument; the result being a coarsened interpretation of the play. (2) The repertory system was based upon the team principle. There were no permanent 'stars' among the actors: the Hamlet of one performance might be a second murderer in the next. (3) Under the old system, theatre managers 'called in' scene-painters, costumiers, composers, lighting experts, and others, to carry out certain separated pieces of work. The repertory system created a corporate art of the theatre – an organic whole, not a casual assemblage of disunited parts. (4) Most important of all for dramatic literature was the fact that repertory directors recognized that a good play might attract only comparatively small audiences. Under former conditions such a play had practically no chance of production, since little if any profit could be expected from it. But in the repertory theatres a few performances of a play with a limited appeal were balanced financially by the production of plays of a more popular type.

The most fruitful early repertory experiment in London was that conducted at the Court Theatre from 1904 to 1907 by J. E. Vedrenne and Granville Barker: Vedrenne as the man of affairs, Barker the man of the theatre. During that Court season thirty-two plays (new and old, native and foreign) were staged. The outstanding feature was the unanticipated popularity of Bernard Shaw. Eleven of his plays were produced, and these accounted for 701 performances out of a total of 988 during the season. The Vedrenne–Barker programme included, also, plays by Granville Barker himself (*The Voysey Inheritance*), John Galsworthy (*The Silver Box*), Ibsen, Euripides (in Gilbert Murray's translations), Maeterlinck, John Masefield, St John Hankin, and others.[1]

Granville Barker (1877–1946) – producer, playwright, and actor during the Court Theatre season – was born in London and at the age of thirteen was sent to the Theatre Royal, Margate, at that time a combination of stock company and dramatic school. In 1891 he made his first appearance on the London stage, and afterwards acted in Ben Greet's and William Poel's Shakespearian companies. He also appeared in Shaw plays, and served as producer to the Stage Society. By the time he began work at the Court Theatre, therefore, Barker was a fully qualified man of the theatre. In a later venture (at the Savoy, 1912) he produced three Shakespearian plays in an original manner. Though *A Winter's Tale* and *A Midsummer Night's Dream* were perhaps unduly strange and fantastic, *Twelfth Night* was

[1] See *The Court Theatre*: 1904–7, by Desmond MacCarthy (1907).

a triumph. The costumes and stage setting were new in style, unobtrusive but sufficient. They were a pleasant 'point of rest' for the eyes of the audience, whose minds were left free to take in the sense and enchanting music of Shakespeare's poetry. Though the work of a stage producer cannot be preserved and immortalized, it is not the least of Granville Barker's achievements that he enabled some thousands of his contemporaries to hear, for the first time, Shakespeare as he should be heard. These performances were taken at a pace about one-third faster than had been customary on the modern stage, and the gain was obvious.[1]

In later years Granville Barker's appearances in the theatre became rare. For a short time it had seemed that he might become the leading dramatist of his generation. *The Marrying of Ann Leete* (1899), his first play, appeared before the influence of the Russian dramatist Tchekov had reached England, yet it is probably the most Tchekovian play in English. The censoring of *Waste* (1907) brought Granville Barker into public notice, but *The Voysey Inheritance* (1905) was his finest achievement, and one of the best and richest plays of modern times. It lacks the moral and intellectual fervour of Bernard Shaw, but in almost every other respect *The Voysey Inheritance* displays that joy of creation and super-abundant vitality absent from a great deal of contemporary drama. Granville Barker's people in this play are creatively well nourished; beside them Galsworthy's later characters seem like dyspeptic ghosts around a board of funeral baked meats. Galsworthy had, however, what Barker had not – sustained power of creation. Apart from translations (e.g. of Spanish plays by Sierra and the Quintero brothers) Granville Barker wrote only two long plays between 1907 and 1925: *The Madras House* (1911) and *The Secret Life* (1923). In neither of these did he equal *The Voysey Inheritance*, although the first act of *The Madras House* is excellent. His first marriage to an accomplished actress was ended by his association with a rich American who be-

[1] Granville Barker's lesson on this point will probably be lost, and the loss will be a misfortune. It is as important to preserve the correct *tempo* in a Shakespearian play as in a piece of great music. *Macbeth* played slowly (as Beerbohm Tree, for example, played it) is *Macbeth* murdered in every sense—in poetry, story, and characterization alike. And in the post-Barker period actors have been encouraged to turn Shakespeare's verse into mumbled prose.

came his second wife and drew him away from the stage towards scholarship. The product of that phase was a series of *Prefaces to Shakespeare* which gave him considerable and continuing repute.

What happened in connexion with the Abbey Theatre and the Court Theatre, happened also at the Manchester Gaiety. When Miss Horniman began her venture there in 1908 scarcely any native dramatic material was available. By 1912 there was a 'Manchester school' of dramatists known on two continents. The leading playwrights of the Manchester group were Allan Monkhouse, Harold Brighouse, and Stanley Houghton. More or less by accident the last named came to be regarded as the leader.

Stanley Houghton (1881–1913) was a Manchester business man with an active interest in the theatre. Between 1905 and 1912 he wrote dramatic criticism for Manchester newspapers, and in 1908 his one-act play *The Dear Departed* was accepted for Miss Horniman's company. With this and other pieces he gained local fame, but in 1912 he found himself suddenly and unexpectedly with a London reputation. Miss Horniman had been invited by the Stage Society to give a performance in London, and she chose *Hindle Wakes* by Stanley Houghton for that occasion. The play, which had not previously been performed, was received with enthusiasm by critics and audiences alike, and Stanley Houghton was 'made'. *Hindle Wakes* was put on for an extended season in London and managers pursued the author. He wrote three short plays[1] for Arthur Bourchier, a London actor-manager, but his earlier success was not repeated. Tired of being lionized by London people, and discouraged by the failure of his new plays, Houghton went to Paris, where he died a few months later. The virtue of his two best works, *Hindle Wakes* and *The Younger Generation*, is in their sincerity and unpretentiousness and the fidelity with which they portray Lancashire life and character. It is probable that London was attracted by other things in *Hindle Wakes*. Metropolitan audiences detected a piquant flavour of sexual excitement in Fanny Hawthorn's refusal to marry the young man with whom she had enjoyed a week-end excursion at Llandudno. The true dramatic and literary

[1] *Phipps*; *Pearls*; *Trust the People.*

interest lies mainly, however, in the skilful portraits of the old people of the two families. This is true also of *The Younger Generation*, with its terrifying Puritan grandmother whose religious philosophy can be summed up in her own words: 'There's original sin in every young man and young woman, and it's got to be stamped out of them. Yes, scourged out of them with whips, and burnt out of them with fire if need be.'

Under the repertory theatre system, drama flourished in the English provinces as it had not done since the days of the medieval craft guilds and their cycles of religious plays – with numerous successful dramatic enterprises in the larger towns, and, also, amateur groups working with skill and enthusiasm all over the country in villages, towns, and cities – in Scotland and Wales as well as in England.

After Dublin and Manchester, Birmingham produced a repertory dramatist of distinction. John Drinkwater (1882–1937) was already an acknowledged poet, before (in 1918) his *Abraham Lincoln* was produced. This play, with its idealistic central figure and noble aspirations, came as a tonic to many people distressed by the war of 1914–18 and its brutalities, its threats of reprisals and counter-reprisals. Written at any other time its success with the public might have been no greater than that of Drinkwater's later historical plays (*Cromwell*, *Mary Stuart*, and *Robert E. Lee*). It is, however, a more impressive play than these: a skilful adaptation of biography and history to the conditions of the modern theatre. It is impressive without pretentiousness or grandiloquence; and by the careful selection and utilization of detail[1] Drinkwater created a convincing and admirable personality.

Attracting large audiences for a long period, *Abraham Lincoln* demonstrated that the spoken word (without rhodomontade or the aid of extravagant action) can be made to appeal to a large popular audience. *Abraham Lincoln* went far towards fulfilling a prophecy made by John Galsworthy nearly ten years previously. Writing in 1909 he suggested that the renascent English drama would travel in two main channels, one bearing 'new barques of poetry, shaped, it may be, like prose . . . a poetic prose-drama, emotionalizing us by

[1] As (for example) the passage about Lincoln's disreputable hat in Scene I.

its diversity and purity of form and invention, and whose province will be to disclose the elemental soul of man and the forces of Nature, not perhaps as the old tragedies disclosed them, not necessarily in the epic mood, but always with beauty and in the spirit of discovery'.[1] Yet, for the time being, *Abraham Lincoln* was to remain a solitary pointer, and when a general stirring of interest in poetic drama came it was on the very different model of Auden and Isherwood and their circle, and of T. S. Eliot and Christopher Fry.[2]

6. J. M. BARRIE

The drama of ideas – rooted in England by Bernard Shaw and cultivated by Galsworthy, Granville Barker, and others – had no influence on J. M. (Sir James) Barrie (1860–1937). Like many of his contemporaries he found little that was admirable in twentieth-century standards of life and conduct, but did not enlist as a fighter in 'the liberative war of humanity'. His was not the temperament of a crusading Bernard Shaw who could with enjoyment raise his ethical battle-axe and split skulls. Barrie's only weapons were a faint disarming smile and a dreamy eye. There are no standards of literary judgement applicable to Barrie. It is possible to write either that his world is more delightful than the real world, or that it is unpleasantly sweet and sickly. His plots are preposterous (e.g. *Quality Street* and *Alice Sit-by-the-Fire*); his characters incredible (e.g. Valentine Brown and Phoebe Throssel, Matey and Lob, Richardson, Tweeny, Mary Rose); his dialogue sometimes as creaky as a rusty machine. Since he was out of the main stream of the contemporary intellectual drama, future playgoers and critics alike may value him for his uniqueness. By the time of his birth centenary in 1960 the current had turned strongly against him: not only was the whimsical element in his plays out of fashion but, also, it was modish to examine his personality through the distorting lenses of the Freudians.[3]

[1] 'Some Platitudes Concerning Drama' (*The Inn of Tranquillity*).

[2] See pp. 135 ff. below.

[3] See broadcast by David Daiches reprinted in *The Listener* (12 May 1960): 'The Sexless Sentimentalist'. Though Professor Daiches wrote 'I am not here concerned to psycho-analyse Barrie', he made much of a supposed morbid 'mother-son relationship'.

James Matthew Barrie was born at Kirriemuir (the Thrums of his novels) in 1860 and educated at the village school, Dumfries Academy, and Edinburgh University, where he graduated in 1882. His early days as a journalist (first in Nottingham and afterwards in London) are described under a thin veil of fiction in *When a Man's Single* (1888), a book with many touches of Barrie's individual humour. Between that time and 1900 he wrote several novels and collections of sketches, as well as a biography of his mother (*Margaret Ogilvie*, 1896). He had practically no 'public life', yet official distinctions fell upon him: a baronetcy in 1913; the Order of Merit in 1922; the Rectorship of St Andrew's University also in 1922.[1]

At the end of the nineteenth century Barrie had a large following as a novelist. He had made a few experiments in play-writing, but with no marked success. A quarter of a century later, when his novels were out of fashion, he had become probably the most popular dramatist then living.

His experimental plays (*The Professor's Love Story*, 1895; *The Little Minister*, 1897; *The Wedding Guest*, 1900) show Barrie endeavouring to fit himself to accepted stage conventions, before he began to write in a more personal manner. *Quality Street* (1901) has the atmosphere of Mrs Gaskell's *Cranford*. Set in the Napoleonic period, its maiden ladies are 'old' (according to the judgement of the time) almost before they are past girlhood, and the pathos of the piece comes from the barbarity of a generation which put its women 'on the shelf' if they did not marry in the earliest twenties or before. The 'lavendered' atmosphere of *Quality Street* is robbed of a good deal of the intended pleasant sentiment by the sense of yellowing and slow decay which hangs about its dimity souls.

Social reformers in need of a tract might turn *The Admirable Crichton* (1903) to their own uses. It is an argument for the claims of God's nobleman as against the 'rights' of those who are merely noblemen of the United Kingdom; and its message is in no way weakened by the probability that it was not intended to convey a message. Though this play has several well-rounded and finished characters, it would be rash to say that any one of them is 'probable'. The illusion of life-likeness given by Barrie to his characters comes

[1] His Rectorial Address, *Courage*, was a characteristic piece of Barrieism.

not from their conformity to the human model but from the fact that they are consistent with Barrie's own imaginative world. In a world of fantasy normal human beings are 'out of the picture'. If it is agreed to swallow the camel which is Barrie's universe, it is absurd to strain at the gnats which are his characters. All that can be asked is that the people within the author's created universe shall look as though they belong there.

The cleavage between the actual world and the Barrie world of fantasy does not, however, disable his plays from providing some critical commentary upon life. To Barrie, one of the most interesting spectacles in the two worlds – his own and this – was the familiar tragi-comic contest between man and woman. In the Meredithian sense Barrie was one of 'the pick of men'.[1] He had womanly insight, and a wish to see life and mankind from the woman's point of view. He was the male egoist's least flattering friend, and would not pretend to believe that the world is kept on its way by strong, self-reliant males. He drew at least two portraits of such strong, self-reliant men: John Shand (*What Every Woman Knows*, 1908) and Harry Sims (*The Twelve Pound Look*, 1913) – and their actual strength is no more than that of over-blown air-balls.

The Twelve Pound Look is possibly the best one-act comedy yet written, though it belongs to a period that is now dead, economically and socially. Barrie was a friend and admirer of George Meredith and in this play he observed several of the principles laid down in Meredith's famous *Essay on Comedy*. Except that it has not the rapier-thrusts of wit that Meredith desiderated for ideal comedy, *The Twelve Pound Look* might usefully be appended to the *Essay* as an illustration of the working of the Comic Spirit. Harry Sims, though pompous and ridiculous, is presented without contempt, as Meredith insisted that a truly comic figure should be. Shand and Sims give glimpses of the universal egoist, even as Meredith's Willoughby Patterne gives a glimpse from a different angle. Sir Willoughby is more rarefied and intellectualized than Barrie's two men, and the latter were consequently closer to average humanity, and more useful as corrective agents of male egoism. Barrie, though himself a

[1] 'You meet, now and then, men who have the woman in them without being womanized; they are the pick of men.' – George Meredith, *The Tragic Comedians.*

'glorious, dazzling success', pleaded through Kate in *The Twelve Pound Look* for the 'poor souls' who had not 'got on' and who therefore retained the humane feelings endangered by the worship of success and efficiency.

In two of his later plays, *Dear Brutus* (1917) and *Mary Rose* (1920), Barrie went farther from the world of reality; to Lob's enchanted Wood of the Second Chance, and Mary's Island that Likes to be Visited. There was always something of the emotional trapeze artiste about Barrie. He seemed often to be poised above a bath of tears, and unemotional spectators expected and rather hoped he would overbalance. He avoided that discomfort skilfully, but the strain was trying for the audience. Both *Dear Brutus* and *Mary Rose* impose some such strain, but, again, the laws of the Barrie universe apply, not the laws of earth.

Barrie's last play, *The Boy David* (1936), was a failure in the theatre, a sign that the author had outlived his own audience. Though his greatest success, *Peter Pan* (1904), long continued to be for the children's institution that inherited it a financially valuable property, its hearty juvenilism wore thin. Barrie was stigmatized as an escapist and as a propagator of infantilism. Neither charge was unjustified, but both were counterbalanced by the good that was in him, by the joy he had given to countless children and adults, by his contribution to human understanding, and by his skill in the chosen craft.

7. THE THEATRE BETWEEN WARS

In the years before the war of 1914–18, it had been assumed that the English theatre was at the beginning of an epoch of activity unequalled since the decline of Elizabethan drama. With some half-dozen men of letters writing for the London stage, and with a chain of repertory theatres outside London, this spirit of optimism seemed well founded. But the catastrophe of war brought a radical change. The audience for what may be called the intellectual drama had never been large, and the necessities of national service seriously diminished the number of theatregoers. At the same time, the stress and strain of warfare increased the demand for light (even frivolous) entertainment – revue, musical comedy, and farce. Theatre rents and production costs rose ruinously; and by 1919 a number of the London playhouses had become little more than expensive toys for millionaires, some of whom were without even elementary knowledge of theatrecraft or dramatic literature. Under these new conditions even Bernard Shaw was unable for a long time to get *Heartbreak House* produced in England. Masterpieces were at a discount.

Future historians considering English drama of the decade following the armistice of 1918, will need to take account of the economic conditions governing the London and provincial theatres, and hampering the dramatists. Serious plays had little chance of production unless they were written for a small cast; while expenses of mounting had also to be reduced to a minimum by avoidance of scenic changes.[1] The 'unities' came into their own again, because it was cheaper to observe than to ignore them. About this time, social and educational institutions (both voluntary and State-aided) increased rapidly in number, and play-production formed part of the cultural work in hundreds of local centres. The establishment of the British Drama League in 1919 did much to foster and co-ordinate such activities. Though the amateur movement is outside the scope of a brief literary survey of the period, it should not be overlooked that members of village companies (and of similar organizations elsewhere) were (and are) writing, as well as producing, plays. The trend of English drama was influenced as much by these unnamed dramatists as by professional playwrights.

The conditions ruling in the commercial theatres after 1918 did result in the virtual exclusion from the public stage of at least one dramatist who had seemed important before the war. *The Tragedy of Nan* (1909) and one or two other plays by Masefield had been performed with moderate success, but after the war (apart from a few experimental performances in London) Masefield's new plays got little farther than the private theatre in his home at Boar's Hill, near Oxford. In *Good Friday* (1916) and *The Trial of Jesus* (1925), alternative versions of the same Gospel incidents, John Masefield cramped

[1] Such economies were imposed only upon 'straight' plays. Musical comedies and revues became more garish and expensive than before. Some of these spectacles led to the bankruptcy court, but there was apparently an endless line of footlight-dazzled financiers – the 'angels' – to fill the gaps.

himself by endeavouring to keep close to the scriptural record. Unless an author accepts the artistic necessity of breaking away from a slavish imitation of the original narrative, a play dealing with the life of Christ can hardly escape seeming a weak paraphrase of biblical English. There is some dramatic and psychological interest in Masefield's treatment of Herod, Pilate, and Pilate's wife, but no play can overcome the handicap of a static central figure. Moreover, while the consistent artlessness of medieval dramatists enabled them to handle religious themes unpretentiously, the occasional 'artless' simplicity of Masefield's verse seems only a studied and irritatingly self-conscious trick.

John Masefield's ability as a playwright up to 1925 must be judged by *The Tragedy of Nan*. A comparison of performances by two professional companies of equal standing showed that *The Tragedy of Nan* required exceptionally sensitive interpretation by every actor, and that in the absence of this the dramatist's characters have little individual force of their own. Masefield does not help his actors; he gives them 'voices', which they must clothe in convincing personalities. The vindictiveness of Mrs Pargetter, the fluctuating loves of Dick, the innocence and despair of Nan, Pargetter's frenzy of grief over his broken toby jug, the poetic mutterings of old Gaffer Pearce: all these are speciously effective on the printed page, but they do not easily bear transportation to the stage. Masefield's later secular plays added little to his reputation as a dramatist.

A richer sense of character was shown in Arnold Bennett's plays. The three acts of *Milestones* (1912) cover three generations (1860–1885–1912), knit together in the play by the unifying idea of the stubborn prejudice with which each successive generation meets the spirit of progress and change: in 1860, Sam Sibley opposes iron ships; in 1885, John Rhead, who had been a pioneer in constructing iron ships, is contemptuous of the project for steel ships. That historical sense which served Arnold Bennett well in his novels for building up the panoramic 'time-background', enabled him in *Milestones* to reproduce the tone and colour of the mid-Victorian and late-Victorian periods. The characters are well drawn, with subtle shades of humour and gravity, as the leading figures pass under the moulding hand of Time. *Milestones* (in which Edward Knoblock collaborated) is a solid and brilliant achievement. Nothing else among Bennett's works as a playwright (either alone or in collaboration) touched the *Milestones* level, though mention must be made of his two first-rate comedies, *The Great Adventure* (1913 – a dramatized adaptation of the excellent comic novel, *Buried Alive*) and *What the Public Wants* (1909), a gentle satire on the newspaper world.

One of the most interesting occasions in the London theatre in the early nineteen-twenties was on 14 March 1921, when Clemence Dane's *A Bill of Divorcement* had its first performance. The authoress had previously made her mark as a novelist with *Regiment of Women* (1917), a ruthless analysis of egoism. *A Bill of Divorcement* is, in some respects, of the Pinero type: 'well made' and with a carefully engineered 'great scene'. But there the resemblance ends. Unlike most of Pinero's, Clemence Dane's play faced a real human problem; and her people behave less like stage automata. Yet it cannot be claimed that the characters are altogether exempt from being crippled by the dramatist to fit the exigencies of the situation she contrived. The weakness of the scene between Sydney and Kit in the last act may be due to the necessity of getting Sydney flung emotionally high and dry. If that is so, it is the management of plot that is at fault. But, on the other hand, Kit's caddishness and imbecility may be due to the fact (shown in several of her stories and plays) that Clemence Dane is weak in portraying men. For its freshness and sincerity, however, and for its combination of clever stagecraft and social purpose, *A Bill of Divorcement* was a remarkable beginning for a young dramatist. In her next play, *Will Shakespeare* (1921), cumbersome dramatic machinery[1] and a dismally unpleasant Shakespeare were too heavy a handicap. If Shakespeare, or any other genius of the first rank, is to be brought to the stage, some sign must be given of the genius of the original.

Somerset Maugham resembled, at first, the Society dramatists of the eighteen-nineties, combining the technical methods of Pinero with the verbal mannerisms of Oscar Wilde. His plays (from *A Man of Honour*, 1903, to *Our Betters*, 1923) reflect the changes in taste among playgoers who liked to see on the stage an imitation of the 'high life'

[1] See, for example, the 'shadows' in Act I

of their own day. Whether or not the dregs of Society actually spoke as they are made to speak in some of Somerset Maugham's plays matters little, but a student of modern drama will find it interesting to compare the stage idioms of 1907 with those of 1923. Lady Frederick (1907),[1] a typically tiresome woman-with-a-past, remarks: 'I've done a lot of foolish things in my time, but, my God, I have suffered.' That voice is the voice of all the women-with-a-past who walked sinuously through late-Victorian and Edwardian stage-plays. And when Dick Lomas says (*The Explorer*, 1908): 'Half the women I know merely married their husbands to spite somebody else. It appears to be one of the commonest forms of matrimony', Somerset Maugham bridges the twenty-five years between Oscar Wilde and Noel Coward. Free on the one hand from Victorian ready-made morality, and on the other hand from neo-Georgian licentiousness and cynicism, *Caesar's Wife* (1919) is among Maugham's best plays; while *The Circle* (1921) and *Our Betters* (1923) have been praised for their careful craftsmanship and acute social criticism; the latter has, in fact, been ranked as the best comedy of its kind since Restoration times. *The Breadwinner* (1930) brings the wheel full circle from Ibsen, for, reversing *A Doll's House*, it shows a husband revolting from the bondage of a happy home and family and going out 'to lead his own life'. *The Breadwinner* presents not only the long-overdue revolt of the male, but also the revolt of Middle Age against Youth, and in this particular Somerset Maugham is more convincing as well as wittier than St John Ervine. To the collected edition of his plays Somerset Maugham contributed informative prefaces regarding his own progress as a dramatist, and described how the restrictiveness of the theatre led him at length to abandon the writing of stage plays. But before doing so he delivered himself of two pieces – *For Services Rendered* (1932) and *Sheppey* (1933) – deeply felt and deeply serious in intention. Neither was on the level of his best work, however, for his effectiveness as a critic of life is in inverse proportion to his solemnity. Through wit, humour, gaiety, and an incisive illusion-proof mind, he was capable of more in the way of the correction of absurdities and abuses than when he permitted a deliberate seriousness to dull his natural gifts.

[1] In the play with that title.

Bernard Shaw once said: 'I hate to see dead people walking about.' Noel Coward's early plays must have infuriated G.B.S., for they were full of galvanized corpses – talking and making the motions of living creatures, but corpses all the same, mere shells of men and women. Though for a while Noel Coward seemed to take a cynical delight in his parade of 'hags who've never surrendered to Anno Domini',[1] he was as conscious a moralist as those medieval writers who paraded the Seven Deadly Sins. Yet, in the manner of his day, he snapped his fingers in the faces of the moralists and tweaked their noses in derision.[2] The immediate popularity of his early plays was due to the 'smartness' of the dialogue (an echo of the conversation that many listeners liked to imagine themselves conducting all day and every day) and to the opportunity that these plays gave for the vicarious satisfaction of anti-social impulses. Until he wrote the first-rate comedy, *Hay Fever* (1925), his plays were mainly significant as a symptom of the deadly amorality of a section of the community – the cocktail and dance-obsessed section. The febrile brightness of the then typical Noel Coward play – e.g. *Fallen Angels* (1925), *Private Lives* (1930), *Design for Living* (1933) – was the author's indictment of a type of person that both fascinated and repelled him, as, in a less intelligent way, Marie Corelli had been fascinated and repelled a generation before. Both these writers could react to vice only through their emotions and could do no more than lodge a protest. The contemplation of vice as a factor in human life demanding a reasoned corrective was beyond their powers. Where Marie Corelli was sentimental, Noel Coward was cynical, which, as Wilde said, is merely the sentimental inverted. When he attempted to deal with a wholly serious theme in a directly serious manner, as in *Post Mortem* (1931), Coward's insufficiency became evident. Bitterness and passionate indignation were not enough to carry this play (which postulates one of the war-dead returning unwelcomed even by those who had most bemoaned his death). The theme required more mental control and a better sense of balance and order than were given to it. But apart from *Post Mortem*, Noel Coward's flair for 'good theatre' has rarely been equalled. Material that is negligible in

[1] *Lady Frederick*, by Somerset Maugham.
[2] See 'The Author's Reply to his Critics': *Three Plays*, by Noel Coward (1925).

print may be irresistibly compelling when spoken or sung on the stage in the highly charged mass-atmosphere of the playhouse: *Bitter Sweet* (1929) and *Cavalcade* (1931) bear witness to this fact; many might despise them, but few could resist them. Even though he reached the zone of Mayfair and Monte Carlo, Noel Coward retained for years much of the spirit of the London gamin who is sometimes witty, sometimes wittily and enjoyably vulgar, sometimes merely vulgar. In the sequence of short pieces collectively named *To-night at 8.30* (1936), *Red Peppers* illustrates this in its ranging from grand robust humour to moments of nastiness. In the same collection, *Fumed Oak* is a crude Cowardesque compression of an idea similar to that used in Somerset Maugham's *The Breadwinner*.[1] But, using material drawn from the same lower middle-class (or upper working-class) level, he produced a more sympathetic and better-mannered full-length comedy in *This Happy Breed* (written in 1939; produced 1943), while in the third act of *Quadrille* (1952) he reached a high level of combined comedy and wit.

After the huge popular success of *The Good Companions*, J. B. Priestley's interest in novel-writing was submerged by the attractions of the theatre, in which his career as a dramatist began with *Dangerous Corner* (1932), an exceptionally neat and ingenious piece of play-making. A chance remark by one of the characters soon after the rise of the curtain plunges a happy group of people into a distressful series of discoveries concerning their inter-relationships in the immediate past and their happiness is ruined. At the moment when the play appears to have ended thus in disaster, a momentary black-out is followed by a return to the opening situation and dialogue. The conversation flows along an almost identical channel, but this time the chance remark passes unheeded; the dangerous corner has been safely negotiated, and the curtain falls finally on an assurance that the characters have this time avoided catastrophe. The play never loses grip, notwithstanding the author's inclination (shown again in *Time and the Conways*) to rain too many blows upon his people, and it is a superb example of dramatic craftsmanship. *Laburnum Grove* (1933) and *Eden End* (1934) – the first dealing with a crook who lived between crimes as a respectable suburban house-

[1] See p. 130 above.

holder, the other a study of character in a Yorkshire setting – maintained Priestley's popularity as a playwright, but *Cornelius* (1935) had few admirers, though its aim was more ambitious. It set out to show the effect upon those concerned of a business in decline (a topical subject in view of the prolonged contemporary trade depression then overshadowing many lives), but the office atmosphere and the principal character, Cornelius himself, became mutually destructive on the stage by dividing the interest of the audience. And, further, the author's skill was insufficient to suggest the deadly time-drag which is the most harrowing part of the experience of those caught up in an enterprise drifting towards inevitable failure. Everything in *Cornelius* happens too swiftly: the reduction of the time-scale necessary in a stage play is not adequately compensated, as it can be by a just use of dramatic illusion. With *Time and the Conways* (1937) J. B. Priestley may be said to have begun a new phase – a phase in which, though still announcing his belief that theatre audiences have the right to be entertained, he became more inclined to use the stage as a platform for the expression of ideas. *Cornelius* had been a signpost pointing in that direction. Though *Time and the Conways* was acclaimed by the critics as a highly original masterpiece, the time-theme fumblingly handled there by Priestley had already been treated with a closer approach to profundity in *Berkeley Square* (1928) by J. C. Squire and J. L. Balderston, working on an idea suggested by Henry James's uncompleted story *A Sense of the Past* (published posthumously in 1916). Ideas are the most exciting of adult playthings, but they hardly are so in J. B. Priestley's hands. He was compelled to over-simplify the new conceptions of time in *Time and the Conways* and to imply an easier interpretation of J. W. Dunne's theories[1] than is warrantable. Except when a dramatist is also a great poet, able as Shakespeare was to absorb and transcend philosophy in and through poetry, the theatre is a ramshackle place for the expression of philosophical concepts. Moreover, the value of a play (or of any other work of the creative imagination) is not in proportion to the seriousness or solemnity of its author's intention. An excellent farce may merit

[1] See *An Experiment with Time* (1927), *The Serial Universe* (1938), and *The New Immortality* (1938) by J. W. Dunne.

higher marks than an indifferent morality play. The contrary view is a heresy that obtained wide currency in the 1930s and after, and among its by-products was the scolding delivered by J. B. Priestley in the explanatory epilogue to the printed text of his *Johnson Over Jordan* (1939), which suffered on the stage from over-elaboration and pretentiousness. This play, using (consciously or not) the mode of Expressionism, depicts an ordinary man re-experiencing phantasmally after death the main phases of his mortal life. If instead of employing all the resources of modern stage production the author had trusted to simplicity of presentation, *Johnson Over Jordan* might have ranked as a modern *Everyman*. As it was, the playgoing public was justified in preferring Priestley's own farcical comedy *When We Are Married* (1938), and his scolding was misdirected. Another of his 'serious' plays, *I Have Been Here Before* (1937), though principally a study in the healing of a psychically sick man, utilized the idea of recurrence and intervention (*vide* Ouspensky's *A New Model of the Universe*, 1931). Of the many stage pieces written by Priestley in the 1940s the most successful and satisfying was *The Linden Tree* (1947), a solidly characterized presentation of intellectual integrity in which the Priestley who feels with and understands men and women had the freedom and scope he failed to command in the severer climate of the realm of ideas.

Potentially, at least, the most important writer for the theatre in the fourth and fifth decades of the century was James Bridie (1888–1951), a Scottish doctor (born O. H. Mavor) turned playwright. Though wayward and erratic, he was a true genius. Bridie's work had that touch of fire and intellectual passion found nowhere else among his contemporaries in prose drama than in Bernard Shaw. That fire in James Bridie's plays compels the acceptance of the incredible as possible, as e.g. the poisoning scene in *A Sleeping Clergyman* (1933), and it is a more intense fire than is ever found in Shaw. Its presence is evident in the character of Dr Knox in *The Anatomist* (1931), one of the earliest and most durable of his plays, and at moments in *The King of Nowhere* (1938), a disturbing work rendered unsatisfactory by doubt as to the mental state of its central character (a doubt also present, but not injuriously in the dramatic sense, in *Hamlet*). While less cosmically imposing than some other of

Bridie's works, *Tobias and the Angel* (1931) remained its author's best play. Well constructed, humane, humorous, moving, it commands respect and affection. Old Tobit and his wife, Anna, are drawn with exquisite delicacy; Tobias is the little man who, all through the ages, finds life a trifle too difficult to manage by himself and requires either an angel or a wife to fortify him; the Angel is an impressive figure but also very good fun, and Sara, Tobias's wife, a likeable minx. But Bridie failed to produce the greater plays of which he seemed always capable. An incorrigible trifler with his own talent, he was never content after *Tobias and the Angel* to fit his material into shapely dramatic form, and the later plays became a capricious showing of fragments of genius, as in *Daphne Laureola* (1949), though in *Mr Bolfry* (1943) he got near to achieving a co-ordinated masterpiece.

Among the younger playwrights who reached a wide popular audience in the nineteen-forties, Terence Rattigan was the most notable as a writer of dramatic prose. He graduated from a modish comedy-farce *French Without Tears* (1936) to a well-sustained and tense study of honesty in conflict with injustice in *The Winslow Boy* (1946), and to a near-tragedy in *The Deep Blue Sea* (1952). *Ross* (1960) is an episodic dramatization of incidents in the life of Lawrence of Arabia. By the date of that play Rattigan had become in the eyes of the 'advanced' critics a mere popular dramatist, though unprejudiced judgement recognized him as a skilful one.

Interest in religious drama was revived by the institution at Canterbury in 1928 of an annual festival of music and drama. Beginning with a presentation of John Masefield's *The Coming of Christ*, the committee in later years commissioned new plays for performance in the Cathedral Chapter House. T. S. Eliot's *Murder in the Cathedral* (1935) was followed by *Thomas Cranmer of Canterbury* (1936) by Charles Williams, Dorothy Sayers's *The Zeal of Thy House* (1937) and *The Devil to Pay* (1939), and Christopher Fry's *Thor, with Angels* (1948). Though not of the popular type, *Murder in the Cathedral* afterwards had a long run in London theatres and encouraged T. S. Eliot to experiment further with verse-drama in *The Family*

Reunion (1939). This latter play transferred the theme of the *Eumenides* of Aeschylus to a modern English country house, and in its verse-style sought to close the gap between poetry and modern conversational prose by a flattened rhythmical speech which fell at times into an arrangement of words bald as verse and stilted as prose. *The Family Reunion* is an example of material pressed into an alien mould, and a showing-up of the fallacy that poetic drama could be forced into existence. But T. S. Eliot nevertheless created a vogue for consciously unpoetic poetry, and as an antidote to lush romanticism and imitation Shakespearianism the vogue performed some service. Yet in also creating a dread of natural exuberance and verbal richness – traditional characteristics of many esteemed earlier English poets and playwrights – the Eliot manner may be considered a lowering and devitalizing influence. In the early nineteen-fifties, however, it had come to be regarded as little short of heresy to deny the highest merit and virtue to Eliot's work, and his standing among intellectualist disciples and unintellectual fashionables alike was reinforced by his further plays *The Cocktail Party* (1950) and *The Confidential Clerk* (1954), though the irreconcilables remained sceptical and unawed.

When Christopher Fry's *The Lady's Not For Burning* (1948) blazed into the prevailing greyness, it seemed likely to become the beacon of a new era of poetic glory in which words would again be released into magnificence. The drabber critics chided Fry for his verbal energy and resource, and for what was alleged to be the lack of dramatic content in his plays; but theatre audiences drawn from all social and intellectual levels delighted enthusiastically in the language, and found enough of story and action to entertain and satisfy. This play has something of Marlowe's dialectical abandon, united with something also of the intellectual acrobatics of the metaphysicals; and while there is much exquisite grace of expression there is also the earthy salt of colloquialism. The verse in *The Lady's Not for Burning* and in *Venus Observed* (1950) runs

> *with a careless and forgetful music*
> *Looping and threading, tuning and entwining.*[1]

[1] *Venus Observed*, II, ii.

After *Venus Observed* Fry tended to bridle his unique gifts and to hark back to the Eliotesque manner in which he had experimented earlier. This retraction led those who had disfavoured his 'looping and threading, tuning and entwining music' to declare that *A Sleep of Prisoners* (1951) was his best play. The controversy of which he became the unwilling centre must be left for settlement in the future on the basis of his total work, though it may boldly be said now that for a moment of time Christopher Fry brought light and air as well as music and warmth into the frigid charnel-house of contemporary verse drama, but that he lapsed into the contemporary mode in *The Dark is Light Enough* (1954) and *Curtmantle* (1961).

8. DRAMA IN THE 1950s

The death of Bernard Shaw at the end of 1950 created a vacuum in the English theatre which no playwright then practising appeared qualified to fill. Coward, Priestley, Eliot, Fry had no new surprises to spring, and during the first half of the decade there was nothing that aroused more than routine interest. The theatres had the usual succession of long-run popular successes and short-run interesting failures. It remained as true as in Dr Johnson's time that 'the drama's laws the drama's patrons give'. While Shaw had not by any means accepted that dictum wholeheartedly, he had allowed that if the drama's patrons were to accept what he thought it good for them to have, he must on his side observe the law that the primary purpose of the theatre is to entertain, and that what else it may be qualified to provide must come through the medium of entertainment. The result in his case is that from among the two dozen or so full-length plays he wrote it is probably safe to guess that at least a dozen will survive to become an accepted part of the main body of English drama.

Looking dispassionately from the angle of the early 1960s at the new plays of the 1950s only a venturesome observer would prophesy that any one has a survival value. Those whose observation is not critically dispassionate will incline to the opposing view that in the 1950s an important revolution was effected in English drama and was productive of more than evanescent masterpieces.

The revolution – important or not – can be said to have begun with the London production of Samuel Beckett's *Waiting for Godot* in 1955. Beckett had been James Joyce's secretary; he lived mainly in Paris, writing as fluently in French as in English, and was obviously much influenced by Joyce though he did not adopt Joyce's verbal style. It would be vain to attempt to say what Beckett's plays are 'about' or what they 'mean', for they belong to what has been labelled 'the theatre of the absurd'. What happens in *Waiting for Godot* does 'not constitute a plot or story' but is 'an image of Beckett's intuition that *nothing really ever happens* in man's existence'.[1] Estragon and Vladimir, who might be described as kind-of-tramps, wait by a tree on a country road which might be described as a kind-of-limbo. To them enter Pozzo, a kind-of-despot, carrying a whip and driving Lucky, a kind-of-slave, tethered by a rope. They mistake Pozzo for Godot, from whom they hear later through Boy, a kind-of-Greek-drama-messenger who has been sent to tell them that Godot will come tomorrow, not today. But Godot does not come at all. Who is Godot? Is he God? But this question and all questions are futile in the theatre of the absurd, where all answers are both possible and impossible and questions and answers are alike equally absurd, because life itself is meaningless. *Waiting for Godot* is a kind-of-play, though in the traditional sense not a play at all but an abstruse metaphysical disquisition.

The fact that *Waiting for Godot* attracted audiences for an unexpectedly large number of performances was evidence of a tendency among audiences to pay more regard to whatever might be the current mode – which veered from Eliot to Fry to Beckett to Osborne to Pinter to Wesker – than to any significance or merit in the work patronized.

With *Waiting for Godot* the reign of the do-it-yourself drama began. Scores of amateur writers, finding that a spate of words about anything might win approbation in the theatre, tried their hand. Construction was out, characterization was out, style and decency of language were out. Commitment was in.[2]

[1] Martin Esslin, *The Theatre of the Absurd* (1962), pp. 293–4.

[2] For an extended discussion of the matter in relation to current poetry and fiction as well as drama, see John Mander, *The Writer and Commitment* (1961).

In the 1920s and 1930s 'social consciousness' was the current term for the 'commitment' of the 1950s, for even in its limited sense of partisan propaganda 'commitment' was no new thing. In a liberal and humanitarian sense – as commitment to the furtherance of whatever things are good for humanity unlimited – it was as old as the literature of classical antiquity.

The conflicting strains of 'commitment' and 'the absurd' made it often difficult to discover what it was that the playwrights of the 1950s were commited *to*; while the decay of craftmanship, coupled with a state of affairs in which a 'directors' theatre' usurped the place formerly taken by an 'authors' theatre', tended to remove plays from the scope of literature. One of the most acclaimed plays of the 'fifties, Shelagh Delaney's *A Taste of Honey* (1958), 'was accepted for production at Theatre Workshop and went through the process of adaptation and elaboration which is usual there' – and it is worth noting that the author 'was not present until nearly the final run-through (when, it is recorded, *she noticed no differences until they were pointed out to her*)'.[1] Theatre Workshop was started at the Theatre Royal, Stratford, east London, in 1956, by Joan Littlewood, a director of exceptional talent and authority who had had wide experience in the provinces. Although she was enthusiastically receptive and encouraging to new authors, what she received from them on paper were rarely plays of fully fledged merit, but mostly material upon which she was able to exercise her stage-shaping hand and mould into director's successes – as was done with *A Taste of Honey*. Another producer, Ann Jellicoe, regarded the script of her own play, *The Sport of My Mad Mother* (1956), much as a choreographer regards the notation for a ballet – not as something with intrinsic value as set down on paper, but as mere written signs of something yet to be created in live performance. This is an acceptable attitude towards stage drama, in relation to which a printed text is redundant; but in so far as this attitude is accepted a play is released from consideration as literature.

Almost simultaneously with the institution of Theatre Workshop in east London, the newly-formed English Stage Company opened at

[1] See John Russell Taylor, *Anger and After* (1962), Ch. 3. The italics are mine.

the Royal Court Theatre in Sloane Square, Chelsea. For several years to follow, it performed a function for the 'new drama' similar to that the same theatre had performed for the new drama of Bernard Shaw and others half a century before.[1] Its main impact was made with John Osborne's *Look Back in Anger* in May 1956, set in a littered one-room flat in a Midland town, the 'home' (or living-quarters) of James Porter[2] (about twenty-five) and his wife Alison ('roughly the same age'). It is impossible to estimate how far the success of the play was due to the hypnotizing effect of Alison's movements in her protracted spell at the ironing board, or to the imitable loutishness of Porter, or to a genuine sense of revolt. While Porter can be taken as either a contemptible creature or as one harshly treated by the world of his time, it is difficult to avoid the conclusion that this anti-hero was to his creator, deep down, a hero. Although the characters seemed 'so modern' in 1956, the rhetorical outbursts of Porter and Alison are almost melodramatically old-fashioned – Victorian claptrap inside out. It is his whining self-pity, however rhetorically dressed, that makes him contemptible in the eyes of an older, morally more robust and more self-reliant generation. Did it come about by a turn of fate or simply through personal inadequacy and spinelessness that this university graduate could find nothing better to do than keep a sweet stall and rail against and bully his all-too-docile wife? Was it perhaps socially and humanly unfortunate that *Look Back in Anger* was first played in Chelsea, where beatniks could find on their doorstep a mirror held up to local nature and feel, in an ecstasy of mass self-dramatization, 'Jimmy Porter is US'? If the play had first appeared nearer the centre of London it might have been more calmly judged.

By 1960 Harold Pinter and Arnold Wesker had come to be seen as potentially more fruitful than Osborne. Pinter's *The Caretaker* (1959) ran for many months in the West End, applauded by audiences who appeared to be seeing a different play from the one probably in-

[1] See above, p. 119.

[2] He is always called 'Jimmy' in the play, a symptom of a curious form of inverted snobbery, rooted in the habit of the period, whereby a peculiarly democratic virtue was assumed to lie in the diminutives of first names, so that William became a more acceptable 'comrade' if called Bill.

tended by the author. To them, Davies the imbecile tramp was an uproariously comic creature, though he is in truth pitiable and tragic. But whether found amusing or discomforting, Davies is a genuine creation, not lived up to by the others, Aston and Mick, though they too are apparently more than a little mad. But as Pinter is pregnant with the symbolic and the absurd, interpretation is disputable. A critic has said that 'The world of Harold Pinter is shadowy, obsessed, guilt-ridden, claustrophobic and, above all, private. You are expected to find your way through it without signposts, clues or milestones.'[1]

In 1960 Arnold Wesker completed 'the Wesker trilogy' – *Chicken Soup with Barley* (1958), *Roots* (1959), *I'm Talking about Jerusalem* (1960). In these plays there is nothing of the inconsequence of the theatre of the absurd, nor of the personalized misfit mentality of Osborne. While he is entirely committed to the view that the people of his own working class are deprived of the good things of life by various kinds of exploitation, Wesker sees their own shortcomings and is not misled into class-conscious romanticism; they are 'debauched by materialism and its by-product cynicism, but also by inherent weaknesses in their own character'.[2] Of the many playwrights of the 1950s it is Wesker more than any other who seemed by the end of the decade to be still in process of development.

Many influences from abroad – both continental and American – affected contemporary English drama in varying degrees after the Second World War, and of these the plays and theories of the German Bertolt Brecht were strongly evident. His *Galileo* (1955) may not improbably be considered the forerunner of Robert Bolt's *A Man for All Seasons* (1960), a biographical treatment of Sir Thomas More, and of John Osborne's *Luther* (1961). It is also conceivable that John Arden's *Sergeant Musgrave's Dance* (1959) owes something to Brecht's *Mother Courage* (1938).

[1] Milton Shulman, reviewing Pinter's *The Dwarfs* (*Evening Standard*, 19 September 1963).

[2] Robert Muller, Introduction to *I'm Talking about Jerusalem*.

A number of forces now work against the writing of plays with the quality of balanced presentation of characters and ideas traditionally accepted as dramatically essential. Too much propaganda, too much theorizing, and too much 'talking about' have the effect of distracting the playwright's attention from playwriting, and of fixing in his mind the illusion that in his professional capacity he is important outside the theatre. A playwright is important within the theatre, not in the pulpit nor on the political platform. Where, even, are Bernard Shaw's lay sermons of yesterday? He lives as a playwright, not as a sociologist. 'We are not politicians,' Joan Littlewood has said; 'we are clowns.' Not politicians and (may it be added?) not scavengers. The intrusion of gutter language into a number of contemporary plays and the frequent preoccupation with homosexuality and vice may be new in detail but not in general trend, for in *Vertue's Commonwealth* (1603) an otherwise unknown Henry Crosse wrote: '. . . a Play is like a sink in a town, whereunto all the filth doth runne: or a bile in the body that draweth all the ill humours unto it'.[1] Nor is the irruption of disrespectful youth 'new': 'Common plays and such like Exercises . . . bring Youth to such an impudent familiarity with their betters that often times great contempt of Masters, Parents, and Magistrates followeth thereof.'[2]

[1] Quoted from Alexander B. Grosart's edition (1878), p. 117.
[2] *Memorials of the Guild of Merchant Taylors*, edited by C. M. Clode (1875), vol. I, p. 578.

CHAPTER IV

POETRY

1. SURVIVORS AND PRECURSORS

When the twentieth century opened, Tennyson had been dead nine years, and there was a widespread impression that English poetry had died with him. Alfred Austin, Tennyson's delayed successor as Poet Laureate, was ludicrously inferior; and although two of the greater nineteenth-century poets, Swinburne and Meredith, lived on until 1909, their best poetry had appeared before the death of Tennyson. Robert Bridges (1844–1930), the most notable 'active' poet alive in 1901, was then fifty-six. He had written several unactable poetic dramas and many fine lyrics, but he had to wait for years before, on his appointment as Poet Laureate in 1913, he began to receive even limited recognition of his standing as a poet. Though his poetic dramas are undramatic, involved and obscure, his lyrics are crystal clear. A strict sense of form and purity of outline made it impossible for him to admit into his poetry the luscious qualities that might have made him popular between 1876 and 1898, his period of full production. He is always serene: feeling is *contained* in his verse rather than expressed by it. His emotion is 'recollected in tranquillity', and this tranquil air is present in his landscape pieces also. The external features of his nature poetry are in contrast to Wordsworth's descriptions of the wild magnificence of northern England. Bridges's landscapes are of the south country, 'bathed in a warm and comfortable glow';[1] and when he contemplates the seas, they are benign seas,

Whereon the timid ships steal out
And laugh to find their foe asleep,
That lately scattered them about,
And drave them to the fold like sheep.[2]

[1] See his *Eros and Psyche* 'March', stanza 24.

[2] *Shorter Poems,* Book I, No. 12.

The retiring genius of Bridges, serviceable to him as a poet, disqualified him from popular esteem as Laureate,[1] but if he could ever have been supposed to care what opinion the general public held of him, *The Testament of Beauty* (1929) might be regarded as his revenge on those who had referred to him as 'the dumb Laureate'. His output was small between 1913 and 1929, but the publication of his philosophical poem of over 4,000 lines compensated the paucity of ceremonial odes. *The Testament of Beauty* sold more copies, it was said, than any poet's work since Byron's, and critics wrote that it was the most important addition to English poetry of its type since Wordsworth's *The Prelude* (1850). Bridges had long been endeavouring, without real success, to naturalize classical metres in English. In some of his later short poems, he believed, the results of experiments with a loose adaptation of the alexandrine (iambic hexameter line) were promising enough to justify a more ambitious attempt. The opportunity came when, long after his eightieth birthday, he was moved to give expression to his reflections upon man and the universe. Bridges's 'loose alexandrines' might be described as free verse controlled by a modulated echo of metrical discipline. There is, in *The Testament of Beauty*, a 'standard' line, say, for example,

We sail a changeful sea through halcyon days and storm[2]

to which every line has an ultimate metrical reference, but the freedom with which that reference is used, and the confident personal skill with which the 'loose alexandrines' are handled, can be seen in any half-dozen lines of *The Testament of Beauty*. If not used with the 'conversational ease' that T. S. Eliot aimed at, they nevertheless have such ease of thought as is possible when the thought itself is often a difficult mental wrestling with a wayward and directionless world. Much of Book I (*Introduction*) is a discussion of the limitations of Reason –

this picklock Reason is still a-fumbling at the wards[3]

– and the poet looked to the growth of a *mature* 'accord of Sense, Instinct, Reason, and Spirit'[4] (which the Greeks had experienced

[1] John Masefield succeeded him as Laureate in 1930.
[2] Book I, lines.
[3] I, 463.
[4] I, 708 ff.

only in the charming unstable 'grace of childhood') operating through Christ as the WORD OF GOD[1] to bring mankind to stability and peace. Book II (*Selfhood*) and Book III (*Breed*) treat of 'the two Arch-Instincts of man's nature'. With excessive simplification we might call them (*a*) the self-Self – the self-protecting assertive personality; and (*b*) the racial-Self – the impulse towards propagation. Both in II and III, however, the digressions and discussions of incidental matters occupy more space than the topics-in-chief. The reference (in the section discussing pleasure in food) to the voluptuary and epicure who

indulgeth richly his time untill the sad day come
when he retireth with stomach Emeritus[2]

is a touch of fun. Humour of a quieter kind also wrinkles the surface from time to time. Book IV, named *Ethick* – mainly a discourse on the 'sense of Duty in man' – leads up to the doctrine that

In truth 'spiritual animal' wer a term for man
nearer than 'rational' to define his genus;
Faith being the humanizer of his brutal passions,
the clarifier of folly and medicine of care,
the clue of reality, and the driving motiv
of thatt self-knowledge which teacheth the ethick of life.[3]

Though, in his long retirement near Oxford, Bridges was not a man of affairs, his eye was as much on the world about him as upon ancient philosophers, to whom he looked indeed for the light by which present discontents could be illumined –

See how cross-eyed the pride of our world-wide crusade
against Nigerian slavery, while the London poor
in their Victorian slums lodged closer and filthier
than the outraged alien; and under liberty's name
our Industry is worse fed and shut out from the sun. –
In every age and nation a like confusion is found.[4]

Bridges died, aged eighty-five, less than six months after *The Testament of Beauty* was published, and in that last poetic utterance

[1] I, 771 ff. [2] III, 118–19.
[3] IV, 1132–37. [4] IV, 356–61.

he spoke with a voice of serene assurance for the guidance of an age of despair. His poem was not unanimously praised, however, especially when its first imposing effect had ceased to awe.

Some of those who demurred at the choice of Bridges as Laureate would have nominated Rudyard Kipling (1865–1936), who had at various times produced suitable verse for national occasions. His poems were read even by those for whom poetry was otherwise repellent, and the Empire thrilled to the simple marching measures of Kipling's Boer War anthem, 'The Absent-Minded Beggar'. But there were many others who found Kipling's verse intolerable. These were antagonized by his militant imperialism, his hotch-potch of brutality and sentimentality, his banjo rhythms, and his addiction to a pseudo-Cockney utterance which was his rendering of English soldiers' speech. Throughout his career the shadow of partisan disfavour continued to fall upon him, although as imperialistic fervour died down he ceased to be either a popular idol or an object of detestation. This change was advantageous, for Kipling's prose and poetry continued to be widely read, but in a more dispassionate atmosphere, and by the middle of the century the mists of prejudice had cleared sufficiently to establish him as a classic of the second rank.[1]

Soldier and sailor rhymes predominated in Kipling's earlier collections of verse, and among these are his most characteristic (though not the most beautiful) poems. By making the uneducated British fighting man articulate, Kipling brought a new element into English poetry. With its dropped consonants and distorted vowels, its sprinkling of foreign words picked up on active service, and its technical jargon, this rude and ungainly speech is difficult to accommodate to the mood of poetry, though on general grounds it is as defensible as the Dorset dialect of William Barnes or the Scottish peasant speech of Burns. There is, however, a reasonable complaint to be made against Kipling in this connexion. He was a cultured Anglo-Indian (born in Bombay, the son of the Curator of Lahore Museum), and though he travelled widely and studied the British

[1] The rehabilitation was led by *A Choice of Kipling's Verse, made by T. S. Eliot, with an essay on Rudyard Kipling* (1941).

soldier at close quarters, 'Cockney' was virtually a foreign tongue to him. In his use of this dialect, therefore, he was performing a literary trick, rather than employing a natural medium of expression: the self-conscious man of letters can be detected behind the tatter of illiterate sounds. A born Cockney knows that a 'foreigner' is speaking, and suspects that the fellow is trying, condescendingly, to talk down to his level. It is worth noting, however, that a no more admirable mock-Cockney came into vogue in the 'proletarian drama' of the 1960s: e.g. *Fings ain't wot they used t'be* by Frank Norman (and Theatre Workshop collaborators).

In an unpublished letter, C. E. Montague referred to Kipling as 'a fifth-form genius', and as a craftsman in verse his equipment was that of a master-in-embryo. He did not always use his technical gift to advantage, and when the weeding-out process is undertaken there is much doggerel to remove. But over against his ready tendency to drop into jog-trot verse must be set the almost Miltonic impressiveness with which he marshalled the pageantry of names – names of people and places,[1] of ships,[2] flowers, and herbs.[3] The power at the command of a skilful craftsman in verse is also shown in 'Boots'. The sickening and deadly state of semi-idiocy produced in a marching column of exhausted soldiers is conveyed with exact effect by the deliberate processional monotony of hammered syllables. If it were true, as William Morris believed, that 'craftsmanship is all', Kipling at his best might stand among the leading English poets. Yet the magical something that lies beyond craftsmanship – that intensity of vision which vitalizes the idea and spirit of great poetry – is rare in Kipling. He wrote 'patriotic' poems (such as 'The Ballad of the "Clampherdown"') and 'English' poems (such as 'The Way Through the Woods'). Ideas of militant patriotism vary from age to age, but by Englishmen in whom the love of England endures it is the *English* poems of Kipling that are likely to be remembered.

His poetry has little metaphysical interest. What served as a philosophy of life in most of Kipling's poetry was the conviction that

[1] 'The Run on the Downs'; 'The Land'; 'The Roman Centurion's Song'; 'The Last Suttee'.

[2] 'Mine Sweepers', etc.

[3] 'Our Fathers of Old'.

Englishmen were divinely charged with the duty of enlightening the world's

fluttered folk and wild –
Your new-caught, sullen peoples,
Half-devil and half-child.[1]

His attitude – partly domineering, partly humble – was that of benevolent despotism. Impatient of the belief current in this century, that every race has the right to be free even though freedom may imply misery and subjection contentment, Kipling wanted the world cleaned up. He preached that the cleaners were not to expect gratitude for their pains; they were to go about their task as 'serfs and sweepers', determined that the work should be carried through, though it be against the will of 'the silent, sullen peoples':

Take up the white man's burden –
And reap his old reward:
The blame of those ye better,
The hate of those ye guard –
The cry of hosts ye humour
(Ah, slowly!) toward the light –
'Why brought ye us from bondage,
Our loved Egyptian night?'

Kipling's doctrine made little headway after the new century began. The passion for self-determination in national and racial affairs was accompanied by the conviction that if the formerly 'subject peoples' preferred to live in Egyptian night, they should not be 'humoured' compulsorily towards the dawn.

While Kipling was writing *Barrack Room Ballads* in the early years of the eighteen-nineties, W. B. Yeats (1865–1939) was laying the foundations of the Irish literary movement, described in the preceding chapter. The full effect of Yeats's work for the Irish theatre was not seen until after 1901, though he was already the author of popular collections of lyrics, *Poems* (1895) and *The Wind among the Reeds* (1899). He continued to produce lyrics as well as plays after

[1] 'The White Man's Burden' (1899).

1901, and in critical opinion his most important poetry dates from 1919 when the volume entitled *The Wild Swans at Coole* came out, showing an increase of poetic power and deepening intellectual quality. In one of the poems of his middle period he complained, 'I am worn out with dreams'[1] – a memorable fragment of self-criticism. It had been pointed out[2] that, comparatively early, Yeats began to cut himself off from a source of poetic energy that had been to him, as to greater poets, remarkably fruitful. As a young man he enriched his poems with concrete images, but these became fewer as the impulse to draw upon personal observation of Nature grew fainter. It appeared as if he, also, fled

And paced upon the mountains overhead
And hid his face amid a crowd of stars.[3]

For what was gained, however, there was a counterbalancing loss of patience to watch for the nearer beauties that once held him: 'wet wild strawberry leaves', 'drowsy water rats', 'mice in the barley sheaves', 'bubbles in a frozen pond'. Carried away as Yeats was by dreams, by theosophy and Eastern mysticism, the faery's song in his own poem, 'The Stolen Child', might have been applied to himself:

Away with us he's going,
The solemn-eyed:
He'll hear no more the lowing
Of the calves on the warm hillside
Or the kettle on the hob
Sing peace into his breast,
Or see the brown mice bob
Round and round the oatmeal-chest.[4]

The nature of the change can be seen by comparing 'The Falling of the Leaves'[5] with 'He Wishes for the Cloths of Heaven'.[6] The second poem (published ten years later than the first) is more tenuous than the other. No poet can escape from earth and make his

[1] *Collected Poems* (1950), p. 152.
[2] See *W. B. Yeats: A Critical Study* (1915), by Forrest Reid.
[3] 'When You are Old' (*Collected Poems*, p. 46).
[4] *Collected Poems*, p. 21. [5] Ibid., p. 16.
[6] Ibid., p. 81.

poetry exclusively from the tapestries of heaven. It is no defence to reply that 'the heavens' embroidered cloths enwrought with golden and silver light' suggests a rare magnificence not to be found in

Yellow the leaves of the rowan above us,
And yellow the wet wild-strawberry leaves.[1]

The magnificence does not compensate the loss of touch with natural things. In moods when ethereal beauties were beyond his reach, Yeats trifled with pretty literary artifices and fragments of Christmas-tree decoration – 'moth-like stars' and 'silver apples of the moon'.

'The Lake Isle of Innisfree'[2] effects a compromise between concrete picturing and dream-like imagining. The cabin of clay and wattle, the bean rows and the honey-bee; 'evening full of the linnet's wings'; the lapping of lake-water – are actualities recalled by the exile. When a more freely imaginative picture is used – as in the lines:

for peace comes dropping slow,
Dropping from the veils of the morning to where the cricket sings,

– the infusion of personal feeling is powerful enough to make the image more substantial than a vague dream-tracery of words. The widespread appeal of 'The Lake Isle of Innisfree' does not depend wholly upon response to sentiment. The studiously careful rhythmical structure is equally effective. Yeats freed himself from the metrical regularity formerly observed, and secured a rhythmical basis with scope for natural speech-stress and the general maintenance of natural word-order. Some use is made of repetition, but little of inversion. There is no rigid syllabic structure, the number of syllables to the line ranging from eight to fifteen. The emotional effect of the poem is also heightened by the subtle interaction of vowel music and consonant values, combining a preponderance of open vowels (sometimes further lengthened by the governing rhythm) with a judicious use of alliteration and sibilants, to suggest the bees and linnets, crickets and lapping water. This might seem, at first, to be nothing but the familiar device of *onomatopoeia*, but

[1] *Collected Poems*, p. 16.

[2] Ibid., p. 44.

that is no more than the stem upon which a variety of other devices is grafted. Few modern poems can have had so much artistry lavished upon them as 'The Lake Isle of Innisfree', but it and much of his work of that period were saturated with the romanticism which Yeats distrusted more and more as he aged. He moved with the current of the times, and though – as his editorial preface to *The Oxford Book of Modern Verse* (1937) shows – he was capricious in his views on poetry, he had both sympathy and understanding for the younger generation of poets whose ideals were so different from those of his own youth. Again and again in the poems of his last years the continuing vigour of his mind and senses was in revolt against the enfeeblement of his body. To anyone who might 'think it horrible that lust and rage/Should dance attendance upon [his] old age' he replied 'What else have I to spur me into song?'[1] His progress as a lyrical poet can be gauged from a comparison of the Innisfree poem (1895) with the more complex 'Byzantium' (1930), the first having a plastic loveliness, the other a beauty that is not less but only less immediately apparent. It was, particularly, the more abstruse beauty in Yeats's poems during his last phase that aligned him with the poets of the new age and won applause and devotion from them and from contemporary critics and scholars. But what posterity will choose to preserve from the five hundred pages of his collected poems is open to question. His later austere complexity will not inevitably continue for all time to blot out his early and more widely comprehensible romanticism and attachment to simpler things.

A. E. Housman (1859–1936) was remarkable for the perfection of his poetic workmanship, astonishing in one who had little time to give to poetry, for he was pre-eminently a classical scholar fully engaged from 1892 as Professor of Latin in the University of London and later at Cambridge. His output was small – but it would be difficult to find a weak line, for the exactitude of his scholarship was matched by the metrical precision of his versification. Everything was winnowed with scrupulous care, and he admitted nothing superfluous or merely decorative in form or style. While there is no excess, at

[1] 'The Spur', *Collected Poems*, p. 359.

the same time there is no insufficiency: everything is adjusted and adequate for its purpose. Housman made effective use of vowel quality and the balance of vowel sounds, but he depended much upon explosive consonants – B, T, D, P, K, M – especially when used in the final position.[1] The simplicity of his vocabulary is shown by an analysis of 'Bredon Hill',[2] which contains 191 words: two of these are trisyllables; twenty-seven disyllables; the remainder (162 words) are monosyllables. Housman had the secret of creating beauty by rigid exclusion of ornament. One of his most beautiful poems, 'Loveliest of Trees',[3] contains only one epithet of beauty, and no adjectives of colour. The exquisite picture is built up by means of four principal words – three nouns and one adjective: *bloom*, *white* ('wearing white for Eastertide'), *snow*, and *loveliest*.

In regard to the content of his poetry, Housman had a superficial likeness to Hardy, but his philosophical outlook resulted in an altogether different attitude. Hardy lived entrenched behind his sombre defences, Housman was out in the open, serene amid the battle – undismayed because entirely without hope:

I pace the earth, and drink the air, and feel the sun.
Be still, be still, my soul; it is but for a season:
Let us endure an hour and see injustice done.[4]

Hardy was too sensitive to be actively a rebel; Housman too resolute in an heroic despair. His theoretical attitude towards poetry, enlivened by indications of the actual making of his own poems, was outlined in his Leslie Stephen lecture at Cambridge in 1933 on *The Name and Nature of Poetry*. The besetting fault in the total body of his verse is a certain monotony of tone and mood, a graveyard preoccupation which will not be fully accounted for until a thorough study of his mind and personality can be undertaken.

2. THOMAS HARDY

Between 1871 and 1896 Thomas Hardy (1840–1928) published the prose works which placed him alongside Meredith as one of the two

[1] E.g. 'Reveille' (*A Shropshire Lad*, 1896).
[2] *A Shropshire Lad.*
[3] Ibid.
[4] Ibid. (XLVIII).

outstanding novelists of the late Victorian period. The hostile reception given to *Jude the Obscure* brought Hardy's career as a novelist to an end. Although his later books were immoderately attacked on account of their bitter dissent from orthodox moral and religious standards, Hardy's reputation was already secure when, deliberately, he closed the first phase of his writing life. He then went on to build a second reputation, and a third. It is the second and third phases of his work that belong to twentieth-century literature.

Thomas Hardy (born at Upper Bockhampton, in Dorset) was descended from an old Jersey family that migrated to England before the end of the sixteenth century. A Thomas Hardy who died at Melcombe Regis in 1599 was an ancestor of Nelson's flag captain, Admiral Sir Thomas Hardy, from whom, in turn, the novelist and poet traced his descent. Hardy's father was a builder, his mother the daughter of a Dorsetshire small landowner, and the centuries of settled English tradition in Hardy's ancestral record undoubtedly stimulated and sustained his interest in the ancient English kingdom of Wessex. Hardy's Wessex is much more than a scenic setting for his stories and poems; it is the dominating Over-Character brooding constantly above his works, and casting its changeless shadow upon the author as well as upon the people in his books. He lays reiterated emphasis upon the unaltering aspects of large tracts of Wessex. Egdon Heath is 'a face upon which time makes but little impression'[1] . . . 'a tract of country unaltered from that sinister condition which made Caesar anxious every year to get clear of its glooms before the autumnal equinox'.[2] The men and women of Hardy's Wessex, though living in the nineteenth century, are subject to 'curious fetichistic fears' and touched by a 'lumber of superstitions, folk-lore dialect, and orally transmitted ballads'.[3] The tragedies that fall upon them are often due, in Hardy's interpretation, to the intrusion of modern customs and new habits of mind. Themselves the product of association between the past and the present, these Wessex people are 'harnessed by the irrepressible New'.[4] The decorative veneer of civilization and progress lies uneasily upon them. Grace Melbury turns upon her father with the cry, 'I wish you had never, never

[1] *The Return of the Native*, Book I, Ch. I. [2] Ibid., Book I, Ch. VI.
[3] *Tess of the D'Urbervilles*, Ch. III. [4] *The Return of the Native*, Book I, Ch. I.

thought of educating me. I wish I worked in the woods like Marty South! I hate genteel life. . . . Cultivation has only brought me inconveniences and troubles.'[1] The timeless, changeless spirit of Wessex speaks in her, revolting against newness and 'cultivation'. For the full significance of Hardy's Wessex to be realized, it must stand in the consciousness of readers like an eternal Presence, both in the poems and in the prose. Wessex was persistent and symbolic in Hardy's mentality. Unlike Wordsworth, who was for a time possessed by Nature's 'weird hauntings', Hardy never passed on to experience her 'holy calm'. Though he loved Nature he found little consolatory power in her, and her constant appearance to him was probably as it was, temporarily, to Wordsworth in a troubled period:

Growing still in stature the grim shape
Towered up between me and the stars, and still,
For so it seemed, with purpose of its own
And measured motion like a living thing,
Strode after me.[2]

Before his first novel was published (in 1871) Hardy had written poems which remained in manuscript until 1898. These early experiments belong to the years from 1865 to 1869, when he was practising as an architect, and before he turned to literature as a profession. He said he was compelled to give up poetry in 1868, no doubt under economic pressure, and his public career as a poet did not begin until *Wessex Poems* (1898) appeared. But Hardy's prose was always that of a man of acute poetic vision. He records in the novels a thousand and one aspects of Nature – from the tiny twig 'on the bare bough of a tree stretched horizontally against the evening fire' of the western sky, to the immense landscapes of Blackmoor Vale and Egdon Heath. These things are seen through the eye of a poet, and it must have been with delight that he at length turned back to verse.

From 1866 to 1925 there is little change of outlook in Hardy's poetry. A few harmonies are heard in the old man's songs at seventy that were absent from the harsher tunes of the young man of twenty-

[1] *The Woodlanders*, Ch. XXX. [2] *The Prelude*, Book I.

five; but 'Hap'[1] (written in 1866) might have been the seed from which *The Dynasts* grew, for the interpretation of the universe is the same in 'Hap' as it is in the great epic-drama written forty years later. This consistency in Hardy's philosophy is striking – deeply impressive even – because it conveys a sense of something far more potent than merely crabbed and stubborn pessimism. Though the root remained fixed, the tree grew and extended its branches over an area as wide as Europe.

In 'Hap' the 'suffering thing' is one single person, whose joy lies slain and whose best hope had failed. The sufferer questions why this should be; and the only answer that suggests itself to him is that human destiny lies in the hands of a blind and indifferent power which strews joy and pain with a nerveless and purposeless hand:

These purblind Doomsters had as readily strown
Blisses about my pilgrimage as pain.

Hardy puts the same question time after time, in one form or another:

'Has some Vast Imbecility,
Mighty to build and blend,
But impotent to tend,
Framed us in jest, and left us now to hazardry?
Or come we of an Automaton
Unconscious of our pains? . . .'[2]

Sometimes, the poet implied, no answer is given; but when an answer does come, it is with the unvarying suggestion that the world and humanity are all part of one vast unconsciousness – 'an ever unconscious automatic sense, unweeting why or whence'. The most mature statement of this central theme in his poetry is in *The Dynasts*, where the problem of individual suffering merges into the vision of a world in travail. The first few pages of the Fore Scene in the Overworld contain the essence of Hardy's final presentation of his philosophy. 'What of the Immanent Will and Its designs?' asks the Shade of the Earth; and as the scenes proceed, a detailed

[1] *Wessex Poems.* [2] 'Nature's Questioning' (*Wessex Poems*).

response is slowly elicited from the several Spirits – a response with these main keynotes:

It works unconsciously, as heretofore,
Eternal artistries in Circumstance . . .

. . . . .

Thinking on, yet weighing not Its thought,
Unchecks Its clock-like laws . . .

. . . . .

Like a knitter drowsed,
Whose fingers play in skilled unmindfulness,
The Will has woven with an absent heed
Since life first was; and ever will so weave.

Throughout *The Dynasts* The Spirit of the Pities yields the one faint element of hope – so faint as to seem no better than the hope of a climber struggling on a polished mountain of dark glass. In the last Chorus of the Pities (at the end of the After Scene) there is a somewhat stronger final flash of brightness, suggestive of man's ultimate release from the presumed mindless and soulless domination of the Immanent Will:

. . . a stirring fills the air
Like to sounds of joyance there
That the rages
Of the ages
Shall be cancelled, and deliverance offered from the darts that were,
Consciousness the Will informing, till It fashion all things fair.

Except among those who are governed by a dispassionately speculative temper, it is almost certain that the repeated charge of pessimism will continue to be brought against Hardy, though there is no sound reason why pessimism should automatically be regarded as an indictment demanding defence or apology. It is possible for a philosophy of pessimism to be accepted by a man who is completely happy in himself.[1] Yet the view was widely held that Hardy must always have been exccedingly unhappy. If this was so, his unhappiness orginated not in his philosophic pessimism but in his acute

[1] 'The poetical character . . . lives in gusto, be it foul or fair, high or low, rich or poor, mean or elevated. . . . It does no harm from its relish for the dark side of things, any more than from its taste for the bright one, because they both end in speculation.' (Keats's letter to Richard Woodhouse, 27 October 1818.)

sense of pity. He was vulnerable through his emotions rather than through his mind, and was almost morbidly sensitive to pain suffered by other creatures:

Why, O starving bird, when I
One day's joy would justify,
And put misery out of view,
Do you make me notice you?[1]

For one whose sensibilities were so sharp as this poem (and much else in Hardy) suggests, philosophic pessimism must have been a valuable anodyne. Christian fortitude may inure a soul to its own agonies without reconciling it to the sufferings of others. 'Life had bared its bones' to Hardy, and he sought refuge from the 'long drip of human tears'.[2] He found that refuge in what others call pessimism, but he preferred to define it as ' "obstinate questionings" in the exploration of reality', and he regarded this policy of obstinate questioning as 'the first step towards the soul's betterment and the body's also'.[3] In this connexion Hardy called special attention to a line in one of his early poems ('In Tenebris').

If way to the Better there be, it exacts a full look at the Worst

– a courageous doctrine, though comforting to few.

Hardy's first sixty years fell in Victorian times, but his continual 'obstinate questionings' separated him from spiritual affinity with Victorianism. Kipling, a good Victorian, was at the opposite extreme; he was not plaintively interrogative, but acquiescent and dogmatically assertive, as his poem 'Natural Theology' shows:

This was none of the good Lord's pleasure,
For the Spirit He breathed in Man is free;
But what comes after is measure for measure,
And not a God that afflicteth thee.
As was the sowing so the reaping
Is now and ever more shall be.
Thou art delivered to thine own keeping.
Only thyself hath afflicted thee.

[1] 'The Reminder' (*Time's Laughingstocks*).
[2] 'On an Invitation to the United States' (*Poems of the Past and the Present*).
[3] See the 'Apology' prefixed to *Late Lyrics and Earlier.*

Kipling marched with trumpets, affirming that the God of our fathers lives and reigns; Hardy stood brooding by the wayside, imagining 'God's funeral' passing by:

I saw a slowly-stepping train –
Lined in the brows, scoop-eyed and bent and hoar –

. . . . .

And they composed a crowd of whom
Some were right good, and many nigh the best . . .
Thus dazed and puzzled 'twixt the gleam and gloom
Mechanically I followed with the rest.[1]

In the early years of this century, critics were reluctant to allow that Hardy had any claim to be considered seriously as a lyric poet. As further volumes appeared, however, opinion veered, and with the publication of a collected edition (1919) his second reputation began to challenge the first.

Much has been made by some writers of the fact that Hardy was trained as an architect. Though the 'architectural structure of his plots' may have been over-emphasized, he certainly had the architect's ability to deal with massive structures. His best novels are built in grandeur, and he was truly impressive in his power to communicate the brooding spirit of great places – of Egdon, of Stonehenge, of the Vale of Blackmoor. His most memorable characters, also, are conceived on the grand scale. Though Tess is a broken peasant girl she is immense in her power of endurance. Jude is a tragic failure – but he is a *great* failure. Where Hardy had space in which to move freely he created with the power of genius; where he was circumscribed, his creative ability often became cramped and abortive.

To suggest that Hardy needed space is not to imply that he was incapable of using the lyric form with success. He wrote few things more likely to live than the war lyric, 'In Time of "the Breaking of Nations" ',[2] containing only sixty-three words. Is it possible, then, to reconcile this small piece of perfection with the theory that Hardy was essentially a 'spacious' writer? The answer may be reached by reference to another lyric, 'Shelley's Skylark'.[3] In 1887 Hardy was in

[1] 'God's Funeral' (*Lyrics and Reveries*). [2] *Moments of Vision.*
[3] *Poems of the Past and the Present.*

the neighbourhood of Leghorn, where Shelley wrote 'To a Skylark' in 1820. Most people think of Shelley's bird as a creature immortal in itself, alive and ever in flight. Not so Hardy. He thought of it as a thing perished; it

Lived its meek life; then, one day, fell –
A little ball of feather and bone;

and is now 'a pinch of unseen, unregarded dust'. It was when Hardy permitted himself a spacious *vision* – allowing room for his spirit to move freely – that he created with the power of unquestionable genius. 'In Time of "the Breaking of Nations"' has for its theme little less than the whole aim and direction of the active human spirit, and in that unbounded field of vision Hardy was able to exercise the full scope of his mind and art. The fewness of the words in no way reduces the magnitude of the achievement; rather it enhances it, by fulfilling one of the requirements of great poetry – that it should hold 'an ocean of thought in a drop of language'. In 'Shelley's Skylark', on the contrary, Hardy harnessed his vision to a speck of dust. This is a fault common to a large number of his lyrics, and it applies with particular force to the sequence of fifteen *Satires of Circumstances.*

Never at any time is Hardy's poetry intoxicating or magical. Occasionally it approaches profundity, or rises towards a guarded exultation;[1] but its chief characteristic is a 'satisfying flatness'. It is 'satisfying', because it presents the interesting spectacle of a mind continually probing and exploring; while its 'flatness' is produced by the perisistent pressure of the Spirit of Negation. Negations are not exhilarating; and when Hardy's poetry does leave flatness behind, temporarily, it is because affirmation is for a moment in the ascendant.[2] Hardy avoided the charm of verbal felicity. Though his rhymes and metres are extraordinarily resourceful, the effect is often discounted by a wanton angularity of phrase. This combination of ugly word-forms with a carefully considered verse-technique is a curious and recurrent feature in the lyrics. 'The Alarm',[3] for example, suggests Hardy's aural obtuseness and imperfect sense of literary tact, for here (in a narrative poem on a traditional theme)

[1] E.g. 'When I set out for Lyonnesse' (*Lyrics and Reveries*).
E.g. 'In Time of "the Breaking of Nations"'.
[3] *Wessex Poems.*

he put into the mouth of a Wessex peasant soldier of the Napoleonic period such constructions as *antedate, jeopardize,*[1] etc. Elsewhere he borrowed a variety of terms belonging to science and philosophy, subjects unhappily handicapped by a complex jargon. Such features in Hardy's poetry are as disturbing as an ugly wound on an otherwise comely face.

The third of Hardy's reputations rests upon *The Dynasts*. The test of mere bigness is not often apposite in literature, though in relation to the twentieth century it is a significant test. Since the passing of the great Victorians, poets had shown little of that power of sustained production possessed by most poets of the first rank. Between 1906 and 1920 Charles Doughty wrote several lengthy works in verse,[2] but his archaisms and crabbed style deter most people, even those who admire his masterly travel book, *Arabia Deserta*.

The Dynasts is the biggest single imaginative work in English literature since the Victorian age, and is almost certainly the greatest: great in conception and in execution. Originally published in three parts (1904, 1906, 1908) this Epic-Drama of the war with Napoleon is presented in nineteen acts and one hundred and thirty scenes, the action covering ten years, from 1805 to Napoleon's final defeat at Waterloo.

In this crowning achievement, most of the Hardyesque elements that had previously distinguished his novels and short poems are gathered up in a unified form, and applied in an attempt to represent and account for the Human Tragedy. Mention has already been made of the manner in which Hardy pursues, in *The Dynasts*, his interrogation of the universe, conducted here by the Phantom Intelligences which he created 'as spectators of the terrestrial action'. Hardy's purpose was to dispense with both the Greek and the Hebrew theogony,[3] and to substitute a supernatural system accept-

[1] It is interesting to note the comparative effect of Chaucer's use of the word *jeopardize*. In *The Boke of the Duchesse* (line 666) the reader feels no incongruity between the word and the speaker, nor between the word and its surroundings. As in 'The Alarm', so in the earlier poem, *jeopardize* is a rhyme-word; but there is no sign that the exigencies of rhyme, alone, dictated its use by Chaucer.

[2] *The Dawn in Britain*, etc.

[3] As in (*a*) Aeschylus and other Greek tragic poets; and (*b*) Milton's *Paradise Lost*, etc.

able to modern minds capable of 'that willing suspension of disbelief for the moment which constitutes poetic faith'. George Meredith (in the first chapter of *The Egoist*) discusses the question of whether the literary artist should consider life minutely with 'the watch-maker's eye' or 'under the broad Alpine survey of the Spirit'. Hardy does both in *The Dynasts*. Through the Phantom Intelligences the world is observed as under the broad Alpine survey of the Spirit, while through the speech and actions of the human figures – 'the Persons' – smaller 'patches of life' are seen in detail, as under a magnifying glass. Hardy followed historical sources as closely as is consistent with the poet's function: that is to say, he took historical fact as his raw material and created from it a vision of life that is, in essentials, 'truer' than history. The formal historian has no other duty than to record plainly the actions of men through the eyes of a man; his view is earthbound. But the poet is a visionary as well as a clear-sighted human creature. He sees from the heights of imagination as well as from the level of earth; he possesses something of divinity in amplification of his powers as a man. *The Dynasts*, therefore, offers this twofold (or, rather, manifold) view of a 'vast international tragedy' – Europe's life-or-death struggle against Napoleon, 'the Man of inharmonious jars'. Hardy's vision permits the reader to obtain a view which sweeps over insular and continental boundaries, escapes from social class-divisions, and transcends the limitations of human sight. The conflict is seen as it appeared to French and Austrian, English and Russian; to monarch and peasant, marshal and common soldier; to servants, spies, and street women; to spirit messengers and recording angels. Hardy, unlike Kipling, was never associated in the public mind with enthusiastic patriotism, but part of Hardy's purpose in *The Dynasts* was to redress the balance of history by emphasizing what continental historians had disregarded – namely, that England's achievement was vitally important in saving the world from Napoleonic domination.

The man Napoleon is the central figure of the tragic conflict in *The Dynasts*, which might indeed be entitled 'The Tragedy of Napoleon Bonaparte'. The other dynastic personages – kings and queens, military and naval leaders – are not in themselves essentially tragic. Napoleon, on the contrary, as Hardy represents him, is a towering tragic figure, 'the Man of Destiny' in whom is implanted some influence that carries him onward in spite of himself; deluding him with false promises of triumph; luring him at last to defeat and ruin. To the Queen of Prussia, Napoleon says:

Know you, my Fair,
That I – ay, I – in this deserve your pity –
Some force within me, baffling mine intent,
Harries me onward, whether I will or no.[1]

And again, in his soliloquy after the defeat at Waterloo:

A miss-mark they will dub me;
And yet – I found the crown of France in the mire,
And with the point of my prevailing sword
I picked it up! But for all this and this
I shall be nothing. . . .
To shoulder Christ from out the topmost niche
In human fame, as once I fondly felt,
Was not for me. . . .
Great men are meteors that consume themselves
To light the earth. This is my burnt-out hour.[2]

This revelation of inward conflict ranks Hardy's Napoleon with the tragic heroes of Greek and Shakespearian drama, though the fundamental Idea of Tragedy is not one and the same in all three.

The further tragic element in *The Dynasts* (the conflict between 'the pale panting multitudes'[3] and the Immanent Will) is of the utmost importance in Hardy's design, and is implicit in his motto on the title-page:

And I heard sounds of insult, shame, and wrong,
And trumpets blown for wars.

There is no space to dwell upon the skill and variety of the versification; the vivid originality and force of the 'stage directions'; the remarkable set of original songs and ballads distributed in the text;[4] or the scenes of rustic comedy,[5] in respect of which (in *The Dynasts* and elsewhere) Hardy has been compared with Shakespeare.

[1] Part II, Act I, Sc. viii. [2] III, 7, ix. [3] 'After Scene.'
[4] See Part I, Act I, Sc. i; I, 5, vii; III, I, xi; III, 2, i; III, 5, vi.
[5] See I, 2, v; I, 5, vii; III, 5, vi.

3. NARRATIVE AND SATIRE

The disparity between popular taste and critical opinion is often seen in an aggravated form in relation to story-telling in verse. Simplification of thought, romantic colouring, and smooth facility in versification – these are qualities which commend a particular type of narrative poetry even to readers who find little pleasure in other kinds of verse. From Scott onward there has been in English literature a succession of story-tellers in verse, and when the larger public has delighted in poetry at all it is usually vigorous narrative poetry that has been bought and read.

Alfred Noyes shared with Kipling the distinction of being one of the few early twentieth-century poets who attracted an eager and loyal audience. It was recorded that Noyes was 'the one modern poet who could make poetry – even the epic – pay!'[1] Yet when interest in contemporary poetry revived, about 1912, he was neglected (and sometimes abused) by those writers and critics who were most desirous of fostering the revival.

While Noyes went along the old familiar road, John Masefield had been experimenting both in life and in literature. Leaving his Shropshire home (where he was born in 1874) he ran away to sea, and memories of that period are given in 'Dauber' (1913). Following some experience as a working sailor

> He took to the road in America, living a free vagrant life, sleeping in barns, working here and there on farms, finally turning up in New York, where he got a job at ten dollars a month in the Colonial Hotel, and earned his money by about sixteen hours' handiwork a day, scouring beer taps, cleaning cuspidors (which we call spittoons) and ejecting turbulent patrons. At about two or two-thirty a.m. he went to his garret, where he read *Morte D'Arthur*, his only book, until he fell alseep.[2]

Once or twice Masefield lifted the veil and allowed himself to be seen 'roughing it'.[3] After working as a gardener and a potman he returned to England and, becoming a journalist, edited the daily 'Miscellany' column in the *Manchester Guardian*. Then he went back

[1] *Contemporary British Literature*, by Manly and Rickert.
[2] A. G. Gardiner (in the *Daily News*, 3 May 1913).
[3] As in 'A Raines Law Arrest' (*A Tarpaulin Muster*, 1907).

to London and settled in Bloomsbury, where he made friends with several well-known writers, including J. M. Synge, the Irish playwright. These two took many long walks through London, engaged in talk which often kept them wandering half the night along deserted streets.[1]

Between 1901 and 1911 Masefield wrote poems, plays, novels, short stories, essays and criticism, all with moderate success; and he was an established writer before the remarkable outburst of acclamation which greeted 'The Everlasting Mercy' on its appearance in the *English Review* in 1911. That long narrative poem in octosyllabic couplets was an attempt to represent in verse, realistically, the spiritual conversion of a prodigal, 'tokened to the devil'. Saul Kane, the central character, tells the story in his own words, and Masefield suppressed nothing: the brutality, the delirium, the foul language – all are there, in the first half of the poem. Later, when Saul Kane has been converted by a Quaker woman, his spiritual ecstasy is described. Amid the earlier blaspheming passages there are poetic ones, but the incongruous mixture would have seemed more effective in a seventeenth-century Puritan tract. It plunges into bathos –

John and Mary died of measles,
And Rob was drownded at the Teasels.
And little Nan, dear little sweet,
A cart run over in the street;
Her little shift was all one stain,
I prayed God put her out of pain

– and it does not justify the many such passages to suppose that Masefield was aiming at the kind of verse Saul Kane himself might have been expected to produce. Bald pedestrian jog-trot and manufactured rhymes also characterize the other long narrative pieces which Masefield wrote in the following years: 'The Widow in the Bye Street' (1912) and 'The Daffodil Fields' (1913). 'Dauber' (1913), though not free from such blemishes, is relieved by fine passages of sea poetry. These poems were written in reaction from picturesque modes of versifying, and caused a sensation by their newness.

John Masefield had done better work in his *Saltwater Ballads* (1902)

[1] See Masefield's poem, 'Biography'.

and *Ballads and Poems* (1910), in which such popular pieces as 'Sea Fever' and 'Cargoes' appeared; and he was afterwards to write a better narrative poem – 'Reynard the Fox' (1919). This record of a fox-hunt is notable for its Chaucerian thumb-nail sketches of human character in the description of the meet in the first part; and the fox's-eye view of the run in part two. Here the poet is in control of his rhythms and metres, and not their slave as in the earlier narrative poems. By prosodic variation the changing sensations of the fox are imaginatively indicated – his first excitement, his fear, his growing weariness, his relief when

The threat of the hounds behind was gone,

and how (after the scent is found again)

His strength was broken, his heart was bursting,
His bones were rotten, his throat was thirsting;
His feet were reeling, his brush was thick
From dragging the mud, and his brain was sick.

But the fox escapes and the poem ends with a quiet descriptive passage. 'Reynard the Fox' is among the best sustained narrative poems written in the quarter-century. Masefield's appointment as Poet Laureate on the death of Bridges in 1930 was interpreted as the Labour government's recognition of his knowledge of and sympathy with the working classes.

Journalism has been a convenient by-road to literature for many authors; for G. K. Chesterton (1874–1936) as a poet, on the contrary, it proved a blind alley. An inveterate journalist, his eyes and ears strained towards the affairs of the hour; and like all satirical poets below the first rank he treated the insignificant twitterings of minor politicians as seriously as if they were the blasphemous thunders of the lords of hell. His *Collected Poems* (1933) is, therefore, a lopsided affair, with page after page of versified disquisitions upon phrases extracted from current newspapers, magazines, sermons, and speeches. But amid this jumbled mass are a score or so of pieces that no other English poet could have written. The long narrative poems – 'Lepanto', 'The Ballad of St Barbara', and 'The Ballad of the

White Horse' – are less impressive than ambitious: none has a compelling story-interest, but in 'Lepanto' there are passages rousing when declaimed; for example:

Don John pounding from the slaughter-painted poop,
Purpling all the ocean like a bloody pirate's sloop,
Scarlet running over on the silvers and the golds,
Breaking of the hatches up and bursting of the holds,
Thronging of the thousands up that labour under sea
White for bliss and blind for sun and stunned for liberty.

This is stirring verse if not first-rate poetry. Probably few readers or speakers care what the lines are *about* – the syllabic pomp suffices.

Among Chesterton's satirical poems the twelve-line 'Elegy in a Country Churchyard' is so good that the rest of his satires seem trivial in comparison. It has the advantage of a theme that, though 'timed', is likely to remain applicable for generations to come; and it has, also, pity and a fine indignation to raise it above the level of satire that is tinged by partisan prejudice and personal animus. Compared with the 'Elegy' there is an absurd air of humourless inflation about 'Antichrist, or The Reunion of Christendom: An Ode', in which Chesterton attacked F. E. Smith (the first Lord Birkenhead) for a now long-forgotten speech on the Welsh Disestablishment Bill.

The best section of G. K. Chesterton's verse is the group of road-songs and drinking-songs scattered through his novel, *The Flying Inn.*[1] Their combination of wisdom and nonsense, humour and high spirits, is irresistible and unique, and these (together with one impressive serious lyric, 'The Donkey') constitute Chesterton's indispensable contribution to English poetry.

The verse output of Hilaire Belloc (1870–1953) was smaller in quantity than that of his intimate friend G. K. Chesterton, but it includes less perishable stuff. A few of his lyrics (such as 'The South Country') are established firmly in the anthologies. The satirical *Cautionary Tales for Children*[2] – though caustic and critical – are at the same time delightfully absurd. Belloc was also a neat epigram-

[1] These poems, reprinted in *Wine, Water and Song* (1915), are included in *Collected Poems*.

[2] Included in Belloc's collected *Cautionary Verses* (1939).

matist, whether offering a compliment to a friend or directing an arrow at a foe.

Of the younger satirists using traditonal verse-forms, Humbert Wolfe (1885–1940) and Roy Campbell (1901–57) received most attention – the former for *News of the Devil* (1926) and *The Uncelestial City* (1930), and the latter for *The Flaming Terrapin* (1924), and *The Georgiad* (1931). After considerable popularity and acclaim in his lifetime Wolfe was quickly forgotten after his death. Campbell, with a narrower but deeper immediate reputation, survived in his poetry and the odium of his support of the Falangists in the Spanish Civil War was not long remembered against him.

4. RUPERT BROOKE AND THE SOLDIER POETS

When Rupert Brooke died at Skyros in the Aegean Sea on 17 April 1915, he was canonized in the popular imagination, and by the influence of his personality rather than his poetry became a prominent figure in contemporary literature. In the stress of the early months of the First World War, the nation needed a human symbol to keep attention fixed upon the professed idealistic aims for which it had been led into battle. After eight months such a symbol was found in the dead poet, Rupert Brooke – remembered, not as a figure of death but as he was while alive: young, quick, and eager, 'a young Apollo, golden-haired'.[1] His early death while on war-service, his physical beauty, his intellectual gifts, his genius for friendship – these were accepted as marks of 'one who seemed to have everything that is worth having'. So, with little reference to his merits as a poet, Brooke became a sign and symbol of his age – even as, three centuries earlier, another handsome and accomplished young Englishman, Sir Philip Sidney, had been a sign and symbol for the Elizabethans.

Born at Rugby in 1887, Rupert Brooke was the son of a housemaster at Rugby School, where he spent a happy schoolboy life.[2]

[1] He was thus described in a verse epigram by Frances Cornford (see her *Collected Poems*, 1954, p. 19).

[2] The *Memoir* of Rupert Brooke by (Sir) Edward Marsh, prefaced to the 1918 *Collected Poems*, was the chief biographical source until Christopher Hassall's full-length *Rupert Brooke: A Biography* (1964).

Later, at King's College, Cambridge, he became absorbed in amateur acting and in the University Fabian Group. Soon he found the Fabians hard and intolerant, devoid of the imaginative idealism urgent in himself. At that time he affirmed: 'There are only three things in the world: one is to read poetry, another is to write poetry, and the best of all is to live poetry!'

Out of term-time, Brooke lived in a cottage at Grantchester (near Cambridge), of which place he wrote one of his best-known poems. When he left Cambridge, some years were spent in travel – first on the Continent, and afterwards in America and the South Seas.[1] He returned to London in June 1914. Then came the war. He took part in the unsuccessful defence of Antwerp and, at the end of February, sailed for the East, where he died less than two months later.

Rupert Brooke had at first been attracted by the artifices of the eighteen-nineties group of writers, but he quickly reacted against their vitiated hot-house atmosphere, and wallowed in ugliness in order to demonstrate his distate for 'pretty' poetry. He wrote sonnets on seasickness and other unsavoury subjects; and, as a protest against the exclusively romantic view of classical heroes, affirmed in the 'Menelaus and Helen' sonnets that 'the perfect knight' and 'the perfect queen' afterwards degenerated into disgusting senility. He quickly passed out of that phase, however. Sitting at a Berlin café in 1912 he thought of the 'incredibly lovely superb world', and wrote his poem about one of the loveliest places he knew, 'The Old Vicarage, Grantchester'. Though he referred to this poem as 'hurried stuff', others found it as cool and refreshing as the May fields (of which he speaks) to 'the bare feet that run to bathe'. His love of Nature was neither mystical nor metaphysical. He saw and touched and enjoyed; that was enough:

I only know that you may lie
Day long and watch the Cambridge sky,
And, flower-lulled in sleepy grass,
Hear the cool lapse of hours pass,
Until the centuries blend and blur
In Grantchester, in Grantchester.

[1] See his *Letters from America* (1916).

In 'The Great Lover' he wrote of the hundred and one everyday things that gave him joy – plates and cups, dust, wet roofs, woodsmoke, 'the cool kindliness of sheets . . . and the rough male kiss of blankets'. He invested this domestic catalogue with significance and beauty, and turned the commonplace into the strangely new.

Though the five sonnets entitled '1914' were enthusiastically received at their first appearance, their poetic qualities probably did not undergo close scrutiny. When war-time emotions had been forgotten, it became fashionable to decry Rupert Brooke, and to deride those who admired him. On the evidence of the *Collected Poems* it would be rash to describe him as a great poet; yet the '1914' sonnets hint at a growing 'high seriousness' which might have matched his sense of melody with a measure of sustaining thought. Because of its prophetic interest, 'The Soldier' became the one poem inseparably linked with Rupert Brooke's name. It is, for all time, his epitaph – beautiful and tranquil; but its broken, staccato movement (awkward in the sonnet form) places it, as poetry, below the first and third sonnets of the '1914' group ('Peace' and 'The Dead') ('Blow out, you bugles, over the rich Dead!').

It is natural though unprofitable to speculate on what might have been Rupert Brooke's place in English poetry if he had lived on. The marks of greatness in his poems are few, but such marks there are. He saw the world with a clear eye and recorded what he saw with directness and clarity. Yet, however poetic in himself, Rupert Brooke was more important as the occasion of poetry in others; though it is not true, as some have suggested, that the war-time revival of English poetry had its origin in Brooke alone. The emotional necessity of poetry had been independently revealed to the fighting men in Flanders and elsewhere before Rupert Brooke's death.

In glancing at some other soldier-poets who wrote verse between 1914 and 1918, the next to whom it is common to turn is Julian Grenfell (1888–1915). Though a soldier on active service in France, Grenfell was able to capture at least one mood of tranquillity amid the turmoil, and in that mood wrote 'Into Battle'. He wrote other verse, but this is his masterpiece and his memorial, created not out of urgent passions, but through calm communion with unwarlike things. In the midst of fire he could withdraw into himself and find solace, harmony, and fellowship with earth and trees and the grass; with stars and birds and horses. Death to him did not seem a pit into which he would be plunged headlong and despairing; it was a rest to which he would go as confidently as men go each night to bed:

The thundering line of battle stands,
And in the air Death moans and sings;
But Day shall clasp him with strong hands,
And Night shall fold him in soft wings.

. . . . .

The fighting man shall from the sun
Take warmth, and life from the glowing earth;
Speed with the light-foot winds to run,
And with the trees to newer birth;
And find, when fighting shall be done,
Great rest, and fullness after dearth.

This spirit of confidence and tranquillity was unapproached by the other war-time poets. Grenfell preserved his spiritual certitude and moral courage even while realizing all that war meant and all that it probably would mean for him very soon. He was killed soon after.

Siegfried Sassoon was a very different type of warrior-poet. In the early months of the war he served as an officer, but, being invalided home, resigned his commission and, for a time, conducted a propagandist campaign against war. So in *Counter Attack* (1918) he set out to present in brutal verse the realities of war without gloss or evasion. The war-poems of Siegfried Sassoon, therefore, take more account of war as a dirty mess of blood and decaying bodies than as a source of heroic deeds. Many of the verses are a nightmare of horror; if they burnt into the memory they did what the author required. Yet Sassoon was quickly disillusioned of hope that the public conscience would be moved to stop war because a soldier told the truth. Some said that his truths were only the gibberings of a crank, and, in the end, Sassoon re-enlisted and went back to the war which truth could not stop. The verses in *Counter Attack* seldom rise to the level of poetry; but criticism is disarmed by their sincerity and the fact that they were put forward as a contribution not to aesthetics but to the cause of human brotherhood. At least these verses reveal the war-mind of thousands who felt (though they might not have spoken in print) as Siegfried Sassoon did:

You smug-faced crowds with kindling eye
Who cheer when soldier lads march by,
Sneak home and pray you'll never know
The hell where youth and laughter go.[1]

The most discerning of the war anthologies[2] contained poems by nearly a hundred writers, and of these about two-thirds were by soldier-poets. Most of them conformed to the accepted modes of poetry, but Wilfred Owen broke away and tried a form which he considered more suited to the disharmony of war. Before his death in action on 4 November 1918 (at the age of twenty-five), Owen had experimented with assonance and dissonance in place of rhyme, and the jarring effect suggested the clangour of warfare without destroying the normal basis of verse-structure. Wilfred Owen's *Poems* (1920) were scarcely two score in number, and in an unfinished Preface he wrote:

I am not concerned with Poetry.
My subject is War, and the pity of War.
The Poetry is in the pity.

The conjunction of poetry and pity can be noted in his most familiar piece, *Strange Meeting*, in which two dead soldiers ('enemies') speak to each other. The waste of young life, and the tragic pathos of cheated youth struck down on the threshold of 'the undone years': these are the themes that move the lips of the second speaker, who closes the poem with the only request that the living millions could grant to the millions dead, 'Let us sleep now. . . .' In his preface Wilfred Owen wrote also: 'All a poet can do today is to warn.' The warning from him went unheeded, but after the Second World War it was to Owen that a new generation turned as the outstanding poet of his time. The rediscovery was greatly stimulated by the *War Requiem* (1962) in which Benjamin Britten set to music a number of Owen's poems. The Requiem was written for first performance at the dedication of the new Coventry Cathedral which

[1] 'Suicide in the Trenches' (*Counter Attack*).
[2] *Valour and Vision*, edited by Jacqueline Trotter (1920).

replaced the medieval building destroyed by German bombing in the 1939–45 war. Inasmuch as the new cathedral was intended to symbolize the spirit of reconciliation between former enemies, Wilfred Owen's 'Strange Meeting' and 'Anthem for Doomed Youth' were uniquely apposite to the occasion. In a definitive edition of his *Collected Poems* (1963), the editor, C. Day Lewis, wrote of the enigma that lies in the sudden maturing which led in the year 1917–18 to 'a period of intense creative activity' and produced what are probably 'the greatest poems about war in our literature'.

Historians may find it both illuminating and sobering to reflect upon the significance of the fundamental division between the poems of Rupert Brooke and Julian Grenfell at the beginning of the First World War and those of Siegfried Sassoon and Wilfred Owen at its end. But it is not enough to consider Owen as exclusively a war poet. Though it cannot be known what might have been the nature or quality of future work by him, there can be no doubt that he possessed the rare genius that marks the true poet and fuses words into inspired phrases and lines:

By choice they made themselves immune
To pity and whatever mourns in man
Before the last sea and the hapless stars;
Whatever mourns when many leave these shores;
Whatever shares
The eternal reciprocity of tears.

Here (from the poem called 'Insensibility') 'the last sea and the hapless stars' and, more unforgettable, 'The eternal reciprocity of tears' have the meaning-beyond-meaning which distinguishes poetry from prose and makes nonsense of critical exercises in textual analysis: such lines are 'felt in the heart and felt along the blood'; they can convey nothing whatsoever through intellect alone.

5. 'GEORGIAN POETRY'

Poetry given, the problem was to sell it. In the first ten years of the twentieth century, as was also to be the case a generation later, English readers bought very little new verse, and with a few exceptions living poets were not considered by publishers as a commercial proposition. By 1912 Rupert Brooke was satisfied that public neglect was a serious hindrance to the development of contemporary poetry. The desire for a wider audience was prompted both by a hope of increased sales (at best, the writers could have little expectation of a sufficient income from poetry) and by the need of intelligent appreciation outside their own coterie. Mental inbreeding among members of literary cliques blighted many young twentieth-century authors, and a healthy instinct and sound common sense led Rupert Brooke to attempt to break the narrow and vicious circle.

Edward Marsh described[1] how Brooke devised a scheme for stimulating public curiosity. He planned to write a volume of poems and to publish it as the work of 'twelve different writers, six men and six women, all with the most convincing pseudonyms'. Marsh made the counter-suggestion of publishing an anthology by 'flesh and blood poets', and at his rooms in Gray's Inn on 20 September 1912 the suggestion was approved and adopted over luncheon by a party consisting of Rupert Brooke, John Drinkwater, Harold Monro, W. W. Gibson, Arundel del Ré, and Edward (afterwards Sir Edward) Marsh himself. However little future attention may be paid to the neo-Georgians of 1912–25, they did stir the public to buy – and to read – poetry, even before the war threw men back upon elementals expressible only in poetry.

A few weeks before Christmas 1912 Harold Monro (1879–1932) published from his Poetry Bookshop in a Bloomsbury slum a volume in brown paper boards entitled *Georgian Poetry, 1911–12*, edited by E. M. (Edward Marsh). A large circulation had been hoped for, but the actual success went beyond expectation. New impressions were called for month after month, and the sales ran into many thousands. Further volumes of *Georgian Poetry* followed at intervals up to 1922, when (with the fifth collection) the series came to an end, though Mrs Harold Monro issued in 1933 a supplementary volume. By 1922 the fervour of 1912 had died down in most of the poets. One or two of the best had altogether ceased from producing verse; for others, verse-writing had become a habit. The

[1] *Rupert Brooke: A Memoir.*

reign of the Georgians was over and the poetic fire – a little dimmed – scattered.

In those five books the work of forty poets was represented. G. K. Chesterton was in the first volume and John Masefield in that and others, but few other well-known writers appeared. None was more promising than Ralph Hodgson (1871–1962), who seemed a poet of almost unlimited possibility. Hodgson's early poems had emotional force and subtlety of music, and compressed a wide range of pictorial and dramatic effects into a minimum of words. Compassion for animals was dominant, and he expressed this with passion and vision. In 'The Bells of Heaven'[1] he spoke of 'angry prayers'

For shamed and shabby tigers
And dancing dogs and bears
And wretched blind pit ponies,
And little hunted hares.

If humanitarian pity produced the last three lines, poetic vision and understanding created the image of intolerable indignity in the phrase 'shamed and shabby tigers', majestic beasts torn from the boundless liberty of the forest and crushed into cowed manginess by some circus-monger. 'The Bull',[2] a more ambitious poem, is an attempt to present, psychologically and poetically, the history of a leader of a herd, dethroned in his old age and decrepitude by a young rebel. The old monarch stands – bewildered, unhappy, sick – waiting only for death, while vultures hover with patient and remorseless persistence:

See him standing dewlap-deep
In the rushes at the lake,
Surly, stupid, half-asleep. . . .

Dreaming things: of days he spent
With his mother gaunt and lean
In the valley warm and green,
Full of baby wonderment,
Blinking out of silly eyes
At a hundred mysteries.

[1] *Georgian Poetry (III), 1916–17; Collected Poems* (1961), p. 75.
[2] *Georgian Poetry (II), 1913–15; Collected Poems*, p. 77.

He relives, in a dream, the glories of his past, but the dream fades; he wakes from his vision, clouds of flies about him,

And the dreamer turns away
From his visionary herds
And his splendid yesterday,
Turns to meet the loathly birds
Flocking round him from the skies,
Waiting for the flesh that dies.

The rest of Hodgson's poetry must be passed over with no more than mention of his longest and most elusive poem, 'The Song of Honour'[1] – a remarkable piece of rhythmical virtuosity in doggerel metre; 'Eve',[2] lovely in its music and word-pictures; and 'The Gipsy Girl,[3] a masterpiece of compression – the substance of a five-act drama and a psychological novel in twenty lines. Many years of silence followed the publication of Hodgson's slim volume, *Poems*, in 1917. Apart from a few verses in periodicals (mostly American) it was not until 1958 that further work appeared in *The Skylark and other Poems*, followed in 1961 by *Collected Poems*. By then the climate for poetry had changed absolutely.

James Elroy Flecker (1884–1915) was the eldest child of Dr Flecker, afterwards headmaster of Dean Close School, Cheltenham, where the boy was educated before going to Oxford. Following Leconte de Lisle, Hérédia, and other poets of the French 'Parnassian' school, Flecker eschewed personal and emotional verse, and (he said) wrote 'with the single intention of creating beauty'.[4] Except in his oriental play, *Hassan* (1922), he rarely got beyond experimentation. *Hassan*, a store of exotic *bijouterie*, is remembered more for its lyrics than for dramatic qualities. The first London production of *Hassan* was a fine stage spectacle, but apart from the melodious lyrics the play was tedious; and had, moreover, touches of that sensual cruelty which became a feature of imaginative writing in England round about the nineteen-twenties. In Hassan's song to Yasmin (Act I, Sc. ii), 'The War Song of the Saracens' (Act III,

[1] *Georgian Poetry (II)*; *Collected Poems*, p. 66.
[2] *Poems* (1917); *Collected Poems*, p. 64.
[3] *Georgian Poetry (III)*; *Collected Poems*, p. 60.
[4] See J. C. Squire's introduction to *The Collected Poems of James Elroy Flecker* (1916).

Sc. iii), and 'The Golden Road to Samarkand', Flecker came as near as he ever did to his 'single intention of creating beauty'. Too often his verse reeked of the unguent pot and the perfume jar.

The human spirit seeks, from age to age, to free itself from the intolerable bondage of its own civilization; to escape from the hell of complication to the heaven of simple things. Blake found a way out, though no one else has followed him to the end of his path; Wordsworth found another way out – by 'returning to Nature'; and in the twentieth century Walter de la Mare found a different way – by a return to the direct vision of childhood. He was not (except incidentally) a children's poet. If his vision was that of a child, his imagination and intellect were always fully adult. Blake's 'Tiger, Tiger' has a divine incomprehensibility behind its external simplicity, and an equivalent divine incomprehensibility may lie in a score of de la Mare's 'simple' poems – in 'Tillie', 'Miss T.', 'Hide and Seek':[1]

Hide and seek, say I
To myself and step
Out of the dream of Wake
Into the dream of Sleep.

Walter de la Mare's poems explore tirelessly *the dream of Wake*. In that dream, natural and supernatural become one, as muffins and mutton and Miss T. become one; the poet sees the future in the instant, and all experience comes to him preternaturally sharpened and free from mental fog. 'The Scribe'[2] is about the subject of all great verse – God and Man and the universe. Milton made ten thousand lines on the theme; de la Mare made twenty-six lines only. In the 'dream of Wake' he sees the universe as a map laid out; he sees its immensity at a glance; he knows that all Time is not long enough to catalogue what he sees. Why write epics, when an epic can no more justify the ways of God than a lyric can? Why write epics, when a lyric may equally well suggest the boundless immensity of the works of God? –

[1] All in *Peacock Pie* (1913); in *Collected Rhymes and Verses* (1944), pp. 183, 234, 216.
[2] In *Motley* (1918); *Collected Poems* (1942), p. 173.

. . . still would remain
My wit to try – . . .
All words forgotten –
Thou, Lord, and I.

His first poems, *Songs of Childhood* (1902), embodied qualities that came to be recognized as characteristic excellences of his poetry. The subtle and varied metrical music was already in process of development; and he was already a poet of silences and shy solitary creatures. His exquisite craftsmanship was never a mere preoccupation with artifice; nor did the dream quality in his verse make him unaware of 'the smooth-plumed bird . . . the seed of the grass, the speck of stone . . . the wayfaring ant', nor of 'fetlocked horses' and bony, knobble-kneed donkeys. He walked on the common earth; his imagination fed upon solider fare than honeydew; and though he might hobnob with fairies and witches, he never discovered a more enchanting companion than the mangy donkey, 'Nicholas Nye'.[1]

The post-war poems of Siegfried Sassoon (e.g. *The Heart's Journey*, 1928, and *Vigils*, 1935) were delicate and reticently reflective, with a suggestion of far-away muted music. Harold Monro, besides editing *Georgian Poetry*, was himself a poet who progressed from the pleasantly fanciful to a series of poems in which there is deep thought and troubled feeling (*Collected Poems*, 1933).

6. NATURE POETRY

In his will Rupert Brooke endowed three of his fellow-writers. He was aware that daily drudgery left contemporary authors with their minds only half free. The demands of business were responsible for the double-edged epithet 'The Week-end School' – applied to the Poetry Bookshop group. When these poets wrote of Nature, they wrote as town-dwellers who met Nature only from Saturdays to Mondays, rather than as men who knew her in all moods.

A few of the poets succeeded – for a time, at least – in avoiding the handicap, and as nearly as any one might in such circumstances as

[1] In *Peacock Pie*; *Collected Rhymes and Verses*, p. 82.

his, William Henry Davies (1871–1940) dedicated himself to poetry. He saw the external world with an uncultured eye and wrote about it, for the most part in 'non-literary' verse.

The story of his early life is told in *The Autobiography of a Super-Tramp* (1908). Born in Newport, Mon., he had a restless and lawless youth, afterwards living as a tramp and very casual worker in America and England until he was thirty-seven. During a quiet period in youth, while apprenticed to a picture-frame maker, he 'composed and caused to be printed a poem describing a storm at night, which a young friend recited at a mutual improvement class'. Years later, after losing his right foot while 'jumping' a railway train in Canada, he turned again to poetry, and in a public lodging-house in south London composed a blank verse tragedy, *The Robber*. When this had been rejected by two theatre managers, he wrote a long narrative poem, a hundred sonnets, 'another tragedy, a comedy, a volume of humorous essays, and hundreds of short poems'.[1] After further wanderings and privations he accumulated £19, the sum required to publish a book of fifty poems[2] at his own risk. Review copies sent out by the printer produced only two brief notices in provincial papers. Davies then began to post copies to well-known people, inviting them to send him the price of the book. Some did so, including Bernard Shaw, who later wrote an Introduction to Davies's autobiography, and before long the 'super-tramp' established himself among contemporary poets.

The few early pieces retained in the voluminous *Collected Poems* (1942) show that Davies distrusted his own ability, and had then a marked tendency to lean upon stereotyped practices in verse. The 'artless simplicity' of his later work was easy game for parodists, yet in those poems Davies displayed a more characteristic quality than in

I would that drowsy June awhile were here,
The amorous South wind carrying all the vale –
Save that white lily true to star as pale,
Whose secret day-dream Phoebus burns to hear.[3]

[1] *The Autobiography of a Super-Tramp*, Ch. XXI.
[2] *The Soul's Destroyer and Other Poems* (1907).
[3] 'Autumn', from *The Soul's Destroyer*; *Collected Poems* (1942), p. 23.

Although the second-hand furniture of conventional verse lumbers up these lines, to produce poetry of any kind was an achievement in the circumstances Davies describes in 'The Lodging-House Fire', a verse transcription of chapter XXVII of the *Autobiography*. Like Herrick, W. H. Davies was a poet of extreme accomplishment and sophistication wrapped in a deceptive aura of simplicity. His poetry had many moods, but his sheep and grass and cloudlets were refreshing in a jaded world:

When I came forth this morn I saw
Quite twenty cloudlets in the air;
And then I saw a flock of sheep,
Which told me how those clouds came there.

That flock of sheep on that green grass,
Well might it lie so still and proud!
Its likeness had been drawn in heaven,
On a blue sky, in silvery cloud.[1]

Though his acute sensibilities are displayed chiefly in enumeration of the smaller delights of the countryside – sights and sounds and odours – Davies was sensible of the menace of the darker wing of Life. Allowing for obvious metrical diversity, Thomas Hardy might have written the lines in which Davies describes the effect upon him of cities:

When I am in those great places,
I see ten thousand suffering faces;
Before me stares a wolfish eye,
Behind me creeps a groan or sigh.[2]

But whereas Hardy sought persistently in Nature for analogies to compel attention to the 'ten thousand suffering faces' of mankind and 'the long drip of human tears', Davies flew to Nature for solace and forgetfulness, pursuing Joy, eschewing Sadness.[3] The central fact in his poetry is not that he saw little more than externals, but that he was grateful to Nature for hanging a solacing veil between his susceptibilities and the world's pain. He learned in his wandering

[1] 'The Likeness' (*New Poems*); *Collected Poems* (1942), p. 53.
[2] 'In the Country' (from *Farewell to Poesy*); *Collected Poems*, p. 106
[3] See *Songs of Joy* and *Sadness and Joy*.

years what lies behind the veil; and in later life he preferred to look no farther than its surface-pattern. For him, to attempt to reduce Nature to a philosophical system would have been to succumb to the barren earnestness and purposiveness against which he protested interrogatively in 'Leisure' – his apology for idlers:

A poor life this if, full of care,
We have no time to stand and stare.[1]

Edward Thomas (born 1878; educated at St Paul's School and Oxford) published his first book when he was nineteen, and for the next twenty years wrote and edited numerous works in prose. He joined the army and was killed in France in 1917, and in that year appeared the earliest collection of poems under his own name. As 'Edward Eastaway' he had published a few poems previously, but readers were not prepared for the revelation of Edward Thomas as a poet equal to the best of his contemporaries. He was entirely original, and his originality is itself strangely original, though there is nothing freakish, either in manner or matter. The sense of 'newness' given by his poetry came from a feeling that it was written by one whose vision and music were free from glints and echoes of others' work. Though Thomas was a reader and critic of poetry, he neither followed nor reacted. He sang as though he were the first and only poet, and there was a curious absence of conscious literary effort in his choice of material. His instrument was not a harp, nor a trumpet, nor an organ; it was a divine penny whistle, full of delicate, half-sweet, half-troubled music. He speaks of a boy, hidden in a thicket, who

Slowly and surely playing
On a whistle an olden nursery melody,
Says far more than I am saying.[2]

But Thomas's own whistle says more than he may himself have been aware.

In 1925 Edmund Blunden was still a poet of promise. Both Davies and Edward Thomas, though intimate with Nature, were more

[1] 'Leisure' (*Songs of Joy*); *Collected Poems*, p. 140.
[2] 'The Penny Whistle', *Collected Poems* (1922), p. 80.

detached than any thoroughgoing Nature poet can be. Blunden, on the other hand, completely identified himself with Nature, whether in the mire and soggy wetness of a November day in the Kentish fields, or

when the morning ripens and unfolds
Like beds of flowers the glories of the plain.[1]

His first book of verse, *Pastorals*, was published in 1916, a few months after he left school (Christ's Hospital) to take a commission in the army. War service in France, a long sea voyage (in 1921–2),[2] and periods as lecturer in English literature at Tokyo University provided Blunden with varied experience, but the dominant note in his poetry up to 1925 remained true to 'The Preamble' to *Pastorals*:

I sing of the rivers and hamlets and woodlands of Sussex and Kent,
Such as I know them: I found a delight wherever I went,
By plat and by hatch, through acres of hops or of corn.

His master then was Clare (1793–1864), the Northamptonshire poet, and these two share the distinction of writing perhaps the best 'winter poetry' in English. There has been much talk in verse about bright frosty winter days, but the drab saturation of winter is equally true and equally English – and Blunden is completely English. He was, perhaps, too good a poet at the beginning. If *The Waggoner* had appeared in 1930 instead of 1920, and had followed a series of inferior volumes, his admirers might have been more content. As it was, he filled the prose of his *Undertones of War* (1928) with the essence of poetry, and in the poems placed as an appendix to the book seemed not to maintain the splendid level of the prose. Throughout his *English Poems* (1925) there is no ease of utterance, no smoothness, no untroubled melody. Blunden was never a Nature poet in the narrow sense of being content to paint external appearances; and in the later poems there is a stronger metaphysical strain. His poetry 'is not the fruit of facility. I strive for utterance', he said.[3] And he speaks of 'half-ideas, verges of shadows and misty

[1] 'Shepherd' (*Poems of Many Years*, p. 47).
[2] See *The Bonadventure* (1922), a record of the voyage.
[3] Preface to *English Poems*.

brightness'. This difficult wrestling of the poet with his material no doubt explains why his verse has an air of thwarted achievement – as if some obstruction impeded the fulfilment; an impression to some extent confirmed by the address 'To Nature':

O my stern mother, aye, in that name loved,
Who gave me life and all its greenest fields,
And yet to counterchange the simple joy
Gave me this brain, whose luck it seems to be
Ever to labour like a winnowing drudge,
But blind, unknowing if it beats in vain. . . .

His collected *Poems of Many Years* (1957) provides an illuminating view of one man's poetic progress through nearly half a century during which, as the Preface to that volume says: 'I have seen with surprise how beloved examples have abruptly become horrible examples, and how a new day blows its trumpets for writings hard to connect with what *was* poetry just before.' To what extent the contemporary winds of change had affected Blunden's own poetry – and to what extent they had failed to change his fundamental vision – can be assessed by comparing any poem in the first fifty or so pages of the collected volume with any in the last hundred or so.

Victoria Sackville-West – first in her *Orchard and Vineyard* (1921) and later in *The Land* (1926), a long descriptive and meditative poem which does solidly for the Weald of Kent what Edmund Blunden might have done more brilliantly though hardly with the same singleness of purpose. *The Land* attempts no more than was within its author's power to achieve confidently. The persistent and inestimable commonplaces of the English country seasonal round are surveyed by an observer saturated in the essence of England, with no patent philosophical purpose and no striving to impose a metaphysical interpretation. The earth to her was earth, beautiful enough even if an exacting mistress:

the man who works the wet and weeping soil
Down in the Weald, must marl and delve and till
His three-horse land, fearing nor sweat nor droil.

For through the winter he must fight the flood,
The clay, that yellow enemy, that rots
His land, sucks at his horses' hooves
So that his waggon plunges in the mud,
And wheels revolve, but waggon never moves. . . .

The Land is an unsentimentalized record of the English farmer's year, less ambitious than Maurice Hewlett's *Song of the Plow* (1916), which is a minor epic of the English agricultural labourer worthy of revival and remembrance.

7. INNOVATORS AND OTHERS

At the close of the first quarter of the twentieth century there were a score or two of competent verse-makers whose work was received with attention by the critics. Scarcely more than half a dozen of those seemed likely, however, to produce verse with the exciting quality of unexpectedness that belongs to true poetry. Such of the Georgians as continued to be productive were pottering in pleasant and well-tended literary back-gardens, cultivating the same poetic varieties as had given colour to the narrow landscape ten years before. There is little need, at any time, for poets to be startlingly 'new', either in form or substance; yet, though few great poets are anti-traditional, they impart to tradition and commonplace a spirit that transforms tidy back-gardens of thought and imagery into majestic and limitless expanses. If poetry does not (for both poet and reader) smash through the walls of the imprisoning self and lead into new countries – whether beautiful or terrifying – poetry might as well not be written. Nothing is so disturbing in poetry as incomprehensibility; but it is doubtful whether any poet of the first rank has entirely avoided or desired to avoid this quality. Incomprehensibility (not to be confused with incoherence: God is incomprehensible – he is not incoherent) is a quality present in even the 'simple' poems of the great poets. Though it may not be a something that is finally and for ever incomprehensible, it is at least a necessary something that produces growing-pains of the mind and spirit. Inability to suggest anything beyond the immediately comprehensible facts of existence was a limitation in most of the Georgian poetry: it provided no enlargement of experience.

As a lyrist of the countryside almost entirely unaffected by current theories, the Rev. Andrew Young received long-delayed recognition when a further edition of his *Collected Poems* was published in 1950. He had been writing for some twenty years with a devotion to the simplicities of Nature which was not diverted by either the metaphysical or the mechanistic preoccupations of the 'new' poetry. His unpretentious verses run like a refreshing stream through the literary waste-land of the period.

Robert Graves was one of the few 'Georgians' who escaped from the back-garden tradition. He found himself in a large and bewildering (but somehow satisfying) wilderness, where familiar things are strange and new:

The evening air comes cold,
The sunset scatters gold,
Small grasses toss and bend,
Small pathways idly tend
Towards no certain end.[1]

The paths of Graves's mind were as bafflingly full of promise as the paths of an English wood, where the wayfarer is in a state of continuous expectation: anything may appear round the next corner.

'Like a storm of sand I run
Breaking the desert's boundaries;
I go in hiding from the sun
In thick shade of trees.

'Straight was the track I took
Across the plains, but here with briar
And mire the tangled alleys crook,
Baulking desire. . . .'

An illuminating index to Robert Graves's mind is provided by the poem called *In Procession*, where, having spoken of the

[1] 'An English Wood'. In the version given in *Collected Poems* (1938) the last line reads 'Towards no fearful end'.

qualities and powers of

The poets of old
Each with his pen of gold
Gloriously writing,[1]

he proceeds to indicate the abundance of material in his own 'teeming mind': children's rhymes, strange tongues and stranger shapes, land and sea and heaven and hell, all history and all religion. But the poet's task is not only to *possess*; it is, also, to *present*:

Could I show them so to you
That you saw them with me,
Oh then, then I could be
The Prince of Poetry
With never a peer,
Seeing my way so clear
To unveil the mystery.[2]

The poet had had 'marvellous hope of achievement', but also (and on these words the poem closes) 'deceiving and bereavement of this same hope'. To read Robert Graves's poetry then was to feel that one was assisting him to wrestle with Chaos. The Foreword to the *Collected Poems* (1938) is largely a repudiation of Graves's earlier work in verse and prose; he acknowledges his inclination to dwell upon 'discomfort and terror', and remarks, 'I should say that my health as a poet lies in my mistrust of the comfortable point-of-rest.'

In Robert Graves's *Poems 1938–1945*, a further collection of forty short pieces, his Foreword declared: 'I write poems for poets, and satires and grotesques for wits. . . . To write poems for other than poets is wasteful.' A similar declaration could have been made by most other poets of that time, for poetry was moving away from the 'common reader' into a region of the intellectual *élite*, though, as will be seen later, some who belonged to that region claimed to be writing poetry for the masses.

Robert Graves's treatise *On English Poetry* (1922) is a sane and sound piece of criticism – neither slavishly traditional nor aggressively

[1] 'Unicorn and the White Doe' (*Collected Poems*).
[2] These lines are deleted from the *Collected Poems* version.

emancipated. At that time the claims of 'free verse' were being advocated, and in a section devoted to *vers libre*, Graves approved the attitude of a friend who 'denied that there was such a thing as *vers libre* possible, arguing beyond refutation that if it was *vers* it couldn't be truly *libre* and if it was truly *libre* it couldn't possibly come under the category of *vers*'. Since the successes and failures of Walt Whitman in America and W. E. Henley in England with free-verse forms, unmetrical and unrhymed verse has been tried by many. When a definite rhythmical current is substituted for metre, free verse can be impressive and pleasing, but the chief objection to be met is the difficulty of distinguishing between free verse and prose. The only reliable way of determining whether the necessary distinction has been preserved, is to listen sympathetically to *vers libre* read aloud sympathetically by a competent reader. Unless the ear can detect that what is being spoken is not prose, it is useless to maintain that such writing has any advantage over plain prose. But free verse at its best, as in Whitman, makes a great deal of metrical verse seem by comparison a mere tinkle.

The merits and possibilities of *vers libre* were revived as the subject of short-tempered controversy after the war of 1914–18, when the Sitwell family (Edith, Osbert, and Sacheverell) set up as leaders of what was then considered to be an anti-traditional movement. If the Sitwells had been less hardy controversialists, they might have been laughed into silence; but their minds were better armoured than those of their opponents. They had wit, command of a barbed vocabulary, and unbounded self-confidence.

The Sitwells were not wedded to *vers libre*, though they flirted with it. Their revolt went further. A succinct negative statement of their aims was given by Osbert Sitwell: 'You cannot write well in the idiom of the day before yesterday.'[1] They were impatient and scornful of the equipment of contemporary 'traditionalist' poets, as they would have been of any one who offered them a sedan-chair when they required an aeroplane. They demanded both an idiom and a form suitable for the reflection and expression of twentieth-century minds.

Dame Edith Sitwell's early verse is full of hard, bright-coloured

[1] *Who Killed Cock Robin?* (1921).

images; everything is objectified, and abstractions are banished. It is a world of things rather than of thoughts; at the same time it is a world of sensations rather than of appearances. Objects and scenes are often robbed of their visual quality so that they may be given a *sensation quality*. The reader is expected to receive an impression of things – not through descriptions that enable him to recognize them as things known by sight, but by an application of epithets designed to revive the sensations previously experienced in contact with similar objects, or in similar circumstances:

Jane, Jane,
Tall as a crane,
The morning light creaks down again.
Comb your cockscomb-ragged hair;
Jane, Jane, come down the stair.

Each dull blunt wooden stalactite
Of rain creaks, hardened by the light . . .[1]

The frowsy appearance of a lank domestic servant roused at early morning is suggested in the second and fourth lines and elsewhere in the unquoted part of the poem; and the third, sixth, and seventh lines attempt to re-create in the reader the sensations produced by a dismal wet morning in someone reluctantly awakening to resume menial duties. Edith Sitwell's earlier verse is too varied to be comprehended in a single category. It has echoes of older poetry – the traditional ballads, Donne, the Augustans, Wilde, and others[2] – while in pictorial effect a proportion of the poems resemble vivid fashion-plate pictures alternating with kaleidoscope designs.

Later, Edith Sitwell developed into a religious and metaphysical poet, under the stressful and sobering influences of the troubled nineteen-thirties and the ensuing Second World War. *The Song of the Cold* (1945), though containing mainly poems written from 1939 onward, also includes a number of pieces from her early and middle period, and shows her progress from the fantastical to the spiritual – a progress which, in the light of her poetry as a whole, can be seen as orderly and inevitable.

[1] 'Aubade', in *Bucolic Comedies* (1923).
[2] See, e.g., 'The Mother' (1915), reprinted in *Rustic Elegies* (1927).

In verse, Sir Osbert Sitwell did his best work in a series of satirical character-sketches[1] in *vers libre* (occasionally varied by rhymed passages). He also produced successful poems in the impressionistic mode. The following extract from 'Giardino Publico' conveys the sensations of heat, and then of coolness and silence:

Petunias in mass formation,
An angry rose, a hard carnation.
Hot yellow grass, a yellow palm
Rising, giraffe-like, into calm,
All these glare hotly in the sun.
Behind are woods where shadows run
Like water through the dripping shade
That leaves and laughing winds have made.
Here silence like a silver bird
Pecks at the droning heat.[2]

Experiments on somewhat similar lines to those carried out by the young Sitwells had been begun in England and America round about 1914 by a group of verse-writers who took the name of Imagists. They shunned abstractions, aimed at the utmost economy of words, and reduced poetic ornament to a minimum. They wished to produce poems with the sharpness of outline and precision of form which belong to a perfectly proportioned statuette or other carved image: 'An "Image" ', they said, 'is that which presents an intellectual and emotional complex in an instant of time.' Richard Aldington, F. S. Flint, and Ezra Pound were leaders of the group, but the ablest was H. D. (Hilda Doolittle), who in a number of poems crystallized beautifully-moulded images, as in this passage (from 'Loss') describing a young Greek warrior:

I marvelled at your height.

You stood almost level
with the lance-bearers
and so slight.

[1] *England Reclaimed* (1927); *Wrack at Tidesend* (1952).
[2] First version 1922. Reprinted (revised) in *Out of the Flame* (1923).

And I wondered as you clasped
your shoulder-strap
at the strength of your wrist
and the turn of your young fingers,
and the lift of your shorn locks,
and the bronze
of your sun-burnt neck.[1]

The early poems of Charles Williams (1886–1945) received warm praise from Alice Meynell, Sir Walter Raleigh, Robert Bridges, and others of equal discernment. His sonnet sequence *The Silver Stair* (1912) is among the few examples of sustained love poetry in the early twentieth century, and is less impeded than some of his later poems[2] by a tendency to treat human love as a sub-department of theology and philosophy. Charles Williams was akin to Donne and other metaphysical poets in attributing a religious value to love and attaching to it a theological language. He was continuously a poet – complex in thought and ecclesiastical in temper – and no division can be made between his works in poetry, drama (the verse plays *A Myth of Shakespeare*, 1928; *Cranmer of Canterbury*, 1936; *The Rite of the Passion* 1929; etc.), fiction, criticism, and biography.

8. THE NEW METAPHYSICALS

The disruption produced between 1914 and 1918 by the war might not of itself have unseated Romanticism, which had prevailed in literature and in the general conduct of life since the last years of the eighteenth century. It was post-war economic and spiritual depression, and deepening dejection in a world impermeable to optimistic idealism in the nineteen-thirties, that at length overthrew the Romantics and brought in a generation of writers of whom some desired a revival of classicism, others a new era in which the scientific spirit of the modern world should be exalted over all else, while yet others (probably the majority) attended at the rebirth of the metaphysical temper which had been dormant in

[1] In *Sea Garden* (1916).

[2] *Poems of Conformity* (1917), *Divorce* (1920), *Windows of Night* (1925), *Taliessin n Logres* (1939), *The Region of the Summer Stars* (1944).

English poetry since the seventeenth century. These new metaphysicals were often as crabbed and tortuous in expression as the least luminous of their long-ago predecessors, and they displayed an equivalent preoccupation with death. But whereas salvation through Christ and damnation through sin were the alpha and omega of John Donne and of the Puritans, salvation through Marx and damnation through capitalism were favoured as substitutes in the nineteen-thirties. The Communist Manifesto displaced the Thirty-Nine Articles.

There had been intermediate stages, however.

The first volume of poems by T. S. Eliot (1888–1965) was published in 1917, *Prufrock and other Observations*, but it was not until 1922, when *The Waste Land* appeared, that he became a recognized force in poetry, compacting in that poem of some four hundred lines 'an interpretation of a whole condition of society'.[1] Eliot was born in America, but after some ten years' residence in England became a British subject, having developed a typical settler's reverence for British institutions, especially for the Anglican Church. His earlier poems had expressed – as much in the dryness of their form as in their subject-matter – a mood of despair in regard to contemporary civilization, and the poet was obviously facing divergent roads, one leading to the ultimate denial of good in the universe, the other to the refuge of Christian hope. Subsequent writings made it clear that Eliot had become the foremost Christian poet of his day and, in his prose, one of the leading Christian apologists. While at Harvard, at the Paris Sorbonne, and at Oxford, his studies had been both extensive and intensive, philosophy and languages (Eastern as well as Western) taking a principal place. His devotion to traditional culture, the extent and depth of his knowledge, his use in poetry of current imagery and current idiom, and his compression in statement, present the reader of Eliot's poetry with an intertwining complexity. The notes to *The Waste Land* show how vain it would be for 'the average man' to pretend to grasp the poem intellectually, and show, too, how far away poetry had travelled from Wordsworth's ideal of simplicity and intelligibility. Eliot it was who was chiefly instrumental in leading poets back to Donne, not as an

[1] F. O. Matthiessen, *The Achievement of T. S. Eliot* (1930).

imitator, but as bringing a Donne-like mind and spiritual apprehension to bear upon the contemporary world, and re-establishing the 'conceits' of the metaphysicals in modern dress. But whereas Donne's imagination was invariably passionate and consuming, Eliot's was often anaemic and chill.

Nevertheless, T. S. Eliot controlled the main current of poetry and criticism for a whole generation, largely through the hypnotic attraction his writings exercised in academic channels and, through acquiescent teachers, upon a multitude of students, including most of the apprentice poets. However much against his personal desire, he became the literary arbiter of the age. His own poetic output was small, particularly in the twenty years or so between *The Waste Land* and *Four Quartets* (first issued in separate parts 1936–1942). Whereas *The Waste Land* had made its way slowly against opposition, its influence had worked so surely, and at an accelerating pace, that *Four Quartets* was accepted immediately as an indubitable masterpiece. Its ultimate rank in English poetry may depend more on its distinction of language than upon any originality or depth of thought, though it has been credited with remarkable qualities in that respect, to some extent on account of such gnomic commonplaces as 'In my beginning is my end. . . . In the end is my beginning.'

The young poets of the new generation felt strongly the influence not only of Eliot but also that of an earlier poet, Gerard Manley Hopkins (1844-89), whose poems were not issued before his death and became widely known only after his friend Robert Bridges edited a collected edition in 1918. Hopkins, a Jesuit and sometime Professor of Greek at Dublin University, was a technical innovator in verse, and the attractions of his poetry are involved with much intellectual complexity which of itself appealed to young minds almost despairingly conscious of the complexity of the civilization into which they were born, and of which they desired to be interpreters to the masses. 'Poetry for the Workers' became both an ideal and a cant phrase; for poetry, unless it is diluted to the point at which it becomes the doggerel vehicle of sentiment, rarely interests the masses – though among the masses as well as among the classes there are some to whom poetry is a necessity. For these, poetry *qua* poetry suffices; to these, 'Poetry for the Workers' is an impertinent snob-phrase.

The poetry of the nineteen-thirties was saturated in the bloody sweat of that decade. This fact gives it a documentary importance which may seem, as time passes, to outweigh its poetic merit. It was symptomatic rather than prophylactic. The poet turned politician may serve his age as politician, but he may in so doing abrogate his more important function as visionary. While no poet can be unaware of temporalities, he is poet only in so far as he is in constant touch also with the eternities, applying to policy the measure of Truth.

W. H. Auden, Stephen Spender, Cecil Day Lewis, and Louis MacNeice received the largest share of attention among the poets of the nineteen-thirties. Their work with that of numerous others is illustrated in two representative anthologies: *New Signatures* (1932) and *The Faber Book of Twentieth Century Verse* (1953).

No generation has been apt or adroit in assessing the ultimate value (as distinct from the immediate utilitarian significance) of the writings of its contemporaries, and the obstacles in the way of a mature and settled judgement are more than commonly weighty in the modern period. The determined adoption of locutions special to the machine age (and, in some quarters, of a phraseology almost private in character) leaves the critic groping for a standard of reference which only the future can provide. Poetry until recently had remained for the most part still rooted in the pastoral life and still with strong attachments to the traditional heroic ages. The imagery of lyrical poetry underwent little fundamental change from Theocritus to Tennyson, while in epic there is no impassable gulf between Homer and Milton. Yet though nowadays it may still be possible to talk of origins and influences linking present-day poets with their forerunners, the material utilized by the characteristic poets of the age differs as much from the familiar material of the pastoral ages as duralumin differs from gold. How shall we decide as between pylons and poplars, between cantilever bridges and crystalled branches, between the aeroplane and the albatross? In the ages of faith the question might have been settled with the assertion that things of permanence must be preferred to those that are transitory. But though we may hope, who would now declare without a doubt that the poplar will outlast the pylon? And if the criterion of judgement is to be sought in an abstract standard of beauty, what assurance is there that in the present or in the future a majority would agree that an albatross is more beautiful than an aeroplane. The shrinkage and decay of the pastoral life and its correspondences may, at least for a prolonged period, detach man from Nature, so that (except for a few antiquarians) poetry about man's creations would be far more intelligible and thus, presumably, more acceptable than poetry about the Creation.

The material of much contemporary poetry is barren and boring to those brought up in an earlier tradition; a thin whimper displaced both the song of joy and the strong cry of agony. T. S. Eliot wrote (in 'The Hollow Men'):

This is the way the world ends
This is the way the world ends
This is the way the world ends
Not with a bang but a whimper.

If that were to be mankind's epitaph, the doomful twitterings that agitated much of the poetry of the 'thirties would have been justified. But 'The Hollow Men' appeared twenty years before the atom bomb. After 1945 it appeared possible that the world might end with a bang as well as a whimper.

Comment on individual poets of these decades can have little point, for, as more than one critic has noted, their voices lack individuality. But differences of quality can nevertheless be detected. Day Lewis's 'Now the full-throated daffodils' appears to be nearer to an instinctive utterance than some of the determinedly mechanistic earlier pieces which came, indeed, from a passing phase unrepresented in Day Lewis's self-chosen *Selected Poems* (Penguin Books, 1951; enlarged 1947).

Of the intellectualist poets of the 1930s and after, W. H. Auden alone appeared to have found a personal language in the modern idiom and to be capable of accepting its restrictive conventions without loss of poetic stature. Auden settled in the United States after the beginning of the Second World War, and became as much a part of the American literary scene as T. S. Eliot did of the English.[1] But through at least the title of one of his post-war books *The Age of Anxiety* (1948) Auden diagnosed the malady of the period and offered it a self-pitying name. Some of the best poetry of Auden's early period is in the plays written in collaboration with Christopher Isherwood: *The Dog Beneath the Skin* (1935), *The Ascent of F6* (1936), *On the Frontier* (1938).

The Second World War started and was fought in a mood of unheroic determination and endurance which failed to produce any such outpouring of verse as came from the 1914–18 war. Only two soldier-poets – Alun Lewis[2] (1915–44) and Sidney Keyes[3] (1922–1943) – attracted particular, but seemingly only temporarily widespread, attention.

Dylan Thomas (1914–53) gathered a larger general audience than any other contemporary poet through his radio broadcasts. His *Collected Poems* (1952) confirmed the impression made by a succession of smaller volumes that his verse has an exuberant poetic fervour and an abundant responsiveness to natural beauty which offsets a large measure of obscurity in expression. His most substantial, popular and least abstruse work, *Under Milk Wood* (1953), devised for broadcasting, combines prose dialogue and commentary with interspersed verses and is entirely original in conception and achievement, presenting life in a small Welsh town through many individual voices.

After the Second World War ended, much was heard of 'the crisis in poetry'. The 'crisis' had financial roots: the public did not buy poetry; therefore publishers in general were not interested; therefore, also, it was alleged, those who might have written poetry could not afford to do so. It could have been said that poetry will out, money or no money. Attempts were made, however, to cir-

[1] Auden was nevertheless elected Professor of Poetry at Oxford in 1956, succeeding Cecil Day Lewis. Auden was succeeded in 1961 by Robert Graves.

[2] *Raiders' Dawn* (1941); *Ha! Ha! Among the Trumpets* (1945).

[3] *Collected Poems* (1945).

cumvent the 'crisis' by devising a number of schemes for encouraging and supporting poets, and a great deal of verse was written, printed, broadcast, publicly read, and recorded for the gramophone. It seemed that almost the whole of this very large body of verse was *willed* into existence, contrived by cerebral mechanism, not achieved by 'the spontaneous overflow of powerful feelings'. A science of poetry seemed to displace the art of poetry. Far from being a matter of reproach, this was to be expected in a predominantly scientific age; and science had been accommodated to poetry in other times[1] – without obliterating the personality of poets or the individuality of their poetry. Now, on the contrary, poems rarely if ever bore the indubitable imprint of the poet in the poem's substance or in its form,[2] and the appended signature became irrelevant to work that was by nature anonymous. Therefore with no single poet of the younger generation out-topping any other among the many, the naming of names becomes purposeless, except to point to a few – e.g. Elizabeth Jennings, Thom Gunn, Ted Hughes – as representative rather than superior to others.

In so far as a crisis in poetry had arisen, its causes can be found in the divagations of verse writers and critics in the fourth and following decades of the century. Although, time and again, critics on both sides of the great divide insisted that *enjoyment* is the key to the reader's proper reception of poetry, enjoyment is precisely what the bulk of contemporary poetry did not provide. Hence the absence of widespread interest in contemporary poetry. Hence, therefore, the 'crisis'.

The inter-relation of poetry and criticism in this setting invites discussion which would require space stretched to infinity. Some crucial aspects of the problem can be observed in the work – both creative and critical – of two older contemporary writers, Edwin Muir (1887–1959) and William Empson. The former's essays in

[1] See Douglas Bush, *Science and English Poetry* (1950); Donald Davie, *The Language of Science and the Language of Literature, 1700–1740* (1963); and cf. I. A. Richards, *Science and Poetry* (1925).

[2] Dr Johnson's opinion of poetry in his time is apposite here: 'Modern poetry is like modern gardening, everything is raised by a hot bed; everything therefore is forced and everything is tasteless.'

The Estate of Poetry (1962) comment incidentally and illuminatingly on Empson's *Seven Types of Ambiguity*, while Muir's *Collected Poems* (1960) and Empson's *Collected Poems* (1955) present two types of poetry, differently derived, by writers of equal distinction but wide separation of purpose and achievement.

CHAPTER V

ESSAYISTS AND CRITICS

1. MAX BEERBOHM

Max Beerbohm (1872–1956) began in the eighteen-nineties with a little book of less than two hundred pages, exquisitely printed, in which a rivulet of text meandered through a meadow of margin. This, the first of his books, was published as *The Works of Max Beerbohm* (1896). He was then twenty-four years old. Following the *Works* came several volumes of prose, and also his coloured cartoons, witty and delicate examples of the art of caricature. But though it was as 'Max' the caricaturist that he became widely known, it was his literary excellence that gave the caricatures their unique touch. Nearly every picture bears, in minute handwriting, a comment in the artist's ironic prose, and the effect of these phrases upon current foibles and follies was as incisive as a diamond cutting into thin glass.

In *Zuleika Dobson* (1911) Max Beerbohm wrote an Oxford love-story unlike all other love-stories. Zuleika is superb. She had been a conjurer – an appallingly clumsy third-rate conjurer; but she is so beautiful that all Oxford fell in love with her – and Oxford committed mass-suicide because of hopeless unrequited passion! This joyous book is brilliantly loaded with irony and satire, and the coping-stone to the whole crazy, mad, sublime structure is in the last few lines. Zuleika had desolated Oxford: the halls of the colleges were empty, its quadrangles silent, its lecture-rooms more than ever deserted. Zuleika, however, sighed for other worlds to conquer, and on the last page of the book she is ordering a special train – for Cambridge. . . .

When Bernard Shaw retired from the *Saturday Review* in 1898, Max Beerbohm succeeded him as dramatic critic. Almost everything he wrote and drew shows the acute and penetrating critic behind the dandified exquisite, though his critical penetration was not seen fully until *A Christmas Garland* (1912) set the fashion for a revival of the art of parody, which brought in J. C. Squire, E. V. Knox, J. B. Priestley, and others. For some years before the appearance of *A Christmas Garland*, parody had been looked upon as a debased type of writing. That misconception was due to the lack of any parodist of genius, for parody may be (as at its best it cannot fail to be) a valuable form of creative criticism. In modern usage the word 'parody' no longer implies exact imitation, but a form of humorous yet controlled exaggeration.[1] In that quality of *controlled* exaggeration lies the value of parody as criticism. The formal critic is able only to take a pointer to literature, hoping that as he speaks and shifts his indicating wand from place to place on the surface of the work criticized the audience will detect the significance of his comments. The parodist makes no direct comment. Unlike the formal critic, he *creates*: he has ceased to be an analyst, a breaker-down, a separator of part from part; that was his chrysalis stage: he is now a synthesist, a builder-up, a combiner of part with part. He sets to work to make a new thing – similar to the already existing thing, but with differences. The texture is similar, but the peculiarities of patterning are slightly more pronounced. The parodist has a twofold function: (*a*) he must produce writings that are of immediate interest in themselves, even for a reader who knows nothing of the original that is being parodied – that is to say, he must be, in part, a creator; (*b*) he must be an unusually illuminating critic for those who go to him for that service. Every book of parodies should qualify for an unwritten sub-title, 'Criticism without Tears'.

A Christmas Garland is made up of seventeen chapters, each with Christmas as its topic, and each written in the style of some contemporary author – A. C. Benson, Wells, Conrad, Bennett, Shaw, and a dozen others. The title of the Benson chapter, 'Out of Harm's Way', is itself a clue to the prevailing mood in that once widely liked author's writings. A. C. Benson, a pleasant essayist, lived as a college don in cloistered remoteness. His observations of life were

[1] Unless the exaggeration is controlled, judiciously and sensitively the result is *burlesque*, not parody.

made from the safe distance and quietude of a college window to which the noises of the world came muted from far away. Life, for him, had been coloured by autumnal mellowness, as relaxing as Max Beerbohm's captured breath of its spirit:

> The yellowing leaves of the lime trees, the creeper that flushed to so deep a crimson against the old grey walls, the chrysanthemums that shed so prodigally their petals on the smooth green lawn – all these things, beautiful and wonderful though they were, were somehow a little melancholy also, as being signs of the year's decay.

Max Beerbohm's gentle though ruthless hand unveiled the safe obviousness of Benson's reflections; the genial and placid sermonizing tone; the genteel restraint of 'h--g' (for 'hang'), 'b-th-r' ('bother'); the pedantic qualification of statement, and the thoughtful provision of alternative phrases, as though the writer would not permit himself to use definite and settled words for which he might be called to account.

Very different, of course, is 'Perkins and Mankind', 'after' H. G. Wells. Here there is no placidity or autumnal greyness, but the notorious Wellsian determination to be up and doing, never to sit still and submit. The breathless lack of repose in Wells's style is pointedly indicated; in the Wells way, a little plebeian hero moves in country-house circles; there is the familiar note of a mechanized system of social reform; and here, too, is the curious sensation (so well known to H. G. Wells's readers) of mankind suddenly becoming hardly more than a smear of minute organisms on a bacteriologist's microscope slide. The Joseph Conrad parody ('The Feast') shows those peculiarities of manner[1] evident in the early novels, before Conrad accustomed himself to the intricacies of the English language. Max Beerbohm also contrives to display the irony for which Conrad's books are celebrated.

A Christmas Garland, and the several other volumes he published after 1900, made Max Beerbohm one of the few writers of the eighteen-nineties who carried their reputations undimmed into the twentieth century. Though Bernard Shaw, Wells, and others lived

[1] E.g. the inverted positions of adjectives and nouns, with the adjectives usually in twos or threes: 'the silence murmurous and unquiet'; 'tendrils venomous, frantic and faint'.

and wrote in the 'nineties they were not of that period. The typical eighteen-nineties people – Wilde and Dowson, Beardsley, Charles Conder, and others – were, in their better moments, brilliant and hard, gleaming and iridescent, like diamonds and rubies and sapphires and opals. Sometimes their works - books and pictures – were like painstakingly wrought cameos of exquisite design: and their writings might also be compared with creations in several arts other than literature. These men were like painters, jewellers, goldsmiths, and sculptors who had mislaid their proper century, lost their way, and fallen into the wrong country. As contemporaries and countrymen of Benvenuto Cellini, they would have felt more at ease. The larger liberties of the Italian Renaissance period would have enabled them to stab with the utmost grace; to poison quite beautifully; to carve tombs and to fashion goblets for the world to wonder at during centuries afterwards. But their destiny was to live in late nineteenth-century England.

While other writers of the eighteen-nineties were becoming mythical figures, Max continued to flourish. In an age of hurry he never hurried; in a machine age he preserved in his writings and drawings the delicate craftwork of a more leisured and less strenuous time; in an age when most people could write moderately well but few had anything to write about, he was perfect in both manner and matter. And when he was at length induced to broadcast on the radio he was immediately the perfect broadcaster, cajoling the microphone to communicate his delicate nuances. From the senility of youth he grew in vigour and sincerity and humanity, until, in middle life, heart was revealed as well as brain. The 1920 volume of essays, *And Even Now*, has the same perfection of style as the former volumes – each word in its place, not a word too many; but, additionally, it has an admixture of human feeling that set it apart from Beerbohm's youthful work. If 'William and Mary' and 'Something Defeasible'[1] are compared with 'The Pervasion of Rouge',[2] it becomes obvious that the author had travelled far, emotionally, in twenty-five years. He could not, in 1896, have drawn the word-picture of Mary, with her laugh that was like the chiming of silvery bells. Among many good things in *And Even Now*,

[1] Both in *And Even Now*. [2] In *The Works of Max Beerbohm*.

nothing is better than 'No. 2. The Pines', a miniature masterpiece of biography in which Swinburne and Watts-Dunton come vividly to life again. In that sketch Beerbohm anticipated the methods of Lytton Strachey.

As the years passed, Max Beerbohm's prose grew less mannered and artificial than formerly (without losing anything of its economy, rhythm, and balance), while his books grew richer in content, gaining immeasurably by the maturity and sanity of his outlook. He holds a high place among twentieth-century essayists: he is completely original, whereas others carried on the tradition of the early nineteenth-century periodical essayists. He was a creative critic of literature and life, with a generous streak of special genius; a philosophic jester bursting bubbles of snobbery and pretence with wit and irony and satire. He played little if any part in the social and political turmoil of his time; but little escaped his notice. He could portray the mind of a contemporary in a phrase and with a few strokes of the pencil fix both body and soul upon paper. Though not himself a vocally aggressive interrogator, he accurately diagnosed the spirit of the age when, shortly after the war of 1914–18 ended, he drew a cartoon entitled 'The Future as the Twentieth Century sees it'. The picture is of a haggard young man looking disconsolately upon a looming mist; nothing can be seen beyond it, but on the face of the mist – reflecting the dominant quality of the young man's mind – appears a large question mark.

Sir Max Beerbohm (he was knighted in 1939) lived on into the second half of the century, remote in his Italian home at Rapallo, but respected – indeed, revered – in a degree experienced by few writers of his generation.

2. THE MANTLE OF LAMB

Regard for Charles Lamb was never so deep and widespread as in the first two decades of the twentieth century; and no other generation was so infected by his spirit. This was to a large extent due to E. V. Lucas's sustained enthusiasm for Elia.

In this century, as in Lamb's, journalism has nursed and housed literature, its elder brother. More than one well-known essayist began at the instigation of a newspaper editor. This produced at least two interesting effects. *First*, the introduction into the press of writings literary in character helped for a while to raise the standard of journalistic prose. *Second*, the essayists themselves, in 'writing to order' and to fill a limited space, were compelled to submit to a discipline that was serviceable, however irksome. What good work can be done frequently and regularly in narrow space was shown by 'The Londoner' in *Day In and Day Out* (1924), a collection from essays contributed to the *Evening News* during a continuous period of some twenty years. The author was Oswald Barron (1868–1939), the leading contemporary authority on heraldry, genealogy, and armour. As 'The Londoner' he was sound and sensible, bright and witty, often wise. He picked up his subjects anywhere, for the familiar essayist's subject is anything, everything, nothing. In the end, he requires no *subjects* but only *material*, and his material is Life. In 'The Londoner's' volume every page presents some facet of Life; for example:

> There is no saying to what we may come or how we shall earn to-morrow's bread in this world that pitches and tosses in a gale of change. Any day might see my business of selling words fail me: might see me, instead, selling bone collar studs and indiarubber umbrella rings. I hope that I should take that change calmly. Much could be said in favour of the collar stud industry: he who follows it lives under the open sky and sees life.[1]

Edward Verrall Lucas (1868–1938) was born at Eltham, and educated at London University. After working on provincial and London newspapers he became assistant-editor of *Punch*; and subsequently literary adviser and director to a publishing house. He edited a definitive edition of the works and letters of Charles and Mary Lamb (1903–5), and wrote the standard *Life of Charles Lamb* (1905). His remaining works comprised travel-books, essays, books about paintings, and a number of volumes that hover between essay and novel: these last E. V. Lucas called 'entertainments'.

He himself said: 'Lamb lives and will live by virtue of being himself and expressing this self in a series of prose essays unsurpassed

[1] 'Being Good with Children'.

in their charm, prodigality of fancy and literary artifice, marked by profound common sense, and starred with passages of great beauty, dazzling insight and kindly capricious humour.'[1] Lucas could wear the mantle of Charles Lamb, but there are pronounced dissimilarities between the two writers. The robust urbanity and sophistication of Lucas made him unlike Lamb, who, though he knew 'more about what books are worth reading than any one living', wore all his knowledge with a deceptive air of innocence: he was 'all for quietness and not being seen, and having his own thoughts and his own jokes'.[2] Lucas's essays and 'entertainments' are marked by fancy, literary artifice, common sense, and humour. Yet his humour, though in general kindly, is sometimes savage, as in *Those Thirty Minutes*,[3] a satirical dialogue aimed at people who agonize their friends by 'seeing them off' on railway journeys. Lucas's essays entice into many by-paths and give the sense of browsing in a fully informed and liberal mind. That may be said of his 'entertainments' also. *Over Bemerton's* (1908), the best of these, has sentiment, wisdom, humane 'bookishness', and a store of curious knowledge.

As 'Y.Y.' of the *New Statesman*, Robert Lynd (1879–1949) looked at the world week by week for many years, setting down his reflections, now gravely, now with gaiety and gusto. He was a skilled phrasemaker[4] and could describe a Cup Final with his eye on many things besides the game – or on everything except the game;[5] and few funnier things have been written than 'Eggs : An Easter Homily'.[6] Lynd's long indispensability as a contributor to the paper is graphically described in Edward Hyams's *History of the New Statesman* (see above, page 21).

[1] Introduction to *The Best of Lamb* (1914).

[2] The phrases quoted in this passage are from an imaginary conversation – 'My Cousin the Bookbinder' – in *Character and Comedy* (1907), in which E. V. Lucas put descriptions of Elia and his circle into the mouth of the bookbinder cousin mentioned in Lamb's letters.

[3] *Mixed Vintages* (1919).

[4] E.g. 'There is grave danger of a revival of virtue in this country. There are, I know, two kinds of virtue, and only one of them is a vice.' – 'Virtue' (*The Pleasures of Ignorance*, 1921).

[5] 'The Battle of Footerloo' (*The Blue Lion*, 1923).

[6] In *The Pleasures of Ignorance.*

The vogue of the familiar essay had been dwindling in the last ten years of Lynd's career. The paper famine during the Second World War allowed newspapers and periodicals no space for the lighter kinds of writing, and the seriousness of the times destroyed the taste for charming triviality in literature.

In so far as the periodical essay may be said to have survived at all as an article with long-term interest, it became a disquisitory form of book-reviewing, as in Raymond Mortimer's *Channel Packet* (1942), Cyril Connolly's *The Condemned Playground* (1944), V. S. Pritchett's *Books in General* (1953).

3. LITERATURE - AND LIFE

Although it had fostered the familiar essay, the influence of journalism upon literary criticism in the twentieth century grew increasingly unhelpful. The 'new journalism' at the end of the Victorian period had one principal aim – to get rid of stolidity. It succeeded. At the same time it abolished solidity, until the popular press made headlines not only the essence of journalism, but its substance also. The spread of schooling to the whole population had the unforeseen result of depressing the general level of mental independence and discrimination, and the 'educated democracy' became the easy and apparently willing creatures of mass-circulation dailies and weeklies and of commercialized television. The literary quarterlies, monthlies, and weeklies which for a while resisted the enervated spirit of the age, declined in influence and very few survived.

The multiplicity of books was in some measure accountable for the enfeebled tone of mid-twentieth-century book-reviewing, compared with that of the nineteenth century. 'Review the popular. Review some of the good. Ignore the bad' became more and more a standing order. The tradition of Jeffrey and Gifford and Macaulay was left behind. When (infrequently) criticism was caustic, it was usually very brief, and critics sometimes cared more for turning an epigram than for steady judgement. Macaulay destroyed Montgomery by patient and leisured disintegration; Rebecca West, in such circumstances, would have chosen the method of instant detonation, as she did when, set to review a popular novelist's new book, she wrote only: 'Mr A. S. M. Hutchinson has produced another novel. How long, O Lord, how long.'[1]

This was also, in general, the method practised (though less briefly) by G. K. Chesterton (1874–1936), who was nevertheless an able critic, until verbal acrobatics became a pernicious habit, and led him into parody of his own early manner. The deterioration in his style can be seen by comparing Chesterton's books on *Browning* (1903)[2] and *Dickens* (1906) with his *Francis of Assisi* (1923). The *Browning* is ebullient and stimulating, but also clear and helpful. It is probably the best introductory guide for readers troubled by that poet's 'difficulty'. The *Dickens* combines enthusiasm with sanity, and ranks second only to George Gissing's critical study, *Charles Dickens* (1898). *Francis of Assisi*, however, is often a confusion of epigram and paradox, with Chesterton giddily gyrating among words. A phrase or two from *Twelve Types* (1910) will show how much Chesterton could put into a sentence before he became obsessed by verbal exhibitionism:

> In the pacifist mythology of Tolstoy and his followers St George did not conquer the dragon; he tied a pink ribbon round its neck and gave it a saucer of milk.[3]

. . . . . .

> Charlotte Brontë showed that abysses may exist inside a governess and eternities inside a manufacturer; her heroine is the commonplace spinster, with the dress of merino and the soul of flame.[4]

A sound argument against criticism by epigram is that it can be quoted with unintelligent facility by people too indolent to form their own judgements. Chesterton's description of Thomas Hardy as 'the village atheist brooding and blaspheming over the village idiot'[5] became a cheap and senseless gibe on the lips of many who found the phrase smart to quote.

Some of the best literary criticism of the period was produced by writers at variance with the hurried spirit of the age; and especially by those whose vision was not narrowed down to the petty heresy that criticism is a private affray between reviewers and authors.

[1] *New Statesman*, 8 July 1922.
[2] *English Men of Letters* series.
[3] 'Tolstoy and the Cult of Simplicity'.
[4] 'Charlotte Brontë'.
[5] *The Victorian Age in Literature* (1913).

Literary criticism is valueless save when it is also by implication a commentary upon life: the critic's qualifications and standards are proportionate to his own inner experience. His function (aside from the examination of technical and textual questions) is to judge of the quality and degree of Truth (imaginatively considered) in the author's work. Alice Meynell (1850–1922) – herself a severe critic and a reticent creator in poetry and prose – demanded much of anyone who presumed to judge, e.g., Coventry Patmore's odes. What she required in that single relation is what might reasonably be looked for always in every critic: 'precision, and its rare companions – liberty, flight, height, courage, a sense of space and a sense of closeness, readiness for spiritual experience, and all the gravity, all the resolution, of the lonely reader'.[1] What she demanded of others she herself possessed. When she pronounced upon a book, life was her standard and measure – as when she says:

> It is no wonder that the proffer of Browning's optimism, half-heartedly made again on the day of his centenary, did again fail. His 'All's well with the world' is as vain as the pessimist's 'All's wrong with it'. It is out of the range of customary life. Intelligible joy and grief are in the midways, and in the midways there is cause for as much sadness as our human hearts can hold.[2]

Alice Meynell's judgements may not always command assent (she was perverse about Jane Austen),[3] but her sympathies were wider than might be expected of any one so little touched as she was by the grosser delights. In one essay she discusses Job, Genesis, Dante, Boccaccio, Claudel, . . . and concludes thus:

> Monsieur Paul Claudel's *L'Otage* should be ministered to pessimists, or rather to their readers, for tears, and Mr Jacobs for laughter. The age is not without its remedies.[4]

Neither before nor since, probably, has W. W. Jacobs been named in such company. Yet the root of truth (as Alice Meynell well knew) is in that conjunction of names. Poor is the man (and the critic too) whose spirit is so illiberal as to restrain him from being on good

[1] 'Coventry Patmore' (*The Second Person Singular, and other Essays*, 1922).
[2] 'Pessimism in Fiction' (op. cit.). [3] 'The Classic Novelist' (op. cit.).
[4] 'Pessimism in Fiction'.

terms simultaneously with Job and Jacobs, Boccaccio and Francis of Assisi, Milton and Edgar Wallace, Donne and P. G. Wodehouse, though this is a liberal doctrine that received little support in the nineteen-thirties and after, when academic criticism became austere to the point of barrenness and straitlaced to the stage of spinsterishness.

The collected *Essays of Alice Meynell* (1914) show that whether she wrote of Andromeda and Arcturus, of laughter or colour, children or sleep, her touch was delicate and her vision clear. She sees a ragged London boy in Hyde Park on the margin of the Serpentine.

> Clothed now with the sun, he is crowned by-and-by with twelve stars as he goes to bathe, and the reflection of an early moon is under his feet. . . .
>
> It is easy to replace man, and it will take no great time, when Nature has lapsed, to replace Nature. It is always to do, by the happy easy way of doing nothing. The grass is always ready to grow in the streets – and no streets could ask for a more charming finish than your green grass. . . . As the bathing child shuffles off his garments – they are few, and one brace suffices him – so the land might always, in reasonable time, shuffle off its yellow brick and purple slate, and all the things that collect about railway stations.[1]

Alice Meynell's poetry has been said to consist less of sounds than of silences. That is true also of her prose. She was at once passionate and austere; her emotions were severely disciplined, to the end that reticence might prevail.

Association of ideas leads from Alice Meynell to Maurice Hewlett (1861–1923). Hewlett tried for twenty years or so to throw off the restrictions of the popular success that came to him with *The Forest Lovers* (1898), a novel that is among the best of its kind. But Hewlett disliked being labelled as a romatic medievalist. His interest, for a large part of his life, lay in other directions – in poetry, philosophy, and the study of agricultural conditions. In addition to several historical novels[2] he wrote a trilogy[3] about a gipsy-scholar, John Maxwell Senhouse, whose letters to Sanchia Percival[4] express what

[1] 'The Colour of Life' (in the *Essays*).

[2] The *Life and Death of Richard Yea-and-Nay* (1900); *The Queen's Quair* (1904), etc.

[3] *Halfway House* (1908), *Open Country* (1909), *Rest Harrow* (1910).

[4] These were published separately in 1910.

may be accepted in part as Hewlett's own philosophy, based upon the maxim: 'Now abide . . . Poverty, Temperance, Simplicity – these three. But the greatest of these is Poverty' – an attractive doctrine when poverty is voluntary. Hewlett, without being tied to any religious denomination, was, by temperament, part Franciscan, part Quaker. For the last few years of his life he lived among Wiltshire villagers, and testified: 'I who was once rich and now am poor, seriously declare that I had not the gleam of a notion what contentment was until I became as I am.'[1] His long poem, *The Song of the Plow* (1916), is a chronicle of the travail of the agricultural labourer through the centuries; and the cause of the English peasantry filled Maurice Hewlett's thoughts and guided his actions from the 1914–18 war-period onward. During those years he wrote his best work – a long sequence of essays gathered into four volumes. The English spirit – its placidity and depth, its sound common sense, its poetry and idealism – has seldom been better expressed. His style, precisely adjusted to the subject-matter, is clear and luminous, sensitive and serene. The likeness between Hewlett and Alice Meynell came from their quietness of spirit. Hewlett began an essay on Dorothy Wordsworth thus: 'I have often wished that I could write a novel in which, as mostly in life, nothing happens'; and he valued Dorothy's *Journal* because 'the peace of it is profound. . . . This woman was not so much poet as crystal vase. You can see the thought cloud and take shape.' It followed as a natural consequence of Hewlett's love of quietness that even the pages in which he was most proudly English are free from insular arrogance. Imperial greatness made little appeal to him. Amid the doubts and difficulties of the years after the war, Hewlett thought it probable that a time would arrive when 'we shall become . . . once more "a small, hardy, fishing, and pastoral people" '. He looked forward without apprehension to that prospect, saying, 'If a little England was good enough for Queen Elizabeth and Sir Walter Raleigh it is good enough for me.'[3] The dwindling of British power was then still thirty years and more in the future.

[1] 'Our First, and Last' (*Wiltshire Essays*, 1921).
[2] 'The Crystal Vase' (*In a Green Shade*).
[3] 'Our First, and Last' (*Wiltshire Essays*).

Percy Lubbock's *Earlham* (1922) enshrined the English spirit of a passing age. The atmosphere and life of a country household in Victorian times are re-created by the author, who, as a child, stayed at Earlham Hall, the Norfolk seat of the Gurneys, an old Quaker family. Percy Lubbock visited the house again in later life, and as he passed through the rooms and the garden and wandered about the countryside, he re-lived the memories so vividly stirred. To read *Earlham* is like passing a long sunny day shielded from hot sunshine in a cool leafy place. The old virtues – modesty, humility, piety, charity – are seen in the guileless beauty of holiness. Famous figures – Elizabeth Fry, George Borrow – pass across the scene; but these seem insignificant in comparison with 'our grandmother':

> She loved the green window-seat and the rustling shadow of the limes. As she grew old and older, she used to sit there in the window for long hours, alone in the summer evening, till the light faded away. She sat without book or work, drinking in the twilit fragrance, communing in her mind – with what? – with the thought of many beloved dead, whom she had lost and mourned, and with the joy of reunion with them that she saw near at hand now, in a very few years. Her mind was *there* more and more. As the evening darkened she seemed, sitting in the window, to have all but passed already into the light she awaited: it shone in her face, I remember, as she spoke of it. I remember vividly her look as she once exclaimed, in sudden uncontrollable wonder, '*What* will it be? – what will it be like?'

Percy Lubbock in *The Craft of Fiction* (1921) set out to make a critical study of the novel objectively and 'in the round'. He refers to the difficulty of 'seeing' a novel as a unity – in the way that a statue, a picture, or a lyric can be seen. The largeness of novels causes them to enter the reader's mind piecemeal, in a sequence of inconstant pictures. Percy Lubbock took a few representative novels and treated them critically, so as to make it possible for a reader to hold them in the mind as complete and rounded works of art.

The Craft of Fiction and Lascelles Abercrombie's *The Idea of Great Poetry* (1925) stand out among critical works of their day. Whereas

Lubbock's book is principally concerned with problems of form, the field of inquiry is wider in *The Idea of Great Poetry*. Most immediately helpful is the first chapter on Diction and Experience, in which Abercrombie develops the thesis that the function of poetry is the translation into language (and the communication) of unusually intense and vivid experience.

As King Edward VII Professor of English Literature at Cambridge (1912 onwards), Sir Arthur Quiller-Couch influenced many young writers. Before his university duties began, he had written short stories, novels, and some criticism; and a new generation welcomed his *On the Art of Writing* (1916) and *On the Art of Reading* (1920), harvested from the Cambridge lectures. Three achievements must be credited to him: a revival of interest in the English (1611) Bible; a temporarily successful battle against jargon and in support of simplicity in prose style; and *The Oxford Book of English Verse* (1900; enlarged in 1939) – which became a national institution, though its taste was questioned and its editorial laxity deplored by the later and younger school of critics.

4. THE NEW CRITICISM

The notion of literary criticism as a record of 'the adventures of the soul among masterpieces', and of reading as mainly a matter of enjoyment, was a suitable accompaniment to the romantic mood in literature and life. When romanticism went out of fashion in the nineteen-twenties, criticism turned away from the pleasure principle and assumed an austere, scholarly habit, as in T. S. Eliot and his disciples, or took a scientific track, as in the case of I. A. Richards and the young men who studied under him. In the nineteen-thirties the increase of political tension at home and abroad turned literary criticism towards a line of inquiry based upon ideological tests and partaking of the nature of a heresy hunt. Though Eliot's criticism may seem, to the average mind, frigid, monochromatic, and often oppressively oracular, it was rooted in his concern for traditional culture. He called attention to the existence of standards – intellectual and spiritual – in *The Criterion*,[1] in *The Sacred Wood* (1920),

[1] See above p. 9.

The Use of Poetry and the Use of Criticism (1933), and other critical writings. The theories he put into practice as a verse playwright are stated in his *Poetry and Drama*[1] (1951).

I. A. Richards was so hot for mental certainties in *Principles of Literary Criticism* (1925) and *Practical Criticism* (1929) that Pegasus seemed likely to turn into a dray-horse pulling a psychological load. Pure enjoyment became suspect in academic circles and among the coteries.

At the middle of the century no young critic with powers of enlightenment was in view, and among living elders only Eliot and Sir Herbert Read had assured authority. No one equalled in perception and general interest the critical writings of Virginia Woolf, which began with *The Common Reader* (1st series, 1925) and were completed in posthumous collections, of which the last was *The Captain's Death Bed* (1950).

After 1945 the political bias which had coloured literary criticism of the 'thirties died away. The study of literature in the universities became concerned largely with textual problems and with imagery and symbolism. Deductions made painstakingly from the use of imagery in poetry seemed often to be little more than involved statements of the obvious; while the spontaneous symbolism of earlier writers induced among disciples and imitators nothing better than a straining away from direct statement into a complex and contrived obliquity.

Overlapping T. S. Eliot's critical periodical *The Criterion*, which ran from 1922 to 1939, another organ of the 'new criticism' started at Cambridge in 1932 with, as co-founder and editor, F. R. Leavis, a Fellow of Downing College who, years later, became University Reader in English. In 1930 he had published *Mass Civilization and Minority Culture*, which showed a commendable concern with some of the disturbing features of contemporary society, and it was with the defence and maintenance of 'minority culture' through an intellectual élite that *Scrutiny* was militantly concerned throughout its twenty-one years as a quarterly publication until it ceased in

[1] Reprinted in *Selected Prose* (Penguin Books, 1953), which gives a comprehensive survey of Eliot's critical writings from 1917 to 1951.

1953.[1] It was, perhaps, strategically essential that Leavis should project himself and his fellows in *Scrutiny* as martyrs to a cause, with the reiterated complaint that the main body of established Cambridge scholars, and no small part of the literary world at large, was embattled against them. It might be closer to fact to hold that the adoption of a tone of argument at once aggrieved and aggressive, at length intimidated many who at first disapproved *Scrutiny*'s policy of subjecting literature to processes of minute textual examination which demanded exhaustive and exhausting concentration on 'the words on the page' and derided literature as a medium of imaginative stimulus. 'Literature' became more and more circumscribed in the *Scrutiny* circle by being concentrated on a small number of 'approved' authors. F. R. Leavis's *The Great Tradition* (1948) treated only George Eliot, Henry James, and Joseph Conrad, while in *Scrutiny* and elsewhere he was obsessed by D. H. Lawrence.

As the policy filtered down through students and disciples it resulted in an attitude to literature resembling that adopted towards cadavers in anatomy schools. But whereas anatomy students dissect bodies already lifeless, Leavisitism finds literature living and leaves it dead. The harm done was the greater because the minority-culture movement was conducted with missionary fervour and professional zeal. It bred 'leaders' – future teachers and professors – who went out into the academic world and spread the nothing-but-the-words-on-the-page fallacy among students at home and abroad, students who, moreover, did not develop independence of thought but, as a consequence of the policy, transmitted the fallacy.

In *How to Teach Reading* (1932) Leavis wrote: 'It should by continual insistence and varied exercise in analysis, be enforced that literature is made of words, and that everything worth saying in criticism of verse and prose can be related to judgements concerning particular arrangements of words on the page.' And in *How Many*

[1] *Scrutiny* was republished complete in twenty volumes in 1963 by the Cambridge University Press. Volume 20 contained Leavis's new 'Retrospect', which was also published simultaneously as a separate pamphlet. It is not irrelevant to mention that the lack of clarity in Leavis's prose style suggested some absence of attention to words on the page.

Children had Lady Macbeth?[1] L. C. Knights, one of the main contributors to *Scrutiny*, wrote: 'the bulk of Shakespeare criticism is concerned with his characters, his heroines, his love of Nature or his "philosophy" – with everything, in short, except with the words on the page, which it is the main business of the critic to examine'. If that is so, so much the worse for the critic. Instead of the 'total complex emotional response' which the school of Knights and Leavis professed to obtain, this type of criticism cuts off its practitioners from access to the essential Shakespeare whose medium was not 'words on the page' but words from the human mouth. Knights declared that the '"human" appeal . . . is an intrusion which vitiated, and can only vitiate, Shakespeare criticism'. It is, of course, the word 'criticism' which is the vitiating intrusion, for Shakespeare's purpose was not to provide fuel for students and scholars but to make the 'a "human" appeal' by putting human beings on the stage and giving them words with which to create diverse characters. In so far as the theatre audience, then or now, achieves 'a total complex emotional response' (which, in any circumstances, can scarcely be other than an arrogant pretension), it comes through seeing the characters as living men and women and hearing the words which are evanescently spoken. If, as the 'new critics' declare, Shakespeare's characters are not to be treated as human beings, Shakespeare worked in vain and some four centuries of enjoyment of his plays has been founded on error. The temptation to apply to the words-on-the-page critics what Pope wrote of Shakespeare adapters need not be resisted: 'All they want is spirit, taste and sense.'

Leavis observed in *Mass Civilization and Minority Culture* that 'culture has always been in minority keeping'. If literature is to retain its place among the humanities and not be degraded to a mere academic discipline – for which the day's newspapers would serve more appropriately – the true aim of reading poetry and all

[1] 'An essay in the Theory and Practice of Shakespeare Criticism', based upon a paper read before the Shakespeare Association at King's College, London, and published by The Minority Press, Cambridge (1933). The author said that the type of criticism he rejected is 'only slightly parodied by the title of this essay'. The particular criticism rejected by him is A. C. Bradley's *Shakespearean Tragedy* (1904), which nevertheless survived the assaults of the 'new criticism'.

imaginative writing must be the production of a *majority culture* (i.e. a cultured majority) in which the best will come to be recognized as that which is most life-enriching. This will entail a prolonged slow progression in which 'ordinary readers' gather from here and there, often at random and often unconsciously through the widest possible choice of books, cumulative fragments of wisdom and discrimination – that is, of 'culture', no less – which critical and linguistic analysis is powerless to give. By the 1960s this was coming to be growingly recognized, and a saner attitude to reading was displayed in *An Experiment in Criticism* (1960) by C. S. Lewis (1898–1963) and in Graham Hough's *The Dream and the Task: Literature and Morals in the Culture of Today* (1963) – both by Cambridge teachers in the university – though it is necessary to go further towards releasing literature from academic bonds and making it, with no political intent, the possession of the people.

After he died, Hudson's name became familiar to thousands for the first time when the bird-sanctuary was set up in Hyde Park as a memorial to him. Interest was artificially stimulated by a newspaper controversy around Jacob Epstein's sculptured representation of Rima, a semi-human character in Hudson's South American romance, *Green Mansions* (1904). The publicity thus given to Rima persuaded many that *Green Mansions* is Hudson's most notable book – an untenable judgement. Imaginative romance was not his natural field. He was happier in a form which allowed direct transmission of his extraordinarily acute faculty of observation, and in the discursively personal books he is most truly himself, the W. H. Hudson who is different from all other writers.

A Shepherd's Life is the best of Hudson's nature books, though that term is too narrow for writings so full and various as these. He was unlike both Maeterlinck and Fabre: Maeterlinck's bees, he thought, were falsely humanized; Fabre he admired, but he could not himself have been content to watch Nature under the microscope. He differed, too, from Richard Jefferies (1848–87).[1] Jefferies was a sentimentally lyrical writer, and Hudson had no patience with the Jefferies type of naturalist. The snaring and killing of rare birds was an abominable offence in Hudson's eyes, even though committed in the name of science and for the sake of collecting museum specimens. His museum was the open air, and he protested that rare specimens should be allowed to live unmolested. *A Shepherd's Life* is an entrancingly discursive narrative, a series of episodes and digressions grouped loosely around Caleb Bawcombe, an old Wiltshire shepherd from whom Hudson heard most of the stories in the book. Plants, animals, men and women, are the stuff from which *A Shepherd's Life* is made, and everything comes vividly alive in Hudson's prose. He sees activity and intelligence everywhere: in the grasses and herbs on Salisbury Plain, in foxes and rabbits, as well as in Joe the coalman and the old church-cleaner and a host of others. Among many fine things are the passages dealing with sheep-dogs and their ways. This is a book to stand with Walton's *The Compleat Angler* and White's *Selborne*.

Fully one-third of Hudson's writings is devoted to bird-studies:

[1] Author of *The Open Air* (1885), *The Story of My Heart* (1883), etc.

CHAPTER VI

TRAVELLERS, BIOGRAPHERS, AND OTHERS

I. W. H. HUDSON; R. B. CUNNINGHAME GRAHAM

Of millions who have wandered the world and of thousands with travel stories worth telling, only the tens have had the ability to write of their wanderings in enduring form. A man determined to find the extraordinary everywhere is not likely to write fine travellers' tales. The material for travel books, perhaps the richest available for any form of literature, is stubborn to handle. It is not the wonders of the world that have provided travellers with their most memorable material; it is, rather, such simple episodes as might happen equally well in an English country lane, on the Arabian desert, or in the forests of the Andes. A first-rate travel book depends comparatively little upon strangeness or remoteness of locality, and much upon the character and vision of the traveller. A few sentences about fleas (as in Kinglake's *Eothën*), or a paragraph about a drunken schoolmaster on the South American pampas (as in W. H. Hudson's *Far Away and Long Ago*), may help to make a book more worth while than any pretentious volume on the world's marvels.

Both W. H. Hudson (1841–1922) and R. B. Cunninghame Graham (1852–1936) travelled in remote parts of the world, and became stored with wanderers' lore. Yet Hudson wrote some of his most entrancing books about life in the English counties, and Cunninghame Graham about his native Scotland. Many autobiographical glimpses were given by Hudson in other books, but in *Far Away and Long Ago* (1918) he provided a detailed picture of his early years. He does not mention dates, however, and his biographer, Morley Roberts,[1] found it difficult to fix the few that are relevant. Hudson's birthplace was the farm of the Twenty-five Ombú Trees on the grasslands of Argentina, about ten miles from Buenos Aires. Though his grandfather was an Englishman, born in Exeter, his father and mother were both from the United States. They migrated to the Argentine before the birth of their children, of whom William Henry Hudson was the third. He came to England a year or two before he was thirty; he was naturalized in this country thirty years later (1900), and died in London. Though not English either by parentage or birthplace, Hudson was a faithful and devoted lover of England, its soil and people; and he liked to be regarded as a native.

The picture of his childhood on the pampas, in *Far Away and Long Ago*, is more than a plain autobiographical record. It abounds in remembered beauties and wise reflections. He was an old man when he wrote this book, and the play of memory upon the remote years produced 'a wonderfully clear and continuous vision of the past'. Hudson was a man of wide and deep experience, as well as a reader and thinker; he was a 'full man', with a natural sense of what should be said and what left unsaid. Though he cannot be described as a natural stylist, his work has a clear naturalness – so much so, that the same hasty conclusion is sometimes made about Hudson as about even better prose writers than he: namely, that he had *no* style. Yet at his best, Hudson could make a page of prose as satisfying and refreshing as a stretch of downland lying still and calm in the pale golden light of a late autumn evening.[2]

The serenity of Hudson's prose accords with the spirit of the man. Life to him was a source of quiet joy, and his delight in living is worth noting, since many of his contemporaries in English literature were men aggrieved – if not in respect of themselves, then in respect of others who suffer. Hudson's delight in life was not an occasional impulse, but a conviction declared in his works from first to last. In *The Purple Land* (1885), Richard Lamb (a fictitious character) is made to say on the first page, 'What soul in this

[1] *W. H. Hudson: A Portrait* (1924).

[2] See, for example, Hudson's description of the Vale of the Wylye: *A Shepherd's Life* (1910), Ch. XIII.

wonderful various world would wish to depart before ninety! dark as well as the light, its sweet and its bitter, make me lov On the last page of *Far Away and Long Ago*, published thirty-t years after, Hudson speaks of an earlier time when he passed thro a period of spiritual questioning, following a serious illness. physicians had prophesied gloomily in regard to his probable le of life, but they proved to be false prophets. Hudson goes on to

> Barring accidents, I could count on thirty, forty, even fifty years their summers and autumns and winters. And that was the life I desir the life the heart can conceive – the earth life. When I hear people say t have not found the world and life so agreeable and interesting as to b love with it, or that they look with equanimity to its end, I am ap think they have never been properly alive nor seen with clear vision world they think so meanly of, or anything in it – not a blade of grass. In my worst times, when I was compelled to exist shut out from Natur London for long periods, sick and poor and friendless, I could yet alw feel that it was infinitely better to be than not to be.

He was no armchair philosopher: he had known the sweets of l but also its bitterness, and pain, poverty, and loneliness. The sola and assurance that he found in the simple fact of being alive can from his intimate communion with Nature. He was not a reclus however. When considering the loveliness of a landscape, he thoug much of the people among its hills and valleys, and suggested as o of its principal charms 'the sense of beautiful human things hidde from sight among the masses of foliage'.[1]

From early boyhood Hudson was a patient and solitary watche of Nature. Out in the Argentine, while a child, he would often b missed from home, and these unexplained absences disturbed hi mother: 'She would secretly follow and watch me standing motionless among the tall reeds or under the trees by the half-hour, staring at vacancy.' Happily, his mother left him to continue his watching. A friend whom he used to visit in London towards the end of his life told how Hudson would be found standing motionless, with bent back, staring out through the window. Thus he would remain perfectly still for long periods – watching the birds amid the trees in the courtyard.

A Shepherd's Life, Ch. XIII.

the birds of Argentina, the birds of England, the birds of London. His ability as an observer, and the amazing sharpness of his perceptions, is shown by the claim that he was able to recognize, by their songs alone, over one hundred and fifty different varieties of South American birds. He collaborated in *Argentine Ornithology* (1889), the standard work; and in his last years wrote a number of pamphlets for the Royal Society for the Protection of Birds.

Robert Bontine Cunninghame Graham was a more romantic figure than W. H. Hudson. Born in Scotland, the eldest son of a Scottish laird, he was educated at Harrow, and subsequently became a Member of Parliament, a Deputy Lieutenant, and a Justice of the Peace for three counties. Yet he was also at one time a prominent anarchist, and a leader in the great Dock Strike in London in 1887, when on 'Bloody Sunday' he fought the police in Trafalgar Square and went to prison. He also peered into many of the world's remote holes and corners, and his books record out-of-the-way experiences in out-of-the-way places. Like Hudson, he spent some time in South America. One of the best things written about him is the sketch by Bernard Shaw appended to *Captain Brassbound's Conversion*. Referring to Graham's *Mogreb-el-Acksa* (Morocco the Most Holy) (1898), Shaw says he was 'intelligent enough' to steal from that book the local colour he wanted for his play: 'its scenery, its surroundings, its atmosphere, its geography, its knowledge of the East, its fascinating Cadis and Kroo-boys and Sheikhs and mud castles'. There follows a vivid and amusing description of Cunninghame Graham's character and personality.

In his books the several Cunninghame Grahams come to light: the Scottish laird and the Spanish *hidalgo*, the irreverent legislator and the anarchic socialist. This bandit of letters had a word and a blow for every man. He was equally sceptical about aristocrats and anarchists, and could knock the wind out of a popular hero with a single sentence: 'Gladstone . . . though in talk for fifty years, never contrived to say a single thing either original or worth remembering.'[1] Travel sketches and travel stories are interspersed with episodes of Scottish life and character, and the moods of his writings

[1] 'A Memory of Parnell' (*His People*, 1906).

are as varied as the scenes and adventures. There are horror and splendour, beauty and squalor; love and hate, passion and pain; cruelty, pity, cynicism, fear, courage, and irony. His pages are vigorous as life itself. While Hudson is placid and meditative, with passages sweet as bird-song, Cunninghame Graham is turbulent and acrid and explosive, restless as the broken waters of a mountain stream falling over jagged rocks. Nevertheless, when occasion demanded, he could stand away from the picture, efface himself, and reveal the pageant of the East. In *Mogreb-el-Acksa* the curtain is often thus drawn aside; while a shorter piece, 'From the Mouth of the Sahara',[1] is an admirable example of his descriptive method. It gives an impression of the passing hours during a day in the desert, and ends with a description of a veiled holy man riding at evening into Marrakesh: 'The night descended on the town, and the last gleams of sunlight flickering on the walls turned paler, changed to violet and grey, and the pearl-coloured mist creeping up from the palm woods outside the walls enshrouded everything.'

2. HILAIRE BELLOC AND OTHERS

G. K. Chesterton (1874–1936) once wrote that his only claim to remembrance in the future would be that he had taken part in a public debate with Hilaire Belloc (1870–1953). These two ran in harness together on many occasions, and it was a stock joke of the period to refer to them as a hybrid creature, 'the Chesterbelloc'. They collaborated as illustrator and author in a few satirical novels,[2] G. K. C. providing the pictures; but their general community of convictions and interests was more important in their works than any formal collaboration could be. Belloc's influence must be accounted the stronger, since Chesterton moved more and more closely towards the religious medievalism that Belloc propounded from the first. They both re-wrote English history, starting with the thesis that the Protestant Reformation was England's worst blunder, destroying the golden Ages of Faith.[3] The history in these volumes, however, is weighted with too much demonstration, and is no more

[1] In *Success* (1902). [2] *Emmanuel Burden* (1904), *Mr Petre* (1925), etc.

[3] See Chesterton's *A Short History of England* (1917); and Belloc's *History of England* (1925 onwards).

convincing than histories with a Protestant bias which Belloc and Chesterton aimed to supersede. Belloc's interest in current affairs and energy in controversy often diverted him from literature to argumentation, and much of his writing was ephemeral. Two controversies in which he almost unceasingly engaged centred around his advocacy of Roman Catholicism and his antagonism to Jews.

In his creative and imaginative books Belloc was so versatile that he might be put in any category, except that of the dramatists. He was novelist, poet, travel-writer, essayist, critic, historian, biographer and children's writer. Despite G. K. Chesterton's enthusiasm it is doubtful whether Belloc's works will survive for long. If any do so, *The Path to Rome* (1902) will most likely ensure him a place among travel-writers; while *Danton* (1899) illustrates the vitality and living interest of Belloc's methods in biography and history.

Joseph Hilaire Pierre Belloc was born near Paris, the son of a French barrister and an Englishwoman who was descended from Joseph Priestley, the eighteenth-century chemist and Nonconformist republican. After attending the Oratory School at Edgbaston, Birmingham, Belloc returned to France to serve in the army, and he there developed that expert interest in military operations displayed in much of his written work. He settled in England from 1892, and took his degree at Oxford in 1895, with first-class honours in history. Then he served by turns as literary adviser on the *Morning Post*, Member of Parliament (1906–10), and Professor of English Literature at East London College (1911–13).

The Path to Rome describes the author's journey on foot from Toul, down the valley of the Moselle, across Switzerland, over the Alps and down through northern Italy to the city on the Tiber. It tells of hills and valleys, rivers, trees, and churches; of peasants and priests; wine, bridges, and Mass; of poets and songs and beer; of nuns, and wine again. The least pleasant feature of Belloc's prose style is his habit of writing at the top of his voice. In an essay on 'Getting Respected at Inns and Hotels'[1] he advised:

> As you come into the place go straight for the smoking-room, and begin talking of the local sport; and do not talk humbly and tentatively as

[1] *On Nothing and Kindred Subjects* (1908).

> so many do, but in a loud authoritative tone. You shall insist and lay down the law and fly in a passion if you are contradicted.

Belloc followed his own advice elsewhere than in hotels and inns, though there is little to be gained by using 'a loud authoritative tone' in literature. There are many delights, however, in *The Path to Rome*. It is a rambling, gossipy book, written in unornamented but pictorial prose; without much set or formal descriptive comment, yet clearly suggesting the widely differing appearance and character of places and people. There is fantasy, also, of a satirical kind, as in the imaginary conversation between St Michael and the Padre Eterno as they look down from heaven upon this world, 'one far point of light' shining in the void among some seventeen million others.[1] The affairs of the Earth and its people have slipped from the memory of the Padre Eterno. When St Michael reminds him of the making of Earth and Man, the Eternal Father asks why the men are throwing themselves into strange attitudes:

> 'Sire!' cried St Michael, in a voice that shook the architraves of heaven, 'they are worshipping You!' 'Oh! they are worshipping me! Well, that is the most sensible thing I have heard of them yet, and I altogether commend them. *Continuez*,' said the Padre Eterno, '*continuez!*'

As a historian, Belloc dissented from the academic methods current at the end of the nineteenth century. Though he drew upon historical documents and formal studies, these were, for his purpose, only the roughest of raw material. He takes the attitude and point of view of a 'traveller in time', working upon documentary evidence and shaping it by the deliberate exercise of creative imagination. Belloc considered that the historian's first duty was to identify himself directly and intimately with the period upon which he is working. It was not enough, in his opinion, for a twentieth-century historian to interpret a past age in terms of modernism: the historian should not only *look* back, he should *go* back and make the past age his own age for the time being, putting himself, imaginatively, in the position of an eye-witness of the events narrated. A

[1] The idea here treated by Belloc in a vein of high comedy appeared independently the same year (1902), in Hardy's 'God-Forgotten' (*Poems of the Past and the Present*). The fundamental difference in treatment provides an interesting comment upon the two writers.

plea for this method was made by Belloc in *Esto Perpetua* (1906):

> Historians have fallen into a barren contemplation of the Roman decline, and their readers with difficulty escape that attitude. Save in some few novels, no writer has attempted to stand in the shoes of the time and to see it as must have seen it the barber of Marcus Aurelius or the stud groom of Sidonius' Palace.

Belloc then proceeded to write *The Eye-Witness* (1908), 'a series of descriptions and sketches in which it is attempted to reproduce certain incidents and periods in history, as from the testimony of a person present at each'. This method is brilliant and attractive. It is also dangerous, except when used by a writer able to decide with conscientious precision what liberty may be allowed in the imaginative 'restoration' of historical material. Belloc himself, for example, instead of reproducing or summarizing the extant rough notes of speeches made at Danton's trial, expands those notes and puts reconstructed speeches into the mouths of the persons concerned. What is possibly an exact representation and impression of scenes and actions is thus conveyed far better than by formal documentation. Acknowledgment of the advantage gained does not, however, fully meet the objection that the vivid picture may also be a distorted picture. At what stage, in the use of this method, does 'serious' history end and historical fiction begin?

Of the effectiveness of Belloc's method there can be no doubt; he wrote nothing better than the frequently dramatic and moving passages in the histories and biographies. It is fascinating to watch the literary artist painting-in details on a canvas where the main outlines are already drawn. Thomas Paine's 'ignorance of French was such that his speech on Louis's exile was translated for him': taking this piece of documentary evidence, Belloc turns it indirectly to account when describing Paine's meeting in prison with Danton: 'The author of "The Rights of Man" stepped up to him, *doubtless to address him in bad French*.'[1] Again:

> In the morning of the 12th Germinal the Convention met, and *each man looked at his neighbour, and then, as though afraid, let his eyes wander to see if others thought as he did.*[2]

. . . . . .

[1] *Danton*, Ch. VII. [2] Op. cit.

> De Montfort . . . sat erect and firm . . .; *only an occasional shifting of his foot in the stirrup* betrayed the weakness of his broken leg.[1]

Phrases similar in effect to those here italicized occur often, and by such additions to the bare narrative Belloc succeeds in bringing history out of the schoolroom, library, and study, into spacious places where its pageantry and movement can be realized: 'The day had remained serene and beautiful to the last, the sky was stainless, and the west shone like a forge. Against it, one by one, appeared the figures of the condemned. . . . One by one they came up the few steps, stood for a moment in the fierce light, black or framed in scarlet, and went down.'[2]

A product of Belloc's political phase was *The Servile State* (1912), which can be read with interest in the light of 'the Affluent State' achieved half a century later.

A long list could be made of younger contemporary travel-writers, but few of their books are likely to survive by literary merit. Arctic and Antarctic exploration – particularly the voyages of Scott and Shackleton – have an extensive modern literature. F. D. Ommanney's *South Latitude* (1938) is a well-written account of arduous adventure and endurance, and the same writer's *North Cape* (1939) is little less good. Peter Fleming's *Brazilian Adventure* (1933) set a fashion of self-conscious and excessive under-statement, which can as easily become a literary vice as exaggerated self-praise.

Though it has been noticed in the following section among autobiographies, T. E. Lawrence's *Seven Pillars of Wisdom* might also be included among travel books alongside its great precursor, *Arabia Deserta* (1888) by Charles Doughty (1843–1926). Other distinguished writers on travel in the Middle East include Gertrude Bell (1868–1926; *The Desert and the Sown*, 1907, etc.) and Freya Stark (*The Southern Gates of Arabia*, 1936, etc.).

After the Second World War travel books tended to become a commercial product, generated by publishers who commissioned authors to visit and 'write up' specified places. These 'literary holi-

[1] 'The Armies Before Lewes' (*The Eye-Witness*).
[2] 'The Death of Danton' (*Danton*, Ch. VII).

days' produced a number of praiseworthy books but no masterpieces.

A more considerable contribution to travel literature, however, was made by a zoologist, Gerald Durrell,[1] whose excursions abroad in search of animals led to a succession of entertaining books: *The Overloaded Ark* (1953), *The Drunken Forest* (1956), etc.

3. BIOGRAPHY AND AUTOBIOGRAPHY

It has been seen in the preceding section that, by the beginning of the century, writers were questioning the literary manner hitherto accepted as adequate for biography. Hilaire Belloc's main concern, however, was with biography as an aspect of history. A few other writers had felt, vaguely, that something was wrong with the general practice, for in the nineteenth century a dreary utilitarianism settled upon English biography. When a 'Life' was not merely a pious memorial tribute it was usually a repository of facts – a work designed for information, not for delight.

In 1900, English biographies that were also literature could have been counted on the fingers of one hand; sporadic efforts towards change produced little evident result up to 1918. In that year *Eminent Victorians*, by Lytton Strachey (1880–1932), was published. Six reprints were called for in seven months, and it became the talk of Britain and America. Within a few weeks other authors were persuaded that this was the best possible way to write biography, and during the next seven years no other book had so many imitators. The chorus of praise was far from unanimous, however. *Eminent Victorians* was more than an essay in literary method. It was also a lively and impudent challenge to Victorian self-content. Victorians had preferred to 'edit' their great men and women. Victorian biographies, therefore, were often adjusted to the prevalent conviction that it was improper and disloyal to tell the whole truth about the dead. And though the whole truth might reveal nothing discreditable, Victorians still preferred to have the truth softened and sentimentalized.

Lytton Strachey broke into the Victorian stronghold without

[1] Younger brother of Lawrence Durrell (see above, p. 88).

apology. He had salutary things to say; he said them provocatively and without romantic embroidery. In his 'Florence Nightingale'[1] the Lady of the Lamp is put aside in her little niche and a much more impressive creature is revealed – she who transformed the Army Medical Service by the irresistible force of her will operating through and upon others. She *was* the Lady of the Lamp – in her spare moments. At others times she was an Angel of Wrath armed with thunderbolts, which she never hesitated to throw. Although this was the authentic Florence Nightingale, many preferred the less authentic but more picturesque popular version. There is a romantic thrill in contemplating the sister of mercy; there is but a sense of majesty in seeing her as a great administrator locked out of her natural sphere by the 'womanly woman' convention, and forced to use one or two loyal men who were ready to be worked to death (literally) in order that her will might be fulfilled. Knowing her as she was, how could Sidney Herbert and Arthur Hugh Clough doubt that her will was also the will of God, and that their duty was to work to the end for its fulfilment? It is a fine story, finely told by Lytton Strachey.

While it is impossible to separate style from content in *Eminent Victorians*, the book is more remarkable as a literary feat than as a representation of personal history. As tales of men and women, these are absorbing from first to last, whether the subject be Manning, Newman, Arnold of Rugby, Gladstone, or another. Yet there is less in the tale than in the telling. All these lives had been written before – but no similar thrill had previously resulted. The new brilliance and new force came from Lytton Strachey's achievement of his purpose to make biography in England an art instead of an industry.

The preface to *Eminent Victorians* is the manifesto of the New Biography. Lytton Strachey began with a statement of method, arguing that it is a disadvantage for any biographer to know too much about his human subject. Not accumulation of material, but scrupulous selection and ruthless rejection should be (Strachey considered) the primary aim. He himself chose to work upon a period already encumbered by the result of too much and too detailed research. Yet, as he looked through the mass, he saw that available

[1] In *Eminent Victorians*.

material had remained unused, and this (perversely, perhaps, but naturally) seemed to him more important than the rest. It was as though he had entered a mansion and found several cupboards locked and sealed – as a precaution against the risk of a display of family skeletons. Strachey threw open all the cupboards. The contents were interesting, the skeletons few: Gordon drank brandy and read the Bible; Disraeli chuckled in private over 'The Faery' Queen Victoria whom he flattered in public; Dr Arnold believed in the Second Coming; Gladstone was a 'confusion of incompatibles'. Strachey did not suggest any shockingness; nor did he (as some pretended) depreciate the great Victorians. He presented them as men and women 'more various than nature', instead of as inanimate idols. If the historian is wise, Strachey said, 'he will attack his subject in unexpected places; he will fall upon the flank, or the rear; he will shoot a sudden, revealing searchlight into obscure recesses, hitherto undivined'.[1]

Nothing makes English people more uneasy than irony, and irony was Lytton Strachey's most intoxicating draught. For a while biography got briskly drunk upon Lytton Strachey's irony, but the less mature irony of his followers quickly made biography fatuous.

Strachey's prose style is not unexceptionable. Its serpentinings appear to be, at first glance, a part of the general intoxication; but no such conclusion should be hurriedly drawn. If the winding sentences were made straight by reducing the number of adjectives and qualifying phrases, the 'superfluous' words would often carry away with them the irony that runs through every line and is the spirit of Lytton Strachey's prose. In the quotation below, omission of any of the words enclosed within square brackets might result in economy, but it would also injure the design of the essay to which the sentence belongs:

> A minority of [susceptible and serious] youths fell completely under his sway, responded [like wax] to [the pressure of] his influence, and moulded their [whole] lives [with passionate reverence] upon the teaching of their [adored] master.[2]

As Lytton Strachey's pages are read with attention, the feeling

[1] *Eminent Victorians*, Preface. [2] 'Dr Arnold' (*Eminent Victorians*).

grows stronger that most of the adjectives and epithets have been fitted in place with deliberation. As the narrative sweeps onward, every other sentence appears to have a sting in its tail.[1] Strachey has his moving passages, also – as in the final paragraph of *Queen Victoria* (1921).

The calculated effects of Lytton Strachey's books were hardened into a formula by other biographers. The originality of the opening of 'The End of General Gordon',[2] with its sudden 'fall upon the flank' of the subject, was particularly attractive to other writers,[3] with some of whom it became an imitative trick.

Philip Guedalla (1889–1944), if not a disciple of Lytton Strachey, at least shared his principles. Strachey referred to biography as 'the most delicate and humane of all the branches of the art of writing';[4] Guedalla said: 'Biography is the painting of portraits . . . and it is impossible to paint them without a touch of art.'[5] Strachey wrote that the old-style biographies, 'one is tempted to suppose, . . . were composed by the undertaker, as the final item of his job'; Guedalla, that biographies have often been 'dismal products in which the official biographer vies with the monumental mason'.

Lytton Strachey's books not only have literary attraction; they are also informative to ordinary men and women. Philip Guedalla, on the other hand, wrote as though for an audience of experts, and was in constant danger of breaking his shins over his own wit. With him, *manner* was all; with Strachey, only a part. There are facts in abundance behind the scenes of Guedalla's *Palmerston* (1926), but these are seldom allowed on the stage, because the author is monopolizing it most of the time. His performance, dazzling at first, becomes tiresome with repetition, and nerve-racking as he grows hilarious. In the War Office chapter of *Palmerston* the first section closes thus:

The French sentries in their bearskins stiffened to salute, as marshals

[1] E.g. 'When Newman was a child he "wished that he could believe the Arabian Nights were true". When he came to be a man, his wish seems to have been granted.' – 'Cardinal Manning' (*Eminent Victorians*).

[2] *Eminent Victorians.*

[3] Cf. the openings of *Byron: The Last Journey*, by (Sir) Harold Nicolson (1924); and *Parnell*, by St John Ervine (1925).

[4] *Eminent Victorians.*

[5] General introduction to *Curiosities of Politics* series (1925).

> clanked by in blue and gold: and three hundred miles away Palmerston, fresh from Cambridge, touched a civilian hat to the mounted sentries in Whitehall and climbed a dark staircase to plumb the mysteries of the War Department.

This cinematographic device of the 'flash back', calling the audience to 'look here upon this picture, and on this', is enlivening – once. But used at the end of four successive sections in one chapter (and frequently elsewhere in the book), it is embarrassing. Guedalla was capable of sense and brilliance together; but he 'played about' with words, recalling the worst mannerisms of Oscar Wilde, Chesterton, and Lytton Strachey. His sentences also (like Strachey's) lift their tails – but often only to wag harmlessly where they were meant to sting. Though Guedalla was the most skilful and lively of Strachey's followers, he could not avoid the follies and pitfalls of imitation.

Despite these innovators, dull journeywork biographies continued to appear in large numbers annually, and of the whole mass of biographical writing only a few further titles need be given: St John Ervine's *Parnell* (1925), Lord David Cecil's *The Stricken Deer* (1929; a life of Cowper) and *The Young Melbourne* (1939), Duff Cooper's *Talleyrand* (1932), Cecil Woodham-Smith's *Florence Nightingale* (1950).

Though most of the credit for temporarily disestablishing the mortuary-puff type of biography deservedly went to Lytton Strachey, the importance in a similar connexion of Edmund Gosse's *Father and Son* (1907) was emphasized by Sir Harold Nicolson in *The Development of English Biography* (1927). Gosse (1849–1928) was born into the atmosphere of stern piety sustained by the Plymouth Brethren, an English Evangelical Protestant fellowship founded in the early nineteenth century. His father, Philip Gosse, was an eminent marine naturalist who found no difficulty in being at once a scientist and a believer in the literal authenticity of the Bible from cover to cover. *Father and Son* is a precise account of the upbringing of Edmund Gosse in an environment which at an early age he found spiritually stifling, and of the differences on fundamental matters which developed between himself and his father after the death of his mother. The book, Gosse's one masterpiece, gave offence to the many who, in 1907, still clung to the view that parents were sacrosanct and beyond criticism by their children. When that dogma disintegrated, the sensitive affection displayed in *Father and Son* and its literary excellence received general recognition, and its place in literature is assured on its high merit as a piece of writing and on its significance as a pioneer work demonstrating that a love of truth concerning men and women does not imply any lack of love for the men and women themselves.

As the twentieth century proceeded, more and more interest was taken in the make-up of individual character, an interest stimulated by the studies of foreign psychologists, chiefly Sigmund Freud (1856–1939), whose inquiries into the significance of dreams led to the theory and practice of psycho-analysis and the casting-off of inhibitions. Whereas in the nineteenth century personal reticence had been a mark of good breeding, the early twentieth century was much too interested in the motives and mechanism of human conduct to maintain such reticence. Every fragment of information about human behaviour was grasped as potentially illuminating and was substantially gratifying also to that hungry curiosity which gnaws at modern people.

It is of the essence of autobiography that the author's style should have an easy intimacy in harmony with the originating impulse which prompted the writing of the book. Autobiographers fail and stultify themselves if they hold the reader at arm's length, though the record may still have a factual interest.

Oscar Wilde's *De Profundis* (1905)[1] and George Gissing's *The Private Papers of Henry Ryecroft* (1903) have the requisite degree of intimacy in their differing ways, but whereas Wilde's is a book with the shades of the prison house on it – a record of agony but with some attitudinizing – Gissing's is largely a joyous celebration of escape from the humiliations of poverty and drudgery. In *The Journal of a Disappointed Man* (1919) W. N. P. Barbellion (pseudonym of Bruce Frederick Cummings, 1889–1917) analysed his thoughts and sensations with the precision of a scientist, yet it com-

[1] The original edition contained only part of the manuscript written by Wilde. The complete version remained unpublished until 1950.

bines literary attractiveness with exactitude and avoids morbidity, though many of the entries allude to the progress of the incurable disease which was slowly killing the author.

There is a high element of originality and charm in Siegfried Sassoon's sensitive personal records, *The Memoirs of a Fox-Hunting Man* (1928) and *The Memoirs of an Infantry Officer* (1930), but T. E. Lawrence's *Seven Pillars of Wisdom* (1926), notwithstanding the fame of its author and the sensational excitement raised by his book, is a constipated masterpiece. If Lawrence had written this remarkable work before he learned, very deliberately, *how* to write, *Seven Pillars of Wisdom* might well have been as great an original achievement in literature as his desert campaign was in the annals of military history. That he had natural talent as a writer is proved by his letters (*Letters of T. E. Lawrence*, edited by David Garnett, 1938), in which alone posterity will be able to get close to a man who, after his brilliant achievement with the Arabs in wartime, was frustrated in peacetime both from without and within, and was destroyed prematurely (in a motor-cycle crash) by the passion he had developed for speed – a passion through which he appeared at last to find the sole appropriate exercise for his own swift and rare spirit. The posthumous publication of the long-withheld account of his life in the Royal Air Force, *The Mint* (1955), despite its much-publicized frankness, showed again that Lawrence could not establish contact nor reveal his character when he wrote for an audience beyond his own circle.

The Letters of D. H. Lawrence (1932) adds only minor details to the more than lifesize portrait of himself that exists in his own novels, stories, and poems.

Ellen Terry and Bernard Shaw: A Correspondence (1931) was a delightful unheralded surprise. The friendship of the great player and the great playwright was conducted through its deepest and most lyrical phases without a personal meeting; when at length they did meet something died in the letters and the fire dwindled. But the book is a human as well as a literary treasure, and only a proper recognition of her genius as a woman, apart from her notable gifts as an actress, can explain how Ellen Terry in these letters is always, even intellectually, Shaw's equal. That it appears so may be due in part also to Shaw's exquisite tact. There was something in each that, while the correspondence flourished, brought out the best in both – her sensibility and intelligence and wit, his sympathy, understanding, and natural tenderness.

The interest of H. G. Wells's *Experiment in Autobiography* (1934), J. M. Barrie's *The Greenwood Hat* (1937), and Rudyard Kipling's *Something of Myself* (1937) is less in the books themselves than in the contemporary eminence of their writers; even Wells, though telling all, tells virtually nothing. George Moore's *Hail and Farewell* (1911–14) has previously been mentioned (above, p. 70) as a masterpiece of indiscretion.

Havelock Ellis's *My Life* (1940), written at intervals over a period of forty years, was intended to be a major work of art as well as a revealing essay in personal examination. Nevertheless, it is unbalanced in its parts, unco-ordinated, and unrevealing. Havelock Ellis (1859–1939) had become both notorious and famous with his *Studies in the Psychology of Sex* (1910–28), but he was a man of letters as well as a scientist and the author of several first-rate volumes of essays. In more informal moods he jotted down the journal entries which make up the three series of *Impressions and Comments* (1914, 1921, 1924), from which more may be learned of Havelock Ellis himself than from *My Life*.

The outstanding large-scale autobiography of the half-century, Sir Osbert Sitwell's *Left Hand! Right Hand!*[1] (5 vols., 1945–50), is also a notable literary achievement. Written in the grand style, it gives an intimately analytical account of the author himself, a unique characterization of his father Sir George Sitwell, while, as a portrait of the age, historians will find it indispensable. Sir George was later given a whole book to himself by Sir Osbert: *Tales My Father Taught Me* (1962).

It is not boldly venturesome to prophesy that one of the relatively few twentieth-century books likely to attain permanent classic rank is the *Lark Rise to Candleford* trilogy by Flora Thompson (1877–1947). The author was little known outside her family circle before

[1] Individual titles were given to the later volumes: II, *The Scarlet Tree* (1946); III. *Great Morning* (1948); IV, *Laughter in the Next Room* (1949); V, *Noble Essences* (1950),

she published *Lark Rise* in 1939, and completed the trilogy with *Over to Candleford* (1941) and *Candleford Green* (1943). This account of village life in the area where the counties of Northampton, Oxford, and Buckingham impinge, preserves much of the indigenous homebred culture of the late nineteenth century in which personal happiness and family contentment went coupled with hard work and small means. Craftsmanship was still a source of pride, and leisure not yet dominated by commercialized and mechanized amusements. Laura, the leading character in these books, is Flora Thompson herself thinly veiled, and all that is recorded is authentic to her early life and life in her country neighbourhood. *Lark Rise to Candleford* is one of those literary miracles in which a writer is suddenly endowed with a power of expression and an appropriate grace of style – a delayed access of genius applied to the creation of a masterpiece which immortalizes a phase of English life that would otherwise pass from the nation's memory.

4. HISTORY

Although history as a branch of academic study does not come within the scope of the present book, a few twentieth-century historians must be named as masters of the rare art of creating literature in the process of writing history. Sir Winston Churchill (1874–1965) had already achieved distinction as a writer before, at the peak of renown as a statesman, he turned to the production of his great history of *The Second World War* (6 vols., 1948–1954). G. M. Trevelyan (1876–1962), long esteemed as a man of letters in the field of history, found his largest audience with *English Social History* (1944), which persuaded many thousands that history holds more fascination than fiction. Among the younger historians, C. V. Wedgwood (born 1910) has been most successful in continuing the Trevelyan tradition, maintaining the twofold standard of scrupulous scholarship and literary excellence. *William the Silent* (1944) established her reputation before she undertook a larger-scale work on the English Civil Wars period, with *The King's Peace* (1955) and *The King's War* (1958) as the initial volumes.

Its first appearance in a popular paper-back series[1] should not be allowed to obscure S. T. Bindoff's *Tudor England* (1950), in which scholarship is combined with narrative excellence. The biggest historical work of the century is A. J. Toynbee's *A Study of History* in twelve volumes (1935–61). An abridgement in two volumes (1946; 1957) brought this vast work to the notice of a wide public, particularly in the United States where it became a best seller, though the proportion of readers to buyers cannot be known. As a venture in the philosophy of history it became a subject of heated controversy among scholars, though it may well be that only its author was qualified to be a thoroughly instructed reader of its 7,000 pages.

[1] *The Pelican History of England* (Penguin Books).

INDEX